access to history

Rebellion and Disorder under the Tudors 1485–1603 for OCR

GEOFF WOODWARD AND NICHOLAS FELLOWS

SECOND EDITION

HODDER
EDUCATION
AN HACHETTE UK COMPANY

Dedication

Geoff Woodward (1946–2015)

The series of books for the new OCR A level Unit 3 Paper is in memory of Geoff who, firstly as Principal Examiner for the Themes paper from 2001, and then as Chief Examiner, developed and nurtured this unit. We hope that with the new edition of this book we have built on his legacy to offer students the best possible support for their studies.

The Publishers would like to thank the following for permission to reproduce copyright material:

Photo credits: p16 Apic/Getty Images; **p17** Fine Art Images/HIP/TopFoto; **p18** https://commons.wikimedia.org/wiki/ File:DukeofNorthumberland_Penshurst.jpg; **p104** https://commons.wikimedia.org/wiki/File:Edward_Seymour.jpg; **p109** Wellcome Library, London, Copyrighted work available under Creative Commons Attribution only licence CC BY 4.0 http://creativecommons. org/licenses/by/4.0/(detail of Cromwell); **p111** The Print Collector/Heritage-Images/TopFoto; **p149** World History Archive/TopFoto; **p156** Wellcome Library, London, Copyrighted work available under Creative Commons Attribution only licence CC BY 4.0 http:// creativecommons.org/licenses/by/4.0/(detail of Burleigh); **p170** Portrait of Mary I or Mary Tudor (1516-58), daughter of Henry VIII, at the Age of 28, 1544 (panel), Master John (fl.1544)/National Portrait Gallery, London, UK/Bridgeman Images.

Acknowledgements: Harvard University Press, *Reform and Reformation: England 1509–1558* by G.R. Elton, 1977. Hodder Education, *Elizabeth I: Religion and Foreign Affairs* by John Warren, 2002; *England 1485–1603* by Nicholas Fellows and Mary Dicken, 2015. Kent State University Press, *Rebellion and Riot* by Barrett L. Beer, 1982. Manchester University Press, *The Pilgrimage of Grace: A Study of the Rebel Armies of October 1536* by Michael Bush, 1996. Oxford University Press, *English Reformations: Religion, Politics and Society under the Tudors* by C. Haigh, 1993.

Every effort has been made to trace all copyright holders, but if any have been inadvertently overlooked the Publishers will be pleased to make the necessary arrangements at the first opportunity.

Although every effort has been made to ensure that website addresses are correct at time of going to press, Hodder Education cannot be held responsible for the content of any website mentioned in this book. It is sometimes possible to find a relocated web page by typing in the address of the home page for a website in the URL window of your browser.

Hachette UK's policy is to use papers that are natural, renewable and recyclable products and made from wood grown in sustainable forests. The logging and manufacturing processes are expected to conform to the environmental regulations of the country of origin.

Orders: please contact Bookpoint Ltd, 130 Milton Park, Abingdon, Oxon OX14 4SB. Telephone: +44 (0)1235 827720. Fax: +44 (0)1235 400454. Lines are open 9.00a.m.–5.00p.m., Monday to Saturday, with a 24-hour message answering service. Visit our website at www.hoddereducation.co.uk

© 2016 Geoff Woodward and Nicholas Fellows
Second edition © Geoff Woodward and Nicholas Fellows

First published in 2008 by
Hodder Education
An Hachette UK Company
Carmelite House, 50 Victoria Embankment
London EC4Y 0DZ

Impression number	10	9	8	7	6	5	4	3	2	
Year		2020	2019	2018	2017					

Cover photo 'The Execution of Sir Thomas More in 1535' © Antoine Caron/Getty Images
Produced, illustrated and typeset in Palatino LT Std by Gray Publishing, Tunbridge Wells
Printed and bound by CPI Group (UK) Ltd, Croydon CR0 4YY

A catalogue record for this title is available from the British Library

ISBN 978 1471838507

Contents

Dedication

Keith Randell (1943–2002)

The *Access to History* series was conceived and developed by Keith, who created a series to 'cater for students as they are, not as we might wish them to be'. He leaves a living legacy of a series that for over 20 years has provided a trusted, stimulating and well-loved accompaniment to post-16 study. Our aim with these new editions is to continue to offer students the best possible support for their studies.

Introduction

This introduction gives you an overview of the following:
*   ★ The OCR A level course
*   ★ How you will be assessed on this unit
*   ★ The different features of this book and how they will aid your learning

The OCR A level course

This study will form part of your overall History course for the OCR specification, of which there are three unit groups and a topic-based essay. The unit groups comprise:

*   British period study and enquiry (unit group 1)
*   non-British period study (unit group 2)
*   thematic study and historical interpretations (unit group 3).

This book has been written to support your study of the thematic study and historical interpretations unit Y306, Rebellion and Disorder under the Tudors 1485–1603.

This unit considers why rebellions broke out in Tudor England and Ireland and the nature and frequency of the unrest during the period. It examines the reasons for the failure or limited success of the rebellions, the impact that they had on Tudor governments and the extent to which governments were able to maintain stability during the period. There is also an in-depth analysis of the three interpretation depth studies:

*   The Pilgrimage of Grace
*   The Western rebellion
*   Tyrone's rebellion.

How you will be assessed on this unit

Each of the three unit groups has an examination paper, whereas the topic-based essay is marked internally but externally moderated.

Unit group 1	Unit group 2	Unit group 3
The British period study is assessed through two essays from which you answer one, and the enquiry is assessed through a source-based question. This counts for 25 per cent of your overall marks	The non-British period study is assessed through a short essay and one longer essay. This counts for fifteen per cent of your overall marks	The thematic and historical interpretations are assessed through two essays which cover at least 100 years, and one in-depth question based on two interpretations of a key event, individual or issue that forms a major part of the theme. This counts for 40 per cent of your overall marks

For the topic-based essay you will complete a 3000–4000-word essay on a topic of your choice. This counts for twenty per cent of your overall marks.

Examination questions for unit group 3

You will be entered for a specific unit for your A level, and your examination paper will contain only the questions relating to that unit. There will be two sections in the examination paper. Section A is the historical interpretations and Section B is the thematic essay.

In Section A there will be two interpretations about one of the depth studies and one question. The question will be worth 30 marks.

In Section B there will be three thematic essay questions, each worth 25 marks, and you will have to answer two of them. As this is a thematic paper the questions may be drawn from more than one key topic.

Section A questions

Section A questions will be worded as follows:

Evaluate the interpretations in both of the passages and explain which you think is more convincing as an explanation of X. [30]

For example:

Evaluate the interpretations in both of the passages and explain which you think is more convincing as an explanation of the reasons for the Western rebellion. [30]

Section B questions

Examples of questions using some of the more common command terms, and specific requirements for answering each term, can be found at the end of each chapter. The command terms are important. A key to success is understanding what these terms mean and what you have to do.

Command term	Description
Assess	Weigh up the relative importance of a range of themes and reach a supported judgement as to which is the most important across the whole period
To what extent/ how far	Consider the relative importance of the named issue or theme and weigh up its role by comparing it (comparative evaluation) with other issues or themes and reach a balanced judgement as to its relative importance across the whole period
How successful	Consider a range of issues or themes and make a judgement as to how successful each was before reaching an overall judgement about success by comparing each issue or theme

Answering the questions

The A level examination is two and a half hours long. Section A carries slightly more marks than each question in Section B and, therefore, particularly as you will need time to read the interpretations, it would be sensible to spend about one hour on Section A and 45 minutes on each essay in Section B. Before you start any of the questions, make a brief plan. Advice on planning both the historical interpretations question and the thematic essay are given on pages 51 and 54.

The answers you write will be marked against the relevant mark scheme. It would be useful to familiarise yourself with this before the examination so that you are aware of the criteria against which your work will be marked. Mark schemes offer guidance, but they cannot cover everything. If you write something that is relevant and accurate, but not in the mark scheme, you will gain credit for it. You will be rewarded for well-argued and supported responses that show evidence of synthesis across the period (see page 94). Marks will not be deducted for information that is incorrect, but you should remember that incorrect knowledge may undermine your argument.

The different features of this book and how they will aid your learning

The book starts with a chronological overview of the major rebellions which will be explored throughout the four main thematic chapters in the book. This is intended to act as a reference point that can be referred to throughout your study of the main themes.

Each main thematic chapter in the book covers one of the key topics listed in the OCR specification.

Each chapter also has a section on the three named depth studies and provides more detail and, where relevant, discussion of any historical debates about that study in relation to the theme of the chapter. The first chapter will look at the causes of the three named rebellions, the second will focus on the nature of those rebellions, the third will examine their impact, and the final chapter will look at the threat they posed.

At the end of the book is a timeline of the major events (page 194) and suggestions for further reading.

The headings below outline the main features of each main thematic chapter.

Chapter overviews

Chapters start with a brief overview of the theme and a series of bullet points which list the main issues discussed. The structure of the chapter is outlined and a timeline lists the key dates for the events discussed in the chapter.

Chapter sections

The chapters are divided into sections, each addressing one of the bullet points listed in the overview. The section addresses a key question or questions, and is further broken down into a series of sub-headings to help your understanding of the topic. By the end of each section you should be able to answer the key question. Your understanding will be reinforced by a summary diagram for each section.

Profiles

These are brief sections detailing the life and key dates of important people in relation to the topic studied.

Key figures

Concise summaries are given of important people in relation to certain events to do with the topic studied.

Key terms

The key terms that you need to understand in order to grasp the important concepts and issues surrounding the topic are emboldened in the chapter the first time they are used in the book, and are defined in the margin and the glossary at the end of the book.

Key debates

Historians often disagree about the causes or significance of historical events and the role and impact of individuals. Key debates are listed at the start of the chapter and are discussed in the historical interpretations section at the end. Not only will this introduce you to some of the key historical debates about the period you are studying, but by using your historical knowledge and the information in the chapter you will be able to test the views of the historians, which will help you prepare for the Section A examination question.

Chapter summaries

At the end of each chapter there will be a summary of the key points covered in the chapter, which will help with revision.

Refresher questions

There will be a series of refresher questions at the end of each chapter. These will not be examination-style questions, but will be designed to ensure you have a clear understanding of the main points and issues raised in the chapter.

Study skills

Each chapter has a study skills section. In each section one part will develop the skills needed for the thematic essay and the other part will develop the skills needed for the historical interpretations question. There will often be examples of strong and weak paragraphs and the opportunity for you to practise the skills on relevant questions and interpretations.

The Tudor century: an overview

The Wars of the Roses and their impact

The issue of the succession to the English Crown had been a major problem from 1399, when Henry IV seized the throne from Richard II. Although Henry and his son, Henry V, brought some stability, this did not last. Henry V died in 1422 and left a minor, Henry VI, to succeed him but it was when he reached adulthood that problems really began. Henry VI was weak and unable to maintain control of the nobility, and as a result another claimant to the throne, Richard of York, emerged. There then began a struggle between two families with claims to the throne. This conflict has become known as the Wars of the Roses, between the Lancastrians, with Henry VI as its head, and the Yorkists, first under Richard of York, and after his death, Edward. The struggle culminated in 1461 with Edward defeating Henry VI and taking the throne. However, this did not bring stability as Henry regained the Crown briefly in 1470, only to be overthrown within a year by Edward. The death of Edward saw unrest continue as his brother Richard seized the throne from Edward's twelve-year-old heir and was crowned as Richard III.

The continual upheavals and frequent changes of succession created instability and suggested that force rather than legitimacy would determine who should rule. The nobility had become accustomed to fighting to determine who would rule and it had also resulted in them assembling their own private armies, which they used to protect themselves and take advantage of the chaos. They were able to use these armies to intimidate others and even challenge the king and his authority, resulting in parts of the country where royal authority scarcely ran.

This situation further damaged Henry VII's position as king, as not only was his claim to the throne weak despite his Lancastrian background, but he had seized it by force. He also faced by challenges from Yorkists who had seen their monarch, Richard III, defeated at Bosworth in 1485 and by nobles who wanted to maintain the influence they had wielded during much of the fifteenth century. Therefore, for much of his reign Henry's main concerns were to gain recognition, stop Yorkist unrest and lessen the power of the nobility so that the Tudors secured their position. These threats to the Tudor line continued well into the sixteenth century and led to the issue of the succession being a major cause of unrest in the early period.

Religious change

When Henry VII came to the throne in 1485, not just England but all of Europe was Catholic and recognised the pope as the head of the Church. A common religious belief helped to create some unity within the country and people were accustomed to the Church rituals and calendar, all of which had been practised for centuries and brought communities together.

However, Henry VIII's decision to break from the Catholic Church when the pope would not grant him a divorce from his first wife, Catherine of Aragon, led to a number of religious changes during his reign and that of his son, Edward VI, which would overturn centuries of tradition. Although Mary, Henry's daughter, reversed them and returned England to Catholicism, that was short lived as when Elizabeth succeeded her in 1558 she re-established a Protestant Church. The religious turmoil created further unrest from the 1530s onwards as people saw their traditional religious practices, such as pilgrimages, and institutions, such as monasteries, attacked. Even under Mary's reign the restoration of Catholicism did not restore order as those who had become committed to the new faith attempted to prevent her accession or remove her once she had become queen. It was only once Elizabeth was securely established on the throne in the 1570s that religious unrest died away. Catholics' hopes of restoring their faith became dependent on foreign help or desperate plots to assassinate the queen. Events such as the Armada in 1588 served only to further strengthen Elizabeth's position and associate the new Protestant faith with nationalism. As a result, religion became a unifying, rather than divisive factor, as it had also been at the start of the period.

Social and economic changes

For the first time since the Black Death in the fourteenth century, the population of England began to increase steadily and from about 1525 the speed of that rise became more rapid. Although the rise was not as spectacular as more recent growths, it had a dramatic impact, particularly from the 1540s onwards. The larger population increased pressure on the demand for food, which could not always be met and was a major problem during times of bad harvests. This resulted in prices rising dramatically in the 1540s and again during Elizabeth's reign, adding pressure on many ordinary people and increasing the numbers suffering from poverty. The situation was made worse by the conversion of much agricultural land from arable to sheep farming as not only were fewer crops grown, but fewer labourers were required to look after flocks of sheep than tend crops, which created unemployment and added to the problem of poverty. The growing population stimulated the demand for industrial goods, but although it created employment opportunities, it also meant that in times of economic slumps and downturns many became unemployed, as happened in the 1550s and again in Elizabeth's reign.

These problems were made worse by warfare. Henry VIII and Edward VI both debased, or reduced the amount of metal in the coinage, which simply put more money into circulation and further increased prices. Prices more than doubled in the first half of the sixteenth century and as wages did not keep up with this rise the standard of living fell for many. This only added to the number of poor, which was a particular concern in towns where there was a large concentration of poor people, who were seen by the authorities to be a threat to law and order and a source of support for rebellions.

The fall in living standards did encourage many of the commons to support the unrest of 1549, but although the situation in the 1590s was probably worse, there were few disturbances as the government put into place social and economic legislation to try and lessen the impact of harvest failures and poverty. Therefore, although social and economic developments did play a role in unrest in the first half of the period, they were less of an issue as the sixteenth century drew to a close, in part due to government legislation but also because the peasantry realised that rebellion achieved little.

Conclusion

The dynastic challenges that the Tudors faced at the start of the period gradually diminished as possible alternatives either died or were killed. Religious and social and economic change and developments in the middle of the period presented new challenges for the Tudor monarchs. However, Elizabeth's long tenure on the throne allowed Protestantism to triumph and the government to respond to the social and economic difficulties, which therefore reduced the likelihood of unrest.

A chronological overview of the main rebellions

Henry VII (1485–1509)

Henry VII faced five serious revolts, three of which aimed to overthrow him. The summer of 1497 was a particularly critical time. England was at war with Scotland, Henry had to fight the Battle of Blackheath to suppress the Cornish rebellion and at the same time Warbeck was laying claim to the throne.

Lovel 1486

Having survived the Battle of Bosworth, Francis Lovel, a councillor to Richard III, sought to overthrow Henry VII. Lovel took sanctuary in Colchester and then escaped before raising troops at Middleham (Yorkshire) in a bid to overthrow Henry VII. He failed and fled to Flanders.

Stafford 1486

Humphrey and Thomas Stafford had eluded capture after the Battle of Bosworth and taken sanctuary in Colchester Abbey. They then fled to Worcester, escaped again and were finally captured at Culham Church (Oxfordshire). Humphrey was executed.

Simnel 1486–7

Lambert Simnel claimed to be Edward, Earl of Warwick, and therefore had a better claim to the English throne than Henry VII. He won the support of several English and Irish nobles, including Lincoln and Kildare, as well as foreign troops, but was captured on the battlefield of East Stoke. The king made him a servant in the royal household.

Yorkshire 1489

Unwilling to pay taxes to fund a war against France, protesters in Yorkshire, led by Sir John Egremont, killed the Earl of Northumberland before royal troops dispersed them. Some rebels were executed but Egremont escaped to France.

Cornish 1497

Unwilling to pay taxes to fund a war against Scotland, Cornish protesters marched towards London. They were slaughtered at Blackheath, the ringleaders – Audley, Flamank and Joseph – were executed, and the county received a heavy fine.

Warbeck 1497

Perkin Warbeck claimed to be Richard, Duke of York, the younger of the two princes who disappeared in 1483 after being held in the Tower of London. He won support from a few English nobles, notably Sir William Stanley, the Lord Chamberlain, from Cornish peasants still smarting from their treatment at Blackheath, and at varying times, from foreign states. He was captured, imprisoned in the Tower and eventually executed in 1499.

Henry VIII (1509–47)

Although Henry VIII is usually viewed as strongest of the Tudor monarchs, he faced the largest Tudor rebellion, the Pilgrimage of Grace, and the most successful, the Amicable Grant. Unrest also surfaced in Ireland as Henry sought to increase his power there.

Amicable Grant 1525

Unwilling and, allegedly, unable to pay taxes to fund a war against France, protesters in several counties, but mainly in Suffolk, forced the government to back down. No rebels were punished.

Silken Thomas 1534–7

'Silken' Thomas O'Neill began a rebellion in Dublin on hearing of the arrest and imprisonment of his father, the Earl of Kildare, in the Tower of London. Thomas and his five uncles attacked Henry's administration before submitting to an Anglo-Irish army. The leaders were brought to London and executed.

Pilgrimage of Grace 1536–7

Three separate risings in Lincolnshire (led by Dymoke), Yorkshire and other northern counties (led by Aske), and a later brief disturbance in Yorkshire and Cumberland (led by Bigod) challenged Henry's religious reforms. They also had economic, social and political grievances. The Pilgrimage was the largest and longest rebellion in Tudor England and resulted in over 200 executions in 1537.

Edward VI (1547–53)

The years of rule of the boy-king Edward VI were some of the most troublesome of the period. Not only were there two sizeable revolts, the Western and Kett's, but some 26 counties witnessed unrest that summer. There was also the possibility of invasion from France, stretching government resources to the limit.

Western 1549

Cornish and Devon protesters besieged Exeter and demanded an end to Protestant reforms and recent taxes on sheep and wool. Their rebellion lasted for five weeks and was ended at the battles of Clyst St Mary and Sampford Courtenay in Devon.

Kett 1549

Robert Kett led a rebellion in Norfolk against illegal enclosures and agrarian practices adopted by the county gentry. Rebel camps were set up in several market towns in East Anglia, and the principal one at Mousehold Heath was only dispersed after the Battle of Dussindale. Kett and other ringleaders were hanged in Norfolk.

Mary I (1553–8)

Mary Tudor came possibly the closest of all Tudor monarchs to being overthrown. Initially, it even appeared as if she would be prevented from taking the Crown as Northumberland's attempt to put his daughter-in-law on the throne appeared as if it might succeed. Within a year she faced another challenge, from Wyatt, which also came close to overthrowing her.

Northumberland 1553

The Duke of Northumberland attempted to prevent Mary from gaining the throne by asserting the claim of Lady Jane Grey, his daughter-in-law. He and his supporters submitted without a fight at Cambridge. He was taken back to London and executed.

Wyatt 1554

Sir Thomas Wyatt raised troops in Kent in protest at Mary's proposed marriage to Philip of Spain. Planned uprisings in several English counties failed to materialise and Wyatt was captured at Ludgate (London) and subsequently executed.

Elizabeth I (1558–1603)

As the Tudors became more secure, alternative claimants died out and people grew accustomed to their rule. Thus, after 1570 Elizabeth faced only one rebellion of note. Ireland, on the other hand, gave Elizabeth a lot more trouble and she faced more unrest there than any other Tudor monarch.

Shane O'Neill 1558–67

O'Neill resented losing the earldom of Tyrone in Ulster to his brother, and murdered him. He then turned on English settlers and the administration in Dublin. The uprising only ended when he was killed in a brawl with rival clans.

Northern Earls 1569–70

The Earls of Westmorland and Northumberland planned to release Mary Stuart from captivity, marry her to the Duke of Norfolk and force Elizabeth to recognise Mary as her successor. The Catholic earls wanted greater power for themselves in the north and called for the dismissal of William Cecil, the queen's secretary. Few supported the rebellion outside Yorkshire and Durham, and when a royal army approached, the earls fled. Northumberland was later executed but Westmorland was never caught.

Munster 1569–73

James Fitzmaurice Fitzgerald rose up against English plantations in Munster and his colleague Edmund Butler attacked settlements in Leix-Offaly. Over 800 rebels were executed but Fitzgerald escaped to France.

Geraldine 1579–83

Fitzgerald returned from abroad and raised Irish rebels in protest at Elizabeth's religious and political policies. Fitzgerald was killed but the Earl of Desmond assumed command and received aid from Italian and Spanish troops at Smerwick. The rebels were rounded up by an English army and Desmond was executed.

Tyrone 1595–1603

Hugh O'Neill, the Earl of Tyrone, raised support from every Irish province against English rule. Elizabeth underestimated the scale of his revolt, made several unwise appointments and deployed insufficient resources until her military commander, Lord Mountjoy, persuaded Tyrone to submit.

Oxfordshire 1596

In spite of severe economic problems, the only armed uprising in England in the 1590s occurred near Oxford and involved a handful of protesters. The government declared that it was a rebellion and meted out harsh punishments to the leaders.

Essex 1601

The Earl of Essex attempted to raise London in a show of popular support for him against Robert Cecil and the queen's councillors. Despite having the nominal support of many nobles, none was willing to risk his life or threaten the queen and the rebellion collapsed within a few hours. Essex was executed along with a handful of his household servants.

CHAPTER 1

The causes of Tudor rebellions

The Tudor period witnessed fifteen major rebellions in England and five in Ireland, as well as numerous other minor disturbances, particularly in 1549. There were a variety of causes, and this chapter identifies similar and dissimilar causes between historical periods and distinguishes between the more important and subsidiary causes and how they changed over the period. The chapter will consider the difficulties in discovering the motives of the rebels and the extent to which most rebellions were multi-causal. This chapter analyses their causes under the following headings:

★ Political causes of rebellion

★ Religious causes of rebellion

★ Economic and social causes of rebellion

★ Conclusion: why did rebellions occur?

It also considers the debates surrounding three in-depth topics:

★ What caused the Pilgrimage of Grace?

★ Was the Western rebellion a religious rising?

★ How far was Tyrone's rebellion simply a protest against increased government interference?

Key dates

1485	Defeat of Richard III at Battle of Bosworth	1548	Tax on sheep and cloth
		1549	First Edwardian prayer book, Subsidy Act
1534	Subsidy Act	1549	Rebellion in 26 counties
1536	Ten Articles, dissolution of the smaller monasteries	1553	The 'Devise' drawn up
		1555–6	Crop failure
1539	The Six Articles	1596–7	Crop failure

1 Political causes of rebellion

▶ *Why was there so much dynastic unrest in Tudor England?*

Political factors were probably the most important and recurring theme as a cause of Tudor rebellions. They could be inspired by a wide range of issues:

- a desire to overthrow the dynasty
- an intention to change the line of succession borne out of personal vengeance, ambition or principle
- a wish to remove 'evil advisers', nominally in the interest of the country but often out of factional disputes and self-advancement
- a reaction to government centralisation which threatened to destroy traditional ways of life.

Political causes were many and varied. Although they changed in the course of the period, other causes and personal motives were frequently interwoven.

Dynastic issues and the succession

The issue of the succession remained a cause of rebellion throughout the period, but was particularly important at the start of the period because of Henry VII's weak claim to the throne, having gained it on the battlefield at Bosworth by defeating the Yorkist Richard III. It was also an issue under both Mary and Elizabeth as attempts were made to either alter or secure the succession. See Figure 1.1 for an explanation of the Tudor, Lancastrian and Yorkist families.

Henry VII

Henry VII may have won the Battle of Bosworth and established the Tudor dynasty, but his tenure on the throne was far from secure. To his enemies – and he had many – he was a usurper and, if he could overthrow a king, so could they. His very presence on the throne therefore sparked off three dynastic rebellions:

- Francis Viscount Lovel, a former Lord Chamberlain, and his Yorkist associates Humphrey and Thomas Stafford, raised troops in 1486 to kill the king as he progressed to the north of England.
- In 1487, Lambert Simnel 'pretended' to be the Earl of Warwick, a young prince with a strong claim to the throne whom Henry kept imprisoned in the Tower of London. Simnel's Yorkist supporters believed they would gain more from killing Henry than from serving him. The Earl of Lincoln was politically ambitious and dissatisfied with his position at court and role that Henry had assigned him. Being a royal councillor and Lord Lieutenant of Ireland was not enough to satisfy this Yorkist claimant whom Richard III had named as his heir. Others, like Lovel and **Margaret of Burgundy** who funded the troops, were diehard opponents of the king, while Gerald, Earl of Kildare, and the 40 or so Irish nobles who backed Simnel, believed their end would be best served by overthrowing the regime.

 **KEY FIGURE**

Margaret of Burgundy (1446–1503)

Sister of the Yorkist kings, Edward IV and Richard III. She married the Duke of Burgundy and after Henry VII took the throne supported Yorkist claimants against him.

Lancastrians, Yorkists and Tudors

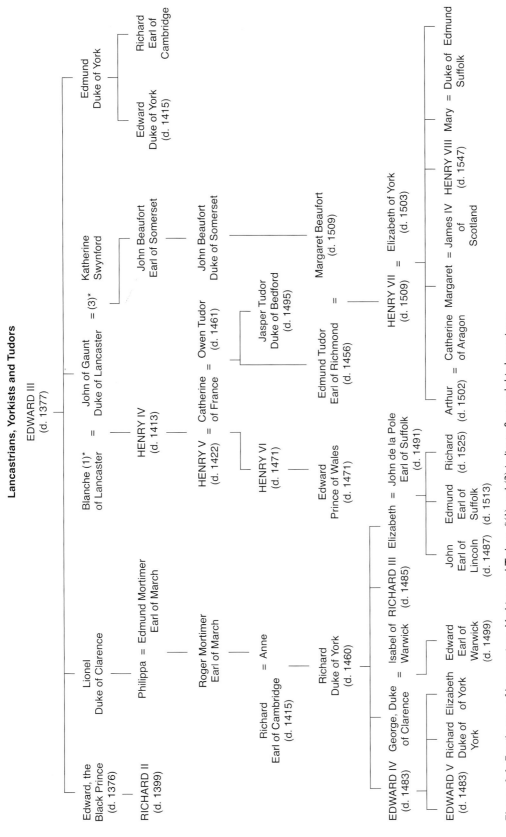

Figure 1.1 Family tree of Lancastrians, Yorkists and Tudors. *(1) and (3) indicate first and third marriages.

- The third dynastic rebellion that Henry faced was led by Perkin Warbeck. He 'pretended' to be the Duke of York, the younger of two princes who had almost certainly been murdered by Richard III. In the early 1490s, Warbeck was backed by France, Burgundy and Scotland, each intent on weakening, if not actively wishing to remove Henry, but when this challenge came to a head in September 1497, all foreign support evaporated.

A mixture of personal and political factors combined to bring about each of these revolts but they had a common link: they wished to remove the king.

Henry VIII

After this initial threat of opposition, Henry VIII faced no dynastic challenge until the 1530s, when he was confronted with the greatest rebellion of the sixteenth century, the Pilgrimage of Grace. Henry's recent divorce from Catherine of Aragon and disinheritance of her daughter Mary had certainly alarmed some northern nobles. Among a wide range of complaints and demands, the rebels wanted Princess Mary legitimised and restored to the line of succession. They were also concerned that Henry might determine the succession by will rather than by parliament and, worse, if he did do this, the title would pass to the Scottish monarchy via his sister, Margaret, who had married the Scottish king, James IV, and produced children.

A portrait of Henry VII painted in 1505 by an unknown artist.

A portrait of Henry VIII painted around 1597–1618 by an unknown artist.

Edward VI and Mary I

Edward VI's '**Devise**' of May 1553 also aimed to exclude Mary from the succession and was largely responsible for the Duke of Northumberland's rebellion. He wished to hold on to power and led an armed uprising in July in favour of his daughter-in-law, **Lady Jane Grey**. In the following year, Thomas Wyatt also sought to influence the succession. He feared the consequences of Mary's planned marriage to Philip of Spain, not least the probable exclusion of Princess Elizabeth from the throne. Although the marriage agreement set clear limits on the extent of Philip's influence in England and defined conditions affecting the upbringing of any children, Wyatt and his supporters placed little trust in the Spanish prince. The rebels never admitted they wanted to overthrow Mary, which was a wise insurance policy should their uprising fail, but the prospect of having a future Spanish monarch ruling England had to be guarded against.

Elizabeth I

Getting the rights of a legitimate claimant acknowledged was one of the main objectives of a revolt facing Elizabeth I in 1569. In this case, 'the preservation of the person of the Queen of Scots, as next heir, failing issue of Her Majesty' was an important cause of the Northern Earls' rebellion, according to the Earl of Northumberland.

KEY TERM

Devise The means by which Edward disinherited his half-sisters, Mary and Elizabeth, in favour of Lady Jane Grey.

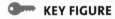

KEY FIGURE

Lady Jane Grey (1537–54)

The great niece of Henry VIII and the granddaughter of Henry VIII's sister, Mary, from her marriage to the Duke of Suffolk.

John Dudley, Duke of Northumberland

1504	Born
1542	Became Viscount Lisle
1547	Became Earl of Warwick on the death of Henry VIII
1549	Crushed Kett's rebellion
	Involved in the removal of Somerset
1550	Appointed Lord President of the Council
1551	Became Duke of Northumberland
1553	Attempted to change the succession and exclude Mary
	Executed

Early career

John Dudley held various posts under Henry VIII, but it was as a soldier during the 1540s that he built his reputation. He was appointed to the Regency Council that ruled following Henry VIII's death. The Duke of Somerset was appointed Lord Protector, but his policies caused unrest in the summer of 1549. This threatened the ruling class and it was Dudley who crushed Kett's rebellion.

Somerset was removed from office in the autumn of 1549 and Dudley replaced him.

Lord President of the Council

Dudley brought stability and ended the costly foreign policies of Somerset.
Historians disagree about Northumberland's conduct while in office. Some see him as a power seeker, others as a typical Tudor statesman who looked to secure his family's position.

Personal advancement

Dudley married off his son, Guildford Dudley, to Lady Jane Grey, Henry VIII's great niece, in May 1553. Edward VI's health deteriorated and this led to the Devise being drawn up, which left the throne to the male heirs of Lady Frances Grey and her daughters. There is debate as to whether this was inspired by Northumberland, to maintain his influence, or Edward, to preserve Protestantism. As Edward's health declined, the Devise was altered so that Lady Jane would succeed. Northumberland had much to gain as his daughter-in-law would become queen. Some have argued that the plot was Edward's idea, claiming that Northumberland would have organised it better, arresting Mary and preventing her from fleeing to her base in East Anglia.

Downfall of Northumberland

Following Edward's death, Jane was proclaimed queen, but Mary raised forces to claim the throne. Northumberland raised troops to confront her, but his forces began to desert and the Privy Council changed their minds and supported Mary. Northumberland abandoned his plan and he proclaimed Mary queen, but he was executed in 1553.

 KEY FIGURE

Mary Stuart or Mary Queen of Scots (1542–87)

Mary had a claim to the English throne as she was the granddaughter of Margaret Tudor, sister of Henry VIII. She was seen as the rightful ruler by many Catholics.

As long as Elizabeth remained unmarried and childless and refused to acknowledge **Mary Stuart**'s claim to the English throne, the succession was in doubt; although whether the rebellious earls wished to bring about Mary's succession prematurely is another matter. They denied treason, of course, claiming that they were 'the Queen's most true and lawful subjects', but given that the penalty for treason was capital punishment, this was to be expected.

The Earl of Essex similarly denied that he wished to harm the queen when he began a rebellion in London in 1601, but he certainly wanted to endear himself to the **heir presumptive**, James VI of Scotland. If Essex could persuade the queen, by force if necessary, to dismiss her advisers and replace them with councillors such as himself, who 'were sympathetic to the prospect of a Scottish monarch', he would be rewarded as the 'kingmaker'.

'Evil councillors'

The accusation that the monarch was surrounded by 'evil councillors' and that he or she preferred to consult 'new' ministers rather than the long-established families of England was a charge frequently made in rebellions:

- In 1497, **Reginald Bray** and **John Morton** were dubbed 'evil advisers' by Cornish rebels.
- In 1525, Suffolk protesters said they were going to 'complain of the Cardinal' (Wolsey) to the king.
- In 1536, Cromwell, Cranmer, Audley and Rich were the targets in ballads and manifestos written by the Pilgrims of Grace.
- In 1554, Thomas Wyatt claimed, 'We seek no harm to the Queen but better counsel and councillors'.
- In 1569, the northern earls held William Cecil responsible for their revolt.
- In 1601, the Earl of Essex aimed to remove Robert Cecil, Elizabeth I's principal adviser.

The claim that 'self-serving upstarts' had deceived the monarch thus appears as a justification for political disturbances throughout the Tudor period.

Each rebel leader appears to have genuinely believed that once royal advisers were removed, then wiser and more effective policies would follow.

If the Pilgrimage of Grace (see page 20) is taken as an illustration, the pilgrims swore an oath to 'expel all **villein** blood and evil councillors against the **commonwealth** from his Grace and his **Privy Council**', and the rebels at York argued that 'persons as be of low birth and small reputation' had exploited their power and 'procured the profits most especially for their own advantage'. It was, of course, true that Cromwell, Cranmer, Audley and Rich were self-made men from politically obscure backgrounds:

- Cromwell had been a merchant and one-time professional soldier.
- Cranmer was a Cambridge academic.
- Audley had been the town clerk in Colchester.
- Rich was a Welsh lawyer.

Lord Darcy was convinced that Cromwell was 'the very original and chief causer of all this rebellion and mischief', whose aim had been to 'bring us to our end and to strike off our heads', although the historian Geoffrey Elton once argued that 'it was the gentry leaders, not the commons, who singled out the hated minister [Cromwell] of the Crown'.

KEY TERMS

Heir presumptive An heir who it was presumed would inherit unless an alternative claimant was subsequently born.

Villein A tenant who was obliged to perform any services that his lord commanded.

Commonwealth The 'wealth' or welfare of the common people.

Privy Council The inner ring of councillors who advised the king.

KEY FIGURES

Reginald Bray (c.1440–1503)
A chief councillor of Henry VII, who looked after the king's estates.

John Morton (c.1420–1500)
Joined Henry Tudor in exile and when Henry became king was appointed Lord Chancellor and then Archbishop of Canterbury. A leading adviser.

Lord Darcy (1467–1537)
Keeper of Pontefract Castle but as he was opposed to the dissolution of the monasteries he handed over the castle to the pilgrims and joined the rebels.

Factions

It was a widely held belief that if there was no parliament and a crisis occurred, then the old nobility should be consulted. Henry VII in fact did do this, holding five Great Councils between 1487 and 1502, but by the 1530s the emergence of a few select advisers, later termed the 'Privy Council', eclipsed this practice and led to the formation of political **factions**.

The Lincolnshire rising and Pilgrimage of Grace

How far events such as the Lincolnshire rising and Pilgrimage of Grace were inspired by disaffected pro-Aragonese supporters at court has been the subject of historical debate. Certainly, Catherine of Aragon's supporters had links with several leading rebels caught up in the rebellion. Among the Lincoln rebels were:

- Sir Robert Dymoke, who had once been her chancellor
- Sir Christopher Willoughby, a knight of the body
- Lord Hussey, chamberlain to Princess Mary.

And in Yorkshire:

- Lord Darcy absented himself from debates in parliament concerning the Act of Succession to avoid arrest.
- Sir Robert Constable fiercely opposed the divorce.

Both became leading pilgrims. This Aragonese faction undoubtedly stood to lose as long as Cromwell remained in favour with the king, but their political grievances were just one of many factors that contributed to the rebellion of 1536.

The reign of Elizabeth I

Factional politics was a principal cause of the two major rebellions in Elizabeth's reign. The northern earls, Westmorland and Northumberland, in 1569, and the Earl of Essex in 1601 were in decline at Whitehall and for similar reasons. Northumberland and Westmorland, together with a handful of southern privy councillors, Arundel, Pembroke, Lumley, Leicester and Throckmorton, schemed to overthrow William Cecil, the queen's secretary. They held him responsible for ill-advised political, religious and foreign policies, and the uncertainty surrounding the succession. Central to their plan was for the Duke of Norfolk, Westmorland's brother-in-law, to marry Mary Queen of Scots, to ensure the continuity of Catholicism. When fear gripped most of the plotters they confessed all they knew and protested their innocence to the queen, but the northern earls unwisely pressed on for personal reasons:

- Westmorland was in financial difficulties and was badgered by his wife to stand up for his beliefs.
- Northumberland, aged 70, was no longer a political force in the north and resented seeing his wardenship of the **middle march** go to a local rival.

The Essex revolt

Political factions were also central to Essex's revolt. Suspended from the Privy Council, banned from the court, charged with treason and in financial difficulties when the queen rescinded his patent to sell sweet wine, Essex's star was falling rapidly in late 1600. 'The queen', he said, 'hath thrust me down to a private life. I cannot serve with base obsequiousness.'

- His clients, such as the earls of Bedford, Rutland and Southampton, still looked to him for patronage but his reputation and credit were in ruin.
- He was up against Robert Cecil who, as Master of the Court of Wards and Chancellor of the Duchy of Lancaster, held all the aces.
- Cecil's clients, like Lord Cobham, Lord Buckhurst and Sir John Stanhope, were in ascendancy and between them dominated court patronage.

In Essex's opinion, Cecil and his clients were 'base upstarts' and 'caterpillars' who were devouring the state's resources for their own profit. Essex planned a demonstration of noble force which he believed the City of London would support and so lead to the queen readmitting him to favour. Essex gambled on his popularity and strength as a factional leader – and lost!

Government intervention

A final political cause of rebellion was the effects that governments had when they began to extend the power of the state into the provinces. As centralisation took hold and the Crown became more omniscient, political and legal privileges were swept away and traditional practices eroded. 'If we may enjoy our old ancient customs', Sir James Layburne of Lancashire declared in 1536, 'we have no cause to rise.' Those most affected by government intervention resided in the more distant parts of England and in Ireland, and as a result these same regions were the areas that were prepared to revolt against Tudor '**despotism**'.

Cornwall and the north of England

The Cornish had no great love for English governments and their rebellions in 1497 and 1549 were partly due to a feeling that they ought to be treated differently from the rest of the country. Similarly, the northern counties consistently complained that they were being ruled by 'strangers', that their wealth was being drained by Londoners, and the traditional nobility had less and less of a say in how the counties north of the River Trent were governed. Stewardships of royal manors, custodianships of castles and the wardenships of the marches were gradually being taken out of their control and manors forcibly given to others by the Crown.

The clergy in the north of England also had grievances. In the 1530s, the ecclesiastical liberties enjoyed by Ripon, Beverley and the Palatinate of Durham were surrendered to the Crown.

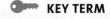 **KEY TERM**

Despotism The government of an absolute ruler who rules without regard for the law.

The uprisings in 1536 (Pilgrimage of Grace) and 1569 (Northern Earls) both petitioned that a parliament should meet in the north, possibly York or Nottingham, to redress local issues, but none was held. The earls in revolt in 1569 made clear their hostility towards the central government when they proclaimed that the aim of their rebellion was 'the restoring of all ancient customs and liberties to God and this noble realm'.

Ireland

Ireland, like the north of England, came increasingly to resent interference from central government in the administration of its affairs. The Tudors had to work with key members of the Anglo-Irish nobility and manage the feuding among rival families as well as possible. Significantly, for the first 50 years of this period, until 1534, the earls of Kildare (a county in Ireland) had acted as the Crown's deputy lieutenants in Ireland, and there were no rebellions. Admittedly, there was considerable corruption and inefficiency, but that was characteristic of the Gaelic way of life during that period, and if it was not ideal at least it worked. Between 1534 and 1603, however, five major rebellions occurred and each can be attributed to political causes.

Silken Thomas's rebellion 1534–7

From 1532, Cromwell started to favour Kildare's rivals for government offices and the current earl began to resent his declining influence in court circles in both London and Dublin. In September 1533, Henry ordered the earl to visit him as he doubted whether he would enforce the break with Rome and **Act in Restraint of Appeals**. The earl replied by sending his wife and in the meantime began to transfer weapons and gunpowder from Dublin Castle to his own estates. A further demand from the king finally brought Earl Kildare to London and once lodged in the Tower, he never left, dying there in 1534. 'Silken Thomas', his son, not surprisingly ignored similar requests to visit London, and he and five of his uncles raised 1000 men in Munster and invaded the **Pale**. Although the rebels called on the Catholic Church for support and condemned Henry's religious reforms, the uprising was primarily political in cause and intent. Thomas's objective was to expel the English administration and become sole ruler of Ireland.

Shane O'Neill's rebellion 1558–67

Shane O'Neill's rebellion between 1558 and 1567 was a complicated affair. He wanted to rule Ulster and was willing to murder his older brother to achieve it, but this only stirred up resentment against him. When he begged forgiveness from Queen Elizabeth, she agreed to recognise him as captain of Tyrone and 'the O'Neill', head of the clan, but he was soon plotting with Charles IX of France and Mary Queen of Scots, and claiming to be the true defender of the faith.

James Fitzmaurice Fitzgerald's first rebellion

O'Neill's rising was quickly followed by two rebellions in Munster led by James Fitzmaurice Fitzgerald. In 1569, he resented attempts by Elizabeth to colonise Ireland and the imposition of **martial law** in the wake of O'Neill's uprising but he was especially aggrieved that his cousin, the Earl of Desmond, had been put in the Tower following a feud with the Butler clan.

Fitzgerald also had a religious pretext, claiming that Elizabeth wanted to introduce 'another newly invented kind of religion', but the main grievance of most rebels was the growing presence of English adventurers in the new **plantations** and their brutal treatment of native Irish.

James Fitzmaurice Fitzgerald's second rebellion

Fitzgerald's second rebellion in 1579 had a more pronounced religious dimension to it, although it was fundamentally about politics. Having returned from Rome and aware of the **Bull of Excommunication** against Elizabeth, he saw an opportunity to rally the Catholic Irish against English rule. Before 1570 no serious effort had been made by English governments to enforce the Protestant faith in Ireland; it would have been unworkable, unwelcome and unwise. Fitzgerald nevertheless played the Catholic card to good effect, but at heart lay his political animosity against the new English settlers and the Dublin administration. Munster, Ulster, Leinster and Connaught rose up in revolt, the pope gave the rising his blessing, and 600 Spanish and Italian troops were despatched to assist.

Tyrone's rebellion: a nation-wide revolt

By the final decade of Elizabeth's reign, it was clear that political tension was gathering once more. The plantations in Connaught and Munster provoked ill-feeling. The new owners:

- raised rents
- claimed land to which they were not entitled
- bribed juries to obtain favourable verdicts.

In addition, government policies of **compositions**, establishing Protestant churches at the expense of Catholics and seizing **attainted lands** from rebels fuelled the resentment.

A system of **garrisons** contained localised disturbances, but Ulster lay largely outside effective English rule. It is ironic that the decision to take Hugh O'Neill, the future Earl of Tyrone, away from Ireland and bring him up in the household of the Earl of Leicester should have backfired so spectacularly. When the earl returned in 1593, he was eager to be recognised as 'the O'Neill', ruler of Ulster. Between 1593 and 1594 he had come to the defence of English garrisons and officials when other clans attacked them, but in his estimation he had not been

KEY TERMS

Martial law Military law that replaces civil law during a political crisis.

Plantations Lands that were confiscated from rebels and granted to English and local landlords at reduced prices.

Bull of Excommunication In 1570, the pope issued a bull of excommunication which freed Catholics from obeying Elizabeth and allowed them to overthrow her.

Compositions Taxes paid instead of having to undertake military service, have soldiers billeted with you, and take part in purveyance or the selling of goods to the Crown at a lower price.

Attainted lands Acts of attainder were passed by parliament on traitors, and their entire property and that of their family were forfeited to the Crown.

Garrisons Fortified towns where soldiers were kept.

adequately rewarded and by 1595 he had had enough. What made his rebellion so different was that it signalled a nation-wide revolt against England that lasted for over eight years. His aim was blatantly political: to expel the new English settlers and Anglo-Irish administration, and to achieve independence.

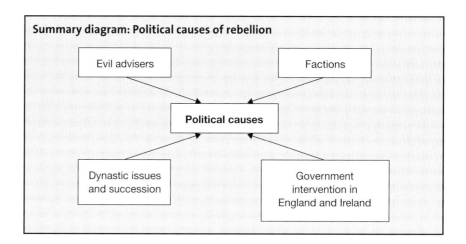

Summary diagram: Political causes of rebellion

2 Religious causes of rebellion

> ▶ Why was religious change the cause of so many rebellions between 1536 and 1569?

The religious changes that begun under Henry VIII signalled a major break with tradition. Generations had been accustomed to traditional Catholic practices and beliefs such as pilgrimages, holy days and purgatory, but their abolition over the course of 30 years created opposition as a centuries-old way of life was attacked, and resulted in a number of religiously motivated rebellions.

Religious devotion was a powerful force in convincing a man that he should rebel against the king. Although the Church upheld law and order and preached obedience to God – for surely rebellion was as much a sin as an act of treason (see page 151) – some clerics nevertheless felt justified in protesting at changes to the traditional Roman Catholic faith, and in 1536, 1549 and 1569, the clergy exhorted true believers to rise up and overthrow Protestant heresy. The rebellions in eastern England in 1549 and Kent in 1554, on the other hand, reflected support for the Protestant faith. In the case of the former, Kett's rebels wanted to advance the Edwardian Reformation more effectively; similarly, in the rebellion of 1554, some of Wyatt's followers were anxious to preserve it in the face of Mary's Counter-Reformation.

Thus, between 1536 and 1569, religious causes played a key role in a number of rebellions. In Ireland, defence of the Church, or more precisely, opposition to Protestant reforms, was the pretext for Kildare's rebellion in the 1530s and four rebellions in Elizabeth's reign, although in each case religion was almost certainly a cloak for political objectives (see pages 22–4).

The Pilgrimage of Grace 1536

The Pilgrimage of Grace is the name given to three separate uprisings, including the Lincolnshire rising, that had overarching causes and which occurred in the northern counties of England.

Religious concerns in northern England

Closing of the monasteries in northern England

In October 1536, uprisings occurred in the adjacent counties of Lincolnshire and Yorkshire which soon spread to most of the north of England. Both had a strong religious undercurrent.

Two sets of ecclesiastical commissioners travelling through Lincolnshire had alarmed many local people: the first was authorised by the Bishop of Lincoln to investigate the condition of the parish clergy; the second was authorised by the government to close down the smaller monasteries (see page 44). Each caused resentment. The rebels from Louth and Horncastle near Lincoln drew up articles requesting that their abbeys should be preserved and wanting guarantees that their parish churches would not be closed as well. They were proud of their 295-foot spire at Louth, completed in 1515, and did not trust the bishop and his chancellor to keep their hands off the church plate and ornaments.

Fears and rumours similar to those in Lincolnshire accompanied risings in Yorkshire. Over 100 monasteries and abbeys were scheduled to be closed and opposition to the dissolution was a dominant factor. The rebels argued that a range of social and economic services would be affected, the poor and children's education would decline, and 'spiritual information and preaching' provided by the monks would disappear. Although such anxieties and claims may have been overstated, the dissolution of the smaller monasteries did motivate many people to protest. In Lancashire, where four monasteries were closed in September 1536, monks encouraged the common people to rise up, protest at the government's religious policy, and assist them in their restoration. Even before trouble broke out in Lincolnshire and Yorkshire, it was suspected that some people in Lancashire were buying up arms.

Heresy

A second concern voiced by rebel groups was that heresy was rife. A diversity of religious beliefs among the king's council and **convocation** was felt by many to encourage heretical ideas, which had to be stopped. Henry no doubt shared this view and had indeed drawn up the **Act of Ten Articles** in July 1536 to clarify the theological position. He would have also agreed that continental reformers such as Luther and Bucer should be identified as heretics, but would

KEY TERMS

Convocation The general assembly of the clergy that usually met when parliament was called.

Act of Ten Articles This Act stressed the importance of baptism, the Eucharist and penance, and put less significance on confirmation, marriage, holy orders and the last rites.

have been surprised to find Rastell and St German named with them as they were both English common lawyers, and he would not condone an attack on his own archbishop Cranmer. Such allegations of heresy, however, reflected the opinions of only a minority of clerics and educated laymen, and interestingly no concern was expressed over the theological attacks on purgatory, which denied its existence.

Government intervention

A third cause of protest was the government's assault on saints, pilgrimages and holy days, which meant a great deal to the people. At Kirkby Stephen in Westmorland, for instance, there was uproar when the priest failed to offer prayers for the forthcoming St Luke's Day, when a fair was scheduled to take place. The Durham protesters carried the banner of St Cuthbert when they marched out of their city and the pilgrims' decision to carry a banner of the Five Wounds of Christ was a further reminder that they were on a pilgrimage, a feature that was later repeated in the Western and Northern Earls' rebellions. English people revered their saints and enjoyed going on pilgrimages, and they were determined to preserve them. The restoration and defence of clerical privileges were also called for; people did not want to pay any more **first fruits and tenths** to the king but they were keen to restore **benefit of clergy** and ecclesiastical liberties. All of these grievances reflected the commons' and clergy's resentment at Cromwell's reforms since 1535. In particular, they resented the part he and Cranmer had played in enacting the divorce and break from Rome, and they wanted the pope restored as head of the Church, claiming that the recent Act of Supremacy was contrary to God's law.

Collectively, these religious issues revealed a wide spectrum of opposition to the Reformation under Henry VIII. Many of the changes had taken place before 1536, but the presence of government and diocesan agents in the autumn brought home to monks, priests, gentry and commons alike the reality of the 'new' reforms.

Different areas had different grievances, which came to be formulated in separate articles as the uprising progressed:

- In Cumberland and the region to the west of the Pennines, there was resentment at **tithes** and the poor quality of many priests (a complaint reminiscent of Kett's rebellion) rather than the closure of the monasteries.
- In neighbouring north Lancashire and much of Yorkshire, the dissolution and the restoration of the true faith were of prime concern.
- In Lincolnshire, it was fear that their parish churches were going to be attacked that evoked their hostility.

The Western rebellion 1549

The reaction of Cornwall, Devon and Norfolk to the Edwardian Reformation in the summer of 1549 demonstrates contrasting experiences and the diversity of belief in the country at that time.

 **KEY TERMS**

First fruits and tenths Taxes on the first year's income of a new bishop and one-tenth of the value of ecclesiastical benefices received by the Crown after the Reformation.

Benefit of clergy The privilege of exemption from trial by a secular court that was allowed in cases of felony to the clergy or to anyone who could read a passage from the Scriptures.

Tithes Payments made by the laity to the parish church of one-tenth of their agricultural profits or personal income.

The Western rebellion was largely the result of religious reforms introduced in June 1549. Thirteen out of 14 articles drawn up by rebel captains at their camp near Exeter show that what they wanted was restoration not reformation, and they marched under the banner of the Five Wounds of Christ.

They rejected everything that was new:

- The English prayer book, which they called 'a Christmas game'.
- The English Bible and the revised liturgy of 1547.
- Apart from the clergy, few would have been able to read or understand the **liturgy** but they knew it was no longer in Latin, and this was unacceptable.

What they did want was:

- the return of papal relics and images
- the restoration of **chantries**
- at least two monasteries in every county
- a Latin Mass that was celebrated with bread only
- a return to the **Act of Six Articles** of 1539.

In this deeply orthodox region, much of the hysteria surrounding the Protestant reforms can be attributed to local priests whom Philip Nichols, a government propagandist, ungenerously called 'whelps of the Romish litter'. There was, however, no direct request to restore the papacy although the first of the Exeter articles, like those of the pilgrims in 1536, challenged the legality of secular authorities to implement religious reform. This, they argued, was the sole right of church councils.

Kett's rebellion 1549

If the Western rebellion was in defence of the old religion, Kett's rebellion was in part a protest at the slow rate of progress Protestantism was making in eastern England.

Unlike other areas of the country, Norfolk had an anticlerical tradition and by 1547 was fertile ground for a proactive Protestant reformation. The Bishop of Norwich, William Rugge, however, was ill-suited to achieve this – he was old and unsympathetic to radical reforms – and there was a strong feeling that the quality of ministers was not good enough to advance the reformation.

The rebels wanted, they said:

- a better educated and resident clergy
- competent teaching of the **catechism and prymer** for children
- good-quality sermons.

If the bishop could not appoint such ministers, then the parishioners would.

There was also resentment at priests who indulged in the property market since they should be devoting their time to spiritual duties, not prosecuting parishioners for unpaid and unfair tithes. The daily services using the new

KEY TERMS

Liturgy An order of church service.

Chantries Chapels where prayers for the souls of the dead were said. Abolished in 1547.

Act of Six Articles This Act upheld the orthodox Catholic faith and remained in force until 1547.

Catechism and prymer A catechism was a book of basic religious instruction in the form of questions and answers; a prymer was an elementary book of religious instruction.

prayer book, conducted under the 'Tree of Reformation' on Mousehold Heath outside Norwich, further testify to the rebels' religious commitment, even if it was economic and social causes that had first brought them to revolt (see pages 40–1).

Wyatt's rebellion 1554

Wyatt's rebellion in Kent in January 1554 took place under the reign of Mary I. Ostensibly, it was caused by secular and political factors yet it also had a religious undercurrent. Significantly, there were no revolts or uprisings in Mary's reign against her Catholic reforms and although it was clear that she intended restoring the old faith and had already reversed many of the Edwardian reforms by the time Wyatt plotted his revolt, he was not a reformer and his agenda was political, not religious. 'You may not so much as name religion', he advised a colleague, 'for that will withdraw from us the hearts of many'.

However, not everyone felt like him. Kent was a strongly Protestant county and had been in the forefront of reform since the 1530s. Many people will have been concerned at Mary's attachment to Roman Catholicism and her intention to marry Philip of Spain. There was also much local support for Protestantism in Maidstone, which supplied 78 rebels, Cranbrook and Tonbridge; and Wyatt's fellow conspirators in Leicestershire (the Duke of Suffolk), Devon (Sir Peter Carew) and Herefordshire (Sir James Croft) had Protestant leanings. Perhaps Wyatt's reluctance to play the religious card was due to his belief that xenophobia would generate greater support nationally.

Invoking the Church certainly worked in some of the Irish rebellions in the later years of Elizabeth's reign, but that was the Catholic Church in a country where the English were detested more than the Spanish. The English, on the other hand, disliked most foreigners and only a minority of Protestants would have felt that the Church and themselves were in danger so early in Mary's reign.

The Northern Earls' rebellion 1569

'Our first object in assembling was the reformation of religion and preservation of the person of the Queen of Scots', declared the Earl of Northumberland under interrogation in 1572. Defence of the Catholic faith, together with personal and political motives, go a long way towards explaining the origins of the Northern Earls' revolt:

- The leading protagonists of the rebellion were Catholic: Northumberland had converted in 1567, and Westmorland was born and bred a Catholic.
- Both men resented the newly appointed Protestant-minded Bishop Pilkington to Durham.
- Rebel proclamations issued at Darlington, Staindrop and Richmond suggest that there was widespread Catholic sentiment. The cause of the rebellion, they declared, was 'a new found religion and heresy, contrary to God's word', which they intended 'amending and redressing'.

Many of the northern aristocratic families had retained the Catholic faith in spite of Elizabethan statutes requiring the regular attendance at church or a fine of 5p a week. Some preferred to pay the fine but others sought protection from justices of the peace (JPs), many of whom were Catholics themselves, and so escaped the law. Wealthier nobles and gentry of course had chapels on their estates and continued to celebrate Mass privately and took communion only once a year at Easter. For ten years the government made no concerted attempt to enforce the **Act of Uniformity** despite the general feeling that little progress had been made in the north to advance Christianity of any kind. Sir Ralph Sadler, a privy councillor who knew the north of England well, informed Cecil in London that 'the common people are ignorant, superstitious and altogether blinded with the old **popish** doctrine, and therefore so favour the cause which the rebels make the colour of their rebellion, that, though their persons be here with us, their hearts are with them'.

The Earl of Sussex, President of the Council of the North, on the other hand, believed that religion was a cloak for political motives, which the earls had used to rally popular support. Recent research has also cast doubt on Sadler's claim that the old faith 'still lay like lees at the bottom of men's hearts and if the vessel was ever so little stirred came to the top'.

Yet many of the rebels are known to have been sincere in their attachment to the old faith:

- Some, like the Nortons from Ripon, the Inglebys of Ripley and Cholmeleys from Whitby, had ancestors who had taken part in the Pilgrimage of Grace.
- The banner of St Cuthbert was taken out of Durham Cathedral and Francis Norton paraded with the Five Wounds of Christ, just as he had done 30 years before.
- Recently returned from the continent were Thomas Markenfeld and Nicholas Morton in anticipation of an armed uprising. Morton appears to have been a prime mover in warning hesitant rebels that if they did not fight there were 'dangers touching our souls and the loss of our country', and left it to them to weigh up the consequences of inactivity.

It is likely therefore that many northern peasants at least revered the old customs, pilgrimages and celebration of holy days, even if they had little understanding of or affection for the Mass. Of course, some tenants and employees of powerful magnates and gentry had little choice in the matter and were forced to follow their masters, but 90 per cent of the known rebels were not tenants of the leaders and presumably joined in for entirely non-feudal reasons.

 **KEY TERMS**

Act of Uniformity An Act that enforced the Protestant prayer book, which was first introduced in 1549, and modified in 1552 and 1559. It imposed punishments on those who did not conform.

Popish A derogatory term for anything that appeared to be Catholic or inspired by the pope.

Summary diagram: Religious causes of rebellion

Year	Name of rebellion	Catholic or Protestant?	Reason	Local or regional?	Religion – main or subsidiary cause?
1536	Pilgrimage of Grace	Catholic	Reaction to the closure of monasteries and other Protestant reforms	Regional in seven northern counties	Main
1549	Western rebellion	Catholic	Reaction to a new English prayer book	Local to Devon and Cornwall	Main
1549	Kett's rebellion	Protestant	Demanded further Protestant reforms	Local to Norfolk	Subsidiary
1554	Wyatt's rebellion	Protestant	Fear of Catholic reformation	Local to Kent	Subsidiary
1569	Northern Earls' rebellion	Catholic	Reaction to Protestant reforms	Regional in four northern counties	Main

 # Economic and social causes of rebellion

▶ *To what extent did the causes of economic and social rebellions change during the Tudor period?*

In the majority of cases, rebellion and disorder were the product of political and religious causes, yet underlying many of the riots and disturbances that afflicted Tudor England throughout the period – some of which became full-blown rebellions – were economic and social tensions. These were the triggers that sparked off disturbances at a local level and, if not well handled, could spiral out of control and become a far more serious rebellion. In contrast, economic and social issues rarely figured overtly in Irish rebellions; and, when they did, they were inseparable from underlying political issues.

Taxation

Government taxation was the single most important cause of popular protest in early Tudor England. In this respect, it was no different from the **Peasants' revolt** of 1381, which followed a decade of financial demands, or **Cade's rebellion** in London in 1450, after a period of heavy taxation. In 1489 (Yorkshire), 1497 (Cornwall) and 1525 (Amicable Grant), taxation was the main cause of rebellion and a contributing factor, albeit minor, in bringing about the Pilgrimage of Grace and the Western rebellion. Tax collectors were often

 **KEY TERMS**

Peasants' revolt In 1381, peasants in Kent and Essex led by Wat Tyler and John Ball marched on London, in protest against a poll tax and calling for the abolition of serfdom.

Cade's rebellion Jack Cade led a revolt in Kent that briefly occupied London before being defeated in battle. The rebels were protesting at high taxes and governmental incompetence.

assaulted and locally people frequently claimed they were too poor or not willing to pay. In 1515, Henry VIII remitted (returned) payments from nineteen Yorkshire towns and villages as they were so impoverished, and according to a survey of 1522, one-third of people in Exeter and Leicester escaped on account of poverty. Generally, around 60 per cent of the adult male population was liable for taxation, but it was levied only occasionally when there was an emergency. Ordinarily the monarch was expected to 'live of his own' and not require parliamentary taxation.

The Yorkshire rebellion 1489

In 1489 and 1497, objections came from Yorkshire and Cornwall, respectively, about having to pay a tax for a war that did not concern them. Parliament had voted to allow Henry VII £100,000 to meet the costs of a campaign against France but the prevailing view in Yorkshire was that the tax was unfair:

- Traditionally, people in the south funded wars against France while the most northern counties met the cost of defending the Scottish border.
- Moreover, the counties of Northumberland, Westmorland and Cumberland had been exempted by the king on account of poverty.
- The protesters were also affected by a bad harvest in 1488 and took exception to the news that the unpopular Henry Percy, Earl of Northumberland, would lead the tax commission.

It has been suggested that the murder of Percy, which had sparked off the revolt, was orchestrated by the king to take over Percy's lands and gain control of the north but there is no extant evidence to support this theory. The earl was very unpopular but so was the prospect of paying taxation.

The Cornish rebellion 1497

The Cornish revolt arose from similar circumstances to those of the one in Yorkshire. In January 1497, parliament had voted for £60,000 to fund a war against the Scots and when news reached Cornwall in May, there was widespread anger. According to the chronicler, Holinshed, the rebels wanted 'to punish those responsible for the tax imposed on the people without any reasonable cause'. They explained with some justification that customarily wars against Scotland were paid by a **scutage** or land tax and only by the four northern counties. Perhaps they recalled the protest in Yorkshire, and if they could get away with not paying a war tax, why not the Cornish? Two councillors were blamed: John Morton, the Lord Chancellor, and Reginald Bray, the king's chief financial adviser who had been responsible for finding ways of increasing revenue from the royal estate in the 1490s.

In fact, the 1497 parliamentary grant was an innovation. The traditional fifteenth (payable by each village or civil parish) and tenth (payable by each borough) were levied as usual at rates that had been set in 1334, but in addition it was agreed that a further grant of £60,000 would be collected if war actually

 **KEY TERM**

Scutage Rather than fight in person for the king in times of war, tenants-in-chief could commute their feudal obligations into a tax known as a scutage or 'escuage'.

broke out and this money would be levied on individuals at rates assessed by royal commissioners. There is nothing to suggest that the Cornish rebels were protesting at the novelty of the tax, but members of parliament (MPs), gentry, merchants and clergy who were most affected would no doubt have had some misgivings. In fact, war did not break out and the second tax was not collected.

The Amicable Grant 1525

On four occasions, the Tudors attempted to levy taxation without parliament's consent: in 1491, 1525, 1544–6 and 1594–9. On each instance England was at war but only once did the levy lead to rebellion. The Amicable Grant was a non-parliamentary tax which commissioners were ordered to collect in the spring of 1525. Objections to paying it were widespread for a number of reasons:

KEY FIGURE

Thomas Wolsey (1472–1530)

The son of a butcher, he rose to be Lord Chancellor, cardinal and Henry VIII's chief adviser. However, his background and wealth made him unpopular with the nobility.

KEY TERM

Laity People who were not clergy.

- In 1522, **Thomas Wolsey** had raised £260,000 in forced loans, which he said would be repaid out of the next parliamentary subsidy. This had not happened and understandably caused resentment.
- In 1523, Wolsey had tried to get parliament to vote a subsidy of £800,000 but it offered only £151,000 payable over four years. The Church was also expected to pay about £120,000.
- The Amicable Grant (which was far from amicable) made excessive demands on the **laity** and clergy alike. Since 1513, Wolsey had introduced tax assessments based on land, income and personal assets, and collected whichever yielded the highest tax.
- Assessments were made by government officials and so ended the principle of paying a fixed rate. The laity were now required to pay a special tax of five per cent if they were rated below £20, 7.5 per cent if rated at between £20 and £50, and 16.5 per cent if rated above £50 a year. Many of the protesters would have been paying tax for the first time at rates they could ill afford.
- The clergy were hit even harder. They were to pay at a rate of 25 per cent of their annual revenue or value of their movable goods worth less than £10, and 33 per cent for those above £10.
- There was a grave shortage of coinage, which is why the government urgently needed to collect the tax, and rising unemployment following a fall in wool prices added to the economic distress.

Protesters in Suffolk claimed, perhaps disingenuously, that 'only for lack of work prevented them from paying'. As they explained to the Duke of Norfolk, 'since you ask who is our captain, for sooth his name is Poverty, for he and his cousin Necessity, have brought us to this doing'.

It seems clear that the grant, coming on top of recent tax demands and at a time of worsening economic conditions, triggered off the rebellion. Any suggestion that the grant may have been unconstitutional – a view put forward by some historians – did not figure in the rebels' complaints.

The Pilgrimage of Grace 1536

Of the many sets of articles drawn up by the pilgrims in 1536, only one concerned taxation. Item 14 of the Pontefract Articles requested 'to be discharged on the quindene [fifteenth] and taxes now granted by act of parliament'. The rebels did not want to have to pay the taxes due from the Subsidy Act of 1534.

Articles presented by rebels in the West Riding of Yorkshire argued that the king was only allowed to collect taxes in defence of the realm, whereas the preamble to the Act claimed that costs incurred in the defence of the realm were the same as if the country was at war and, since the country owed Henry a debt of gratitude, this debt could now be repaid in taxation.

In Lincolnshire, where rebellions in 1536 first began, it may have been rumours that the tax was a prelude to further fiscal exactions, such as a tax on white meat and horned cattle, that alarmed people so much.

In reality, the subsidy's yield of £80,000 was comparatively small and affected only a few people, but many rebels claimed they could not afford it. Although attempts to collect taxes in peacetime would also be made in 1540 and 1553, the 1534 subsidy was the only one that provoked a popular protest.

The Western rebellion 1549

The Duke of Somerset's Subsidy Act of 1549 had a dual objective:

- to raise as much money as possible at a time of acute shortage
- to encourage more farmers to return their lands to tillage.

To achieve these ends, a tax of 1*d.* (0.42p) on a sheep and 1/2*d.* (0.21p) on every pound of woollen cloth was levied on pasture farmers and cloth producers. In practice, the tax hit poorer peasants and tenants most of all as wealthy clothiers and sheep farmers raised their prices to offset its cost. The West Country was, of course, not the only sheep-farming region but Devon was a largely enclosed county and was affected more than most. Moreover, the tax was due to be assessed two weeks after the introduction of the English prayer book and so added to their list of grievances against the government.

Enclosures

The act of enclosing a field with a hedge, fence or ditch, or amalgamating two farms and enclosing them (known as engrossment) was not a major cause of rebellion but it could cause tension between landowners and tenants, provoke local disturbances and riots, and occasionally lead to something more serious. This is what happened in 1536, 1549 and 1596.

The Pilgrimage of Grace 1536

Only one of the articles presented to the 'Lords of the King's Council' at Pontefract in 1536 cited enclosure as a cause of the Pilgrimage of Grace. Item 13 called for:

> *Statute for enclosures and intakes to put in execution, and that all intakes [and] enclosures since 1489 to be pulled down except [in] mountains, forest and parks.*

There was much rioting over illegal enclosures in the course of 1535 and it is likely that this was a common grievance among particular northern rebels. For example:

- over 300 people at Giggleswick in Yorkshire pulled down hedges and dykes
- there were riots at Fressington in Cumberland.

Both areas sent rebels in the following year to attack the lands of the Earl of Cumberland, a notorious landlord who had enclosed his tenants' lands in the Eden Valley and denied them grazing rights. **Husbandmen** at Horncastle in Lincolnshire were also concerned at the encroachment of tenants' rights, although this was a minor grievance among the commons.

Kett's rebellion 1549

Kett's rebellion at first sight appears to have been caused by unlawful enclosures. Articles 1 and 3 of 'Kett's Demands Being in Rebellion' of July 1549 declared:

> *We pray your grace that where it is enacted for enclosing that it be not hurtful to such as have enclosed saffron grounds [that is lands where saffron was grown] for they be greatly chargeable to them, and that from henceforth no man shall enclose any more.*

> *We pray your grace that no lord of the manor encloses the common land.*

The rebellion was triggered by a local incident between two rival landowners, Robert Kett and John Flowerdew. Both had recently enclosed their lands and Flowerdew, Norfolk's **feodary**, was not popular in Wymondham and nearby Attleborough, where rioting began. Kett, who had the presence of mind to dismantle his own fences before the locals did it for him, became the spokesman for the rebels. What had sparked this peasant revolt were allegations that landlords had been deliberately obstructing a government commission that was investigating illegal enclosures. The rebels believed that they would have the backing of the government if they were to take the law into their own hands. Similar riots and hedge-breaking occurred in Sussex, Kent, Cambridgeshire, the Midlands and south-west counties, but it was in Norfolk where riots turned to open rebellion.

Norfolk was a densely populated county, and good, flat, fertile land was scarce. Many tenant farmers actually favoured enclosure because it denied their landlords the ancient right of **folding** their sheep and cattle on the tenants'

KEY TERMS

Husbandmen Small farmers or landowners of a lower social standing than yeomen.

Feodary An officer of the court of wards, which looked after the lands of minors.

Folding Allowing cattle and sheep to graze and manure the land.

arable fields and only opposed enclosure when they were denied this practice. This, in part, explains why Kett was keen to maintain enclosures where saffron, a flower that produced a yellow dye used in the local cloth industry, was grown, so that landlords could not fold their animals on the land and damage such a valuable crop. On the other hand, there was general concern at wealthy landowners, such as lords of the manor who had extensive private estates, pasturing their flocks on common land, which was in short supply.

We have already seen above that Article 3 declared:

> *We pray your grace that no lord of no manor shall common upon the commons.*

Article 29 also stated:

> *We pray that no lord, knight, esquire nor gentleman do graze nor feed any bullocks or sheep if he may spend £40 a year by his lands only for the provision of his house.*

The **overstocking** of common land was a widespread complaint, but one that did not necessarily infringe the law. What was unacceptable to peasants in Norfolk was that when they had turned to the legal system to try to prevent the gentry from putting large numbers of animals on the common land, it had let them down. In the 1540s, Norfolk peasants from Hingham and Great Dunham had prosecuted their landlords for grazing animals on common land, but without success. Magistrates were usually landlords themselves and either knew or sympathised with the landowners involved.

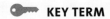 **KEY TERM**

Overstocking Putting too many animals on the land.

1549: The 'year of commotion'

Disturbances occurred in different areas of the country in 1549 when peasants felt they could not get justice lawfully:

- In Somerset, for instance, disturbances occurred when open fields were converted into deer parks.
- At Wilton in Wiltshire, peasants removed Lord Herbert's hedges that he had put up on common land.
- Serious riots in Sussex were only prevented when the Earl of Arundel forced 'certain gentlemen, and chiefly for enclosures' to dismantle their hedges.

Only in low-lying sheep-corn areas in much of the Midlands, East Anglia, southern and south-east England might enclosure become a grievance. Some counties were more affected than others. Northamptonshire, Oxfordshire and Buckinghamshire consistently experienced disturbances. In Leicestershire, 30 per cent of land was enclosed but this was exceptional and nationally only three per cent of most seriously affected counties were enclosed under the Tudors. In most of the country, in areas of forests, fens, moorlands and uplands, enclosure was not a live issue. If enclosures were achieved by mutual consent among neighbours or if enclosures posed no threat to their livelihood, they were likely to be accomplished without objection. And in the opinion of a contemporary writer, Thomas Smith, husbandmen were just as likely to do this as the yeomen and gentry:

> *Every day some of us enclose a plot of his ground to pasture, and were it not that our ground lies in the common fields, intermingled one with another, I think also our fields had been enclosed, of a common agreement of all the township, long ere this time.*

The Oxfordshire rebellion 1596

As population levels started to rise in the second half of the sixteenth century, pressure on land for food and work increased, and the enclosure of common land, whether agreed amicably among farmers or enforced illegally by greedy landlords, was seen by the distressed groups as the cause of their grief. For much of this period, grain prices rose ahead of wool prices and enclosures attracted less critical attention. By the 1590s, however, private profit was replacing communal cooperation.

Allegations that common lands had been fenced off, villagers denied rights of pasturage and land converted from arable to pasture lay behind the food riots in the south-west and south-east of England in 1595 and the enclosure rebellion in Oxfordshire in the following year.

In 1593, the government had felt reasonably confident that restrictions on enclosing open fields, which had been in place for nearly half a century, could be lifted 'because of the great plenty and cheapness of grain'. A run of good harvests and pressure from landowners to bring more marginal and wasteland under cultivation saw new enclosures at Hampton Gay and Hampton Poyle in Oxfordshire.

Yet the government's optimism was misplaced. Three years later, four men gathered at Enslow Hill with the intention of seizing arms and artillery from the home of Lord Norris, the Lord Lieutenant of Oxford, and marching to London. They expected to be accompanied by many more protesters but no one else joined in. Although the Privy Council feared that similar plans existed to seize food supplies and attack gentry and their farms, no further disturbances occurred. In reality, this 'rebellion' was untypical of the second half of the sixteenth century but as the **Midland revolt** in 1607 demonstrated, it did not mean that enclosures could not be a cause of rebellion in the future.

Famine and disease

On average, one in four harvests in Tudor England failed and when this happened mortality rates increased. However, if there was a series of poor or bad harvests, then economic and social problems occurred as well and this could result in open rebellion. The most serious crop failures were in 1555–6 and 1596–7, but the years 1519–21, 1527–9, 1544–5, 1549–51 and 1586–7 were also periods when wheat harvests were poor. Famines usually lasted for two years

 **KEY TERM**

Midland revolt A serious peasant uprising in Leicestershire against landlords who enclosed common fields and converted them from arable to pasture.

before grain prices fell and food, if available, came within the budget of most people's pockets. What is interesting is that apart from the brief flashpoint in Oxfordshire in November 1596, poor harvests, dearth and the resulting famine were not responsible for any other rebellion under the Tudors. In fact, good harvests occurred on the eve of rebellions in 1536, 1546–8 and 1567–9.

The worst harvests in the sixteenth century took place in 1555 and 1556 and coincided with an influenza epidemic that may have killed six per cent of the population, but there were no uprisings or stirrings. Nevertheless, an armed riot could readily be provoked by deprivation and hunger, and, in conjunction with other grievances, could be transformed into more aggressive and prolonged disturbances. William Cecil was in no doubt that shortages of food would lead to unrest, commenting 'nothing will sooner lead men into sedition than dearth of victual'.

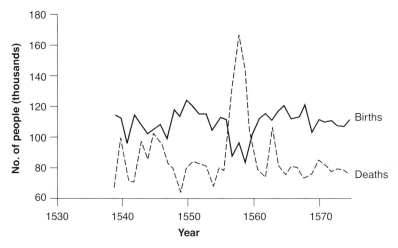

Figure 1.2 Births and deaths in England 1539–70.

Between 1485 and 1528 there were four major outbreaks of plague and the English 'sweat' was particularly virulent during this period:

- The 'great sweat' of 1551 is known to have killed thousands.
- London lost 20,000 people in 1563.
- Bristol suffered badly in 1565 and 1575.
- Hull was hit in 1575–6 and 1582.
- Norwich may have lost as many as ten per cent of its citizens in 1579–80.

It was exceptional, however, for a town to suffer a mortality and subsistence crisis simultaneously. Upland areas, where there was marginal land and often grain shortages, were rarely affected by plague or disease. Conversely, towns and cities, where the population was denser, were prone to spreading contagious diseases but food supplies were generally good due to the proximity to ports and nearby areas of mixed farming. Ninety per cent of the people lived in the countryside and most were concentrated in the south-east and outskirts of

London. Moreover, in times of widespread dearth and famine, starving people made poor rebels and farmers tended to stay at home to look after their cattle or to harvest their crops. In addition, the gentry and landowners, who might have led protests or uprisings, stood to gain from high prices at times of bad harvests, so the likelihood of rebellions occurring was slim.

Food riots did occur in the last two decades of Elizabeth's reign:

- Gloucestershire, Wiltshire and Somerset in 1586
- Kent and Essex in 1595
- Sussex, Norfolk, Kent and the south-west in 1596.

None of these resulted in an armed rebellion.

Inflation

The price rise, especially in the cost of grain, which afflicted much of the Tudor period, was not a major cause of disturbance. In the early Tudor years, population levels were only just recovering from the bubonic plague in the fourteenth century. The country's population stood at around 2 million in 1485. A shortage of labour meant that wages, especially for agricultural workers, were high and land rents comparatively low. Landlords had regularly granted long leases of 99 years, which by the early sixteenth century still had many years to run. Rents were usually fixed according to customary practices and although **entry fines** could reflect market conditions, they were rarely more than two years' rent. There were therefore sufficient employment opportunities in the countryside and towns and standards of living appear to have been rising. These were not conditions likely to give rise to popular unrest, although that was to change.

Impact of price inflation

As the population rose to over 4 million by the end of the sixteenth century, demand for food, work and land increased, which served as an accelerant to **inflation**. Among those who gained were:

- landlords who bought vacant farms at low prices
- landlords who invested in trade or modernised their estates
- freeholders who passed on any increase in prices to their tenants
- clothiers who took advantage of the growth in the woollen cloth market and expanded their businesses
- speculators who invested in property, hoarded grain supplies and profited from changing economic conditions.

The main losers were wage earners, day labourers, journeymen and **tenants at will**, who could be evicted without notice. These people found that their wages failed to keep pace with prices, employment opportunities declined, and waste

 **KEY TERMS**

Entry fine A fee paid by tenants when renewing their lease that allowed them to re-enter their property.

Inflation A rise in prices and an accompanying fall in the purchasing power of money.

Tenants at will Tenants who could be ejected from their land at the will of their landlord when their lease expired.

and marginal land, on which many depended in times of hardship, disappeared. These were the preconditions for economic and social disorder that prevailed in some parts of the country in the 1530s–1550s and 1580s–1590s, and which erupted into violence in 1536 and 1549.

Price inflation in the 1536 rebellion

Both Aske and Kett referred to the impact that inflation was having on the price of land. Indeed, inflation was hitting the north so much that if the monasteries were to close, Aske claimed, 'there should be no money nor treasure in those parts, neither the tenant to have to pay his rents to the lord, nor the lord to have money to do the King service'. There was general anxiety that the dissolution would result in considerable hardship for the poor and for those dependent on charitable giving. On average, as little as three per cent of monastic wealth went towards the poor but this was vital for those people who lived in almshouses and hospitals or who relied on dole money and alms. If Lancashire is taken as an example, Cartmel Priory gave ten per cent of its income in alms and Furness Abbey housed thirteen paupers and doled out £12 a year to eight local widows.

Hospitality for travellers was also particularly useful to 'strangers and baggers of corn' travelling between Yorkshire, Lancashire, Kendal, Westmorland and Durham, and the government's concern to ensure there was adequate shelter and provision for merchants in the north accounts for the temporary continuation of some of the smaller monasteries. Robert Southwell, who was a Lancashire commissioner in 1537, later reflected that there might not have been a rebellion if 'some small part of the demesnes upon their suit to the Council [had been] distributed to the poor'.

Unlike many monastic houses in the south, those in the north of England still played an important part in the lives of many people and, at a time of rising food prices, many poor turned to them in their hour of need.

Table 1.1 The relationship between the rapid rise in the price of foodstuffs and the comparatively slow rise in industrial products and agricultural wages between 1491 and 1570 (1491–1500 = 100 per cent)

Decade	Foodstuffs	Industrial products	Agricultural wages
1491–1500	100	97	101
1501–10	106	98	101
1511–20	116	102	101
1521–30	159	110	106
1531–40	161	110	110
1541–50	217	127	118
1551–60	315	186	160
1561–70	298	218	177

Social issues

The Pilgrimage of Grace

Among Aske's complaints in 1536 was a practice known as rack-renting. On the expiry of a lease, unscrupulous landlords had raised their rents at rates greater than the customary entry fine. In the sixteenth century, rents in the estates belonging to Henry Clifford, Earl of Cumberland, had risen eightfold and tenants unable to pay were evicted. Aske wanted the fine, known in many northern parts as a 'gressum', to be statutorily fixed at two years' rent. Henry Percy, Earl of Northumberland, had also raised the entry fines on his properties in Yorkshire, although his tenants had refrained from turning against him.

Excessive rents also figured among Kett's articles in 1549. Rents had increased by 30 per cent since 1548 and a number of landlords had revived old feudal dues such as **castleward**. Copyholders and freeholders had also complained that they had been forced off their lands. Landlords were accused of buying land and altering tenancy conditions to their own advantage. As a result, common people were denied the right to catch rabbits and fish the rivers.

The right to hunt with handguns and crossbows was also defended in Aske's articles of complaint.

The gentry and lesser nobles had a social grievance of their own. In 1536, the government passed the Statute of Uses, which forced landowners to keep their estates as a single block rather than divide them among several heirs or grant part of an estate to a younger son or daughter. In law, only the eldest son or daughter was entitled to inherit land, and **feudal dues** such as **wardship** were payable to the Crown upon inheritance. In recent times, hard-pressed landowners, keen to evade these dues and wanting to divide up their lands, had transferred the legal ownership of land to **feoffees** by a device known as the 'use'. Aske himself was a feoffee of two sets of estates. Cromwell was equally keen to extract every payment due to the Crown and close this legal loophole, which angered many younger sons of nobles and gentry. They therefore found themselves fighting on the same side as the poorer commoners in 1536, but for different purposes.

Kett's rebellion 1549

Economic and social issues were the principal causes of Kett's rebellion in Norfolk – seventeen out of 29 of his demands were focused on enclosures, rents and landlords – but here the gentry received no sympathy from the rebels and the rebellion was as close to a class war as any in the sixteenth century.

To understand this, we need to recognise that the majority of the land was held by a small number of gentry and lesser nobles. Norwich, the county town, was the second largest city in England with about 13,000 people but its principal source of employment, the worsted cloth industry, was in decline and, as demand for its material fell, unemployment levels rose.

 **KEY TERMS**

Castleward Tenants had once been required to defend Norwich Castle but this military service was later commuted to paying a rent.

Feudal dues Financial rights and powers that the king had over the nobility.

Wardship The Crown acted as the guardian of the son or daughter of a deceased tenant-in-chief until he or she came of age at 21.

Feoffees Property trustees and administrators.

The situation in the countryside was little better. Wheat prices increased by 50 per cent in 1548, enclosures were rife and the people had lost all confidence in the governing classes to protect their welfare. Many of the 46 gentry and merchants who held more than 60 per cent of the land in Norfolk were JPs or had connections to local and county authorities and ensured their interests were well served.

Not surprisingly, the rebels wanted to return to the good old days when Henry VII reigned and to 'redress and reform all such good laws, statutes, proclamations, and all other your proceedings, which have been bid [forbidden] by your Justices of your peace, reeves, **escheators**, and others your officers, from your poor commons'.

A unique feature of Kett's rebellion was a request that 'all bond men may be made free'. **Bondmen or serfs** were a legacy from feudal times and few are known to have existed by the beginning of the Tudor age. The reference, however, may have been to tenants serving on the 40 manors belonging to the Howard family. Thomas Howard, Duke of Norfolk, and his son, the Earl of Surrey, had been arrested in 1546 and their estates administered by the Crown. Perhaps little had changed by 1549 when Kett's request was made. Certainly, tenants were paying high rents, **inquisition fines** were exacted and wardship was levied, but this also happened elsewhere. It is far more likely that the legally minded Kett sought to eliminate an anomaly and safeguard the future tenure of all tenants in Norfolk.

The Western rebellion 1549

Significantly, the Western rebels made no complaints about enclosures or rack-renting although, like everyone else, they were concerned at rising food and wool prices, which made enclosures more profitable. It has already been pointed out that their main economic concern was the novel tax on sheep and wool introduced in 1548.

If their economic problems were not the same or as acute as those facing tenants and landholders in Norfolk, both sets of rebels bore some resentment towards the gentry. In Devon and Cornwall they wished to limit the size of gentry households worth 100 marks (£66) to one servant and expressed concern at how local gentry were enriching themselves by purchasing Church lands. This condemnation seems little more than an attack of envy at the growing wealth of the gentry, but it may also have reflected concern at the perceived loyalty shown by a servant to his lord rather than to the community as a whole.

But whereas the Western rebels wanted to restore the Catholic Church and its lands to the rightful owners and had the support of local clergy and the commons, the Norfolk rebels were intent on narrowing the gap between the privileged few and unprivileged many, which seemed to be widening. Both sets of rebels, however, contained radical elements who professed a desire to 'kill all the gentlemen'. We cannot say whether this was an empty gesture or a serious threat but it served to underline the tension that existed between the commons and the gentry.

 **KEY TERMS**

Escheators County officials responsible for overseeing Crown lands and collecting feudal payments such as wardships and escheats.

Bondmen or serfs Slaves.

Inquisition fines Fees paid for an enquiry and valuation of a deceased person's estate who was believed to hold freehold land in chief of the Crown.

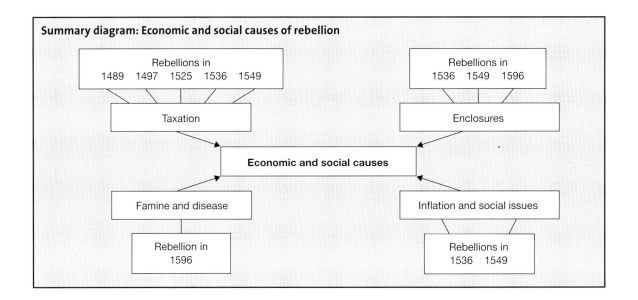

Summary diagram: Economic and social causes of rebellion

 ## Conclusion: why did rebellions occur?

▶ *Why is it so difficult to determine the causes of Tudor rebellions?*

Mono-causal or multi-causal?

It should be clear from the analysis of Tudor rebellions on the preceding pages that only a few had a single cause. Taxation, dynastic and Irish political revolts may be categorised as having predominantly one cause but most rebellions occurred for a number of reasons:

- Religious issues, mainly Catholics vying with Protestants, were evident in most of the uprisings in England between 1536 and 1569, but political factors were also present.
- Dynastic causes were most prominent in Henry VII's reign, yet concern over the succession was a constant theme throughout the period and in later years assumed religious connotations.
- Economic and social problems were most acute in the mid-sixteenth century and underpinned a host of revolts in 1549.

Yet, while it is the historian's task to try to make sense of events and to prioritise their causes, it should be remembered that determining the motives of rebels and their responses to developments is not an exact science. The vast majority of rebels left no record of why they rebelled: we know that some in Yorkshire in 1536 and 1569 were forced by their landlords to take part, some were paid to join in at Maidstone in 1554 and Durham in 1569, and some at Louth in 1536 are known to have participated out of adventure.

Our understanding of why rebellions began is not helped by 'official' accounts sponsored by the government. For example, in 1554 John Proctor claimed in his official *Historie of Wyates rebellion* that the rebels were solely motivated by xenophobia, which is precisely what Mary and her advisers wanted people to believe. Catholicism must not be seen to be under attack, yet it is apparent that a number of rebels were Protestants, some of the gentry saw rebellion as a way of enhancing their political prospects at court and in the county, while unemployed cloth workers who participated had their own social and economic grievances. One cause alone, no matter how 'official' an account may be, does not explain this rebellion.

The role of rumour

Rumour undoubtedly played a key part in bringing about a rebellion. Fear, and the anger which it engendered, lay behind many revolts:

- In Yorkshire in 1536, people believed that their parish plate and jewels were going to be seized, their churches destroyed, taxes imposed on christenings, marriages and burials, and laws passed prohibiting the eating of white bread, geese and chickens. And once an uprising began, news spread to neighbouring areas and triggered further disturbances, often out of solidarity with their fellow commons.
- In 1549, stories circulated the south-west of England that babies would be baptised only on Sundays, which would put the soul of a dying child in peril.
- In King's Lynn in Norfolk, it was alleged that gentlemen's servants had 'killed poor men in their harvest work and also killed women there with child'.

Rumours, once begun, were hard to stop and quickly proved infectious. Fear that Spain would take over the country if Philip married Mary was translated into fact in Kent and Devon on the eve of Wyatt's rebellion. Over 100 Spaniards armed with '**harness, arquebuses and morions, with matchlight**' were reported to have occupied Rochester in the dead of night and it was rumoured in Plymouth that they planned to rape all the women in Devon.

Uncovering the motives

What was recorded in the rebels' demands and in the subsequent depositions and confessions of leaders reflects the interests of the literate minority who may or may not have been speaking on behalf of the majority of those who took part. And, of course, they may have been biased or lying! What remained of the Earl of Essex's declining reputation took a further knock when he later confessed that he had lied under examination. When we try to assess the relative importance of a particular cause in bringing about a rebellion, we should perhaps ask 'importance to whom?' To the gentry, clergy, lawyers or commons?

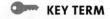 **KEY TERM**

Harness, arquebuses and morions, with matchlight
Body armour, long-barrelled handguns, metal helmets, and fuses to ignite the arquebuses.

If we take the Pilgrimage of Grace as an illustration, the tenants on Clifford's estates in Westmorland were mainly concerned about the unfair rents and entry fines levied by the earl. In Cumberland, the Penrith rebels were most concerned about endemic thieving and robbery. In northern Lancashire, disturbances were inspired more by the threatened closure of monasteries, but people in the south of the county felt less concerned and none of them joined the rebellion. Across the Pennines on the Percy estates in Yorkshire and Durham, tenant–landlord relations were not an issue, and instead peasants joined their landlords in protesting at a range of government policies. At the same time, none of the peasants would have had the slightest interest in the Statute of Uses or the high fees charged by feodaries and escheators. These were the concern of lawyers and gentry. And only the most erudite of theologians would have been in a position to demand the condemnation as heretics of continental reformers such as **Melanchthon** and **Oecolampadius**, but this is what the Lincolnshire clerics insisted Aske should do when he presented his articles at York. Nevertheless, there was much common ground between the different groups and areas of disturbance from which rebels were recruited. 'Each professed to be a rising of the commons', writes the historian Michael Bush (1996), 'each was similarly marked by a concern for both the Faith of Christ and the Commonwealth; each hated the government for being extortionate and heretical.'

Underlying issues and short-term causes

Historians should also try to separate underlying (long-term) issues, which may go back a long way, from short-term causes that usually trigger rebellions. At times this is feasible, although there are difficulties in attempting such an analysis. Rebellions caused by religious reforms, for example, can usually be traced back to the reform itself. The presence of commissioners in 1536 surveying the smaller monasteries in the northern counties led to an immediate reaction, and four days before the new prayer book was due to be used in Bodmin and the day after it was first used at Sampford Courtenay in June 1549, violence broke out in the West Country. The dissolution of the chantries, on the other hand, should remind us that not all religious reforms evoked immediate popular revolts. The Act of 1547 was implemented in the spring of 1548 but no rebellions occurred (in spite of their universal popularity at this time) until the following year, and then only in the western counties.

Social and economic factors often took a long time before they had an impact on society. Population levels had been steadily rising since the end of the fifteenth century, although their real effects were not felt until the 1540s. Pressure for work and demand for food were added to the increasing shortage of land, all of which contributed to the rising cost of living. Contemporaries, looking for immediate causes, understandably focused on enclosures and sheep and blamed the Subsidy Act and enclosure commissions of 1549.

KEY FIGURES

Philip Melanchthon (1497–1560)

A moderate Protestant who succeeded Luther as the leader of the German Reformation.

Johannes Oecolampadius (1482–1531)

A leading Swiss Protestant who implemented reforms in Basel in the 1520s.

In fact, whether or not a revolt broke out usually depended on local conditions and other unrelated factors. Thus, there were riots and disturbances in 27 English counties in the summer of 1549, but only in Devon and Cornwall and Norfolk and Suffolk were there prolonged rebellions. Most riots were local incidents and were suppressed by town and county authorities before they got out of hand.

The decline of feudalism, especially in the north of England, has been seen as an underlying issue in the Northern Earls' revolt, yet particular political and personal factors that triggered the uprising were not present elsewhere in the north. It seems, therefore, that attempts to distinguish between long-term underlying issues and more immediate causes of rebellions can throw light on the interplay of different factors. However, they are also likely to produce a simplistic analysis of a very complex event.

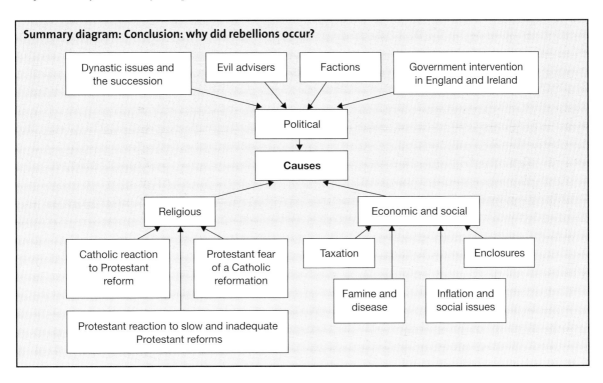

Summary diagram: Conclusion: why did rebellions occur?

Chapter summary

Rebellions during the Tudor period had a number of causes, including political, religious, social and economic, although within each of these broad groups there was a wider range of issues, such as faction, protests against ministers and taxation, that caused unrest. However, in most instances a rebellion had more than once cause, and often the motives of the rebels are difficult to discern, for example, religion was sometimes used as a cloak for political grievances. Moreover, the nature of the causes changed over the period, with political and taxation dominating the early part, religion and social and economic grievances becoming more frequent in the mid-Tudor period, and political and economic grievances being more obvious during the reign of Elizabeth I. However, the pattern was somewhat different in Ireland, where rebellion was often aimed at preventing an increase in the power of Tudor governments, but became increasingly bound up in opposition to religious changes.

 Refresher questions

Use these questions to remind yourself of the key material covered in this chapter.

1 What evidence is there that dynastic rebellions in Tudor England were motivated by personal ambition?

2 How common was the allegation that the Tudors were advised by 'evil councillors'?

3 Were 'evil councillors' simply scapegoats for unpopular government policies?

4 What evidence is there that political factions were a cause of Tudor rebellions?

5 In what ways did government intervention in England differ from that in Ireland as a cause of rebellion?

6 Why was religious change the cause of so many rebellions between 1536 and 1569?

7 What evidence is there that religion was a cloak for politically motivated rebellions?

8 Why was taxation such a frequent cause of rebellion in the period between 1485 and 1550?

9 Why were some areas of the country more affected than others by enclosures?

10 Why was famine not a principal cause of rebellion?

11 In what ways did inflation contribute to the outbreak of rebellions in England?

12 How far were economic and social causes of rebellion interrelated?

13 Under what circumstances did landlord–tenant relations change in Tudor England?

14 What difficulties face the historian in trying to discern the real motives of English and Irish rebels?

In-depth studies and debates

The examination requires you to study three topics in depth and for this unit they are:

- The Pilgrimage of Grace
- The Western rebellion
- Tyrone's rebellion.

This section will go into more detail about the causes of these three rebellions and introduce you to some of the key debates about the causes of each rebellion, so that you will have enough depth of knowledge to be able to evaluate passages that are set on any of these three rebellions.

Key debate 1: what caused the Pilgrimage of Grace?

Elton's view

In 1977, in *Reform and Reformation*, G.R. Elton suggested that the Pilgrimage of Grace was the result of court faction. He argued that the Aragonese faction, who had been defeated at court and in parliament, following the fall of Catherine of Aragon and the break with Rome, appealed to the country at large to stop further changes and raised a popular rebellion to achieve this. According to this interpretation, it was Henry's attempt to end his marriage to Catherine that had started the problems, which were exacerbated by his centralising policy that undermined the feudal ties in the north. The men who led the rebellion were the very men who had lost out as a result of this policy. To support his argument, Elton noted that the leading figures in the rebellion, such as Lord Hussey, had links with Catherine and her daughter Mary. These men had been replaced by Cromwell and Richard Rich, and this view is given further credibility by the attack on Cromwell, Rich and Cranmer in the Pilgrim's Ballad.

There is certainly sufficient evidence to suggest that men such as Hussey had a motive to organise the rising:

- The increasing government centralisation had seen men such as Hussey, Darcy and Constable lose influence.
- The north appeared to be excluded from decision-making, hence the rebel demand for a parliament in the north.
- The Percy family, who were on the rebel side, had lost influence in the north, with Henry Percy pressured to name the king as his heir and therefore disinherit his son.
- The Clifford family, who had done well during the reorganisation, remained loyal to the king.
- The rebels demanded the restoration of Mary to the succession.
- The organisation of the rebellion suggests that it was not spontaneous.

Contrary views to Elton's

Other historians have challenged Elton's thesis. Although most have argued that the rebellion was multi-causal, some have stressed the importance of social and economic factors, while others have stressed religious grievances, which appear to be the dominating factor in the rebels' demands. In arguing that economic factors were important, historians have noted that the demands contained a number of economic grievances such as:

- complaints about the 1534 Subsidy Act
- complaints about enclosure, which was a problem in some of the more heavily populated areas of the Lake District and the West Riding of Yorkshire
- complaints about entry fines.

There were also rumours about new taxes on sheep and cattle, while the harvests of 1535 and 1536 were poor, adding to the potential for discontent. Some historians have also suggested that the dissolution of the monasteries should be seen as an economic issue, as they played a vital role in the local economy and provided help in times of distress, so their removal would have been disastrous.

In terms of arguing that religion was the most important cause, perhaps the clearest case was put forward by Christopher Haigh, writing in *English Reformations, Religion, Politics and Society under the Tudors*, published in 1993. In this book, Haigh argued that although the demands of the rebels, as expressed in the Pontefract Articles, contained a range of issues, the secular demands were a late addition to the religious grievances. According to his account, it was not the break with Rome and the abolition of papal authority that were responsible for the rising, but the suppression of the smaller monasteries and other religious grievances that caused the rising.

Haigh's view that religion was the most important cause is given further credence by:

- The banner of the rebels depicted the five wounds of Christ.
- The pilgrim's oath contained the statement that they were undertaking the pilgrimage in the name of Christ.
- The religious grievances were at the head of the rebels' demands and made up nine out of the 24 demands.
- There were complaints in the demands against some reformist bishops, such as Cranmer, and some European reformers, such as Martin Bucer.
- Traditional religious practices, such as saint's days, were under attack and the abolition of holy days was unpopular.
- The new taxes on baptism, burial and marriage were unpopular, particularly among the poorer elements who could not afford them.
- The rising occurred immediately after the closure of some of the smaller monasteries.

- The area in Lancashire that was the first to rise was around the dissolved monasteries.
- Rumours of further religious changes, such as the closure of some parish churches, worried many.

Key debate 2: was the Western rebellion a religious rising?

Most accounts of the Western rebellion have explained it as a religious rebellion, hence it has also been known as the Prayer Book rebellion. There is certainly a great deal of evidence that suggests it was a religious rising, as the evidence from Christopher Haigh on page 55 shows, but also:

- The demands of the rebels were heavily religious, demanding the restoration of many old religious practices, including the restoration of the Six Articles, the ceremony and ritual of Catholicism and holy bread and water.
- The rebels attacked the Protestant belief in communion in both kinds.
- The rebels wanted the return of Cardinal Pole, although as a political leader.
- They demanded the return of two traditional clerics: Richard Crispin and John Moreman.

However, as the extract on page 55 from Barrett L. Beer suggests, there is certainly some justification for seeing the rising as more socially and economically driven:

- The demands were drawn up by clergy, so were bound to have a religious dimension.
- The original demands have not survived, but from other evidence we know that they contained social and economic concerns.
- The actions of the rebels suggest that the gentry were the enemies of the rebels as:
  - they attacked and robbed the gentry on St Michael's Mount
  - at Bodmin they shouted 'Kill the Gentlemen'
  - the rebels killed William Hellyons, the only member of the gentry who resisted
  - they attacked Trematon Castle, plundered it and put its owner in jail.
- Government forces also appeared to show that the rebellion had a class element by setting fire to rebel defences at Crediton, prompting Beer to note that 'the charred barns and houses stood as a grim reminder of the widening cleavage between the landowning gentry and the masses of working men and women'.
- During the siege of Exeter, the city government was concerned that the poorer elements within the city would let the rebels in, so they organised poor relief, sold firewood cheaply and distributed food at a low cost or free to the poor.
- The leader of the royal army warned the government about the nobility exploiting the peasantry.

Should the rising be known as the Prayer Book rebellion? ?

However, it might be possible to link the religious and social grievances of the rebels. It was, after all, the gentry who had gained from the Reformation, obtaining land following the dissolution, and this may explain why the rebels wanted a limit to the number of servants they could employ and the restoration of some of the monastic lands they had gained. Moreover, it was also the gentry who had implemented the unpopular religious changes.

The unpopularity of the gentry, for whatever reason, be it religious or economic, may therefore explain why they were not only unable to maintain order, but were a target for the rebels.

Key debate 3: how far was Tyrone's rebellion simply a protest against increased government interference?

Elizabeth faced more unrest in Ireland than any other Tudor monarch, and Tyrone's rebellion, 1594–1603, lasted longer than any other rebellion and was probably the most threatening as the rebels defeated the English forces at Yellow Ford in 1597.

The rebellion had a number of possible causes, with some arguing that it was government interference, particularly the plantation policy in Connaught and Munster, which provoked unrest. This resulted in increased rents, while it also saw the establishment of Protestant churches, adding a religious dimension to the rising. Irish chieftains therefore saw their whole system under threat and they lost further trust in the English deputies. However, others have argued that Elizabeth neglected Ireland:

- War with Spain meant that money was short and therefore expenditure on Ireland was low.
- The Deputy in Ireland, Fitzwilliam, was too old to keep order and this led to factional disputes in Dublin.
- This allowed clan warfare to develop, with cattle-raiding and summary executions.

There were also two other contributory, but interlinked factors that should be considered when trying to assess the causes:

- Hugh O'Neill, Earl of Tyrone, came to power in Ulster and began to train an army. He was in contact with Spain from 1590 and after aiding English garrisons in the early 1590s changed sides as he did not feel that he was sufficiently rewarded.
- England needed to secure Ireland against Spain and prevent the Spanish from using it as a base from which to invade England. However, Tyrone was able to raise the whole country against English rule.

Tyrone's motives appear relatively clear:

- expel the English settlers and government
- achieve independence.

Study skills: thematic essay question

How to plan the essay

The title of the unit, 'Thematic study', makes it clear that the essay section should be approached thematically rather than chronologically, particularly if you want to reach the higher mark range. In answering essay questions, you are required to make connections, comparisons and links between different elements of the period and aspects of the topic. In the opening paragraph you should try to establish a hypothesis based on the question; this should be tested in the main body of the essay before reaching an overall judgement. This is much easier to do if you approach the essay through a thematic structure. In your answer you will need to cover the whole period, and answers should look to establish patterns of change and continuity and similarity and difference.

Given the large amount of material that you will have to handle, it is very important that you spend time planning your answer. As the essay should adopt a thematic structure, it makes sense if the plan follows the same format and is therefore not chronological, going through the reigns of each monarch, or just a list of dates.

In developing your skills to answer essay questions for units 1 and 2, you will have considered the wording of a question. Although you will also have looked at planning an answer, the requirements for these types of question are, as was suggested above, somewhat different, as you will need to establish the themes you will consider.

Consider the question below:

> 'Religion was the most important cause of unrest in England in the period from 1485 to 1603.' How far do you agree?

In this essay you would need to consider a range of causes and weigh up their relative importance against that of religion in creating unrest. Drafting an essay plan will establish the themes you will consider, but will also provide you with an outline of the argument, or thesis, that you will follow.

Consider the example essay plan below:

Religion: This was only important in the period after the break with Rome and was not a cause after 1569. Even within the period 1536–69 it was not always the main cause and may have been the cloak for political causes, as in the Pilgrimage of Grace or Northern Earls' rebellion.

Factional: Present throughout the period, with Yorkist rebellions under Henry VII, linked to religion under Henry VIII with Aragonese faction, similar with Northumberland and Wyatt and again with Northern Earls, but with Essex his rebellion was due more to being excluded from favour.

Dynastic: As with factional throughout, but change in nature from overthrow under Henry VII and Edward VI/Mary to secure under Elizabeth.

Taxation: Important in period to 1549, but decline in importance afterwards, often the only cause of rebellions such as Yorkshire or Cornish, but also subsidiary in Western and Pilgrimage.

Enclosure: Important in 1549 (Kett) and again in 1596 (Oxfordshire), but subsidiary cause in 1536 (Pilgrimage of Grace), limited role across the period as a whole.

Social: Most important in 1549 (Kett and Western) with hint of class war, but also important in 1536 (Pilgrimage of Grace) and 1596 (Oxfordshire).

Conclusion: Importance of factors changes across the period, religion not most important cause across the period as at best only 1536–69 and at times subsidiary or part of multi-causal, whereas faction and dynastic present throughout.

The plan does not simply list the reasons, but offers a comment about their importance, and the conclusion offers a clear line of argument which has been supported in the previous paragraphs. Planning an answer will help you to focus on the actual question and marshal the large amount of knowledge you have, in this case about the causes of rebellion. It should prevent you writing all you know about the causes and stop you going through the period monarch by monarch, or rebellion by rebellion, and explaining the causes of each individual rebellion so that no comparison is made.

How to write the opening paragraph

Having planned your answer, you are in a position to write the crucial opening paragraph, in which you should set out your line of argument – establish your thesis – and briefly refer to the issues you are going to cover in the main body of the essay. This will help you to remain focused on the actual question. In establishing your thesis, it might be helpful to consider the following questions:

- What was the situation at the start of the period?
- What was the situation at the end of the period?
- Were there any parts of the period where there was considerable change or does the pattern remain the same throughout the period?

These questions will help you to remain focused on the key elements being tested in this unit: continuity and change.

The following is an example of a good opening paragraph to the question:

‘Religion was the most important cause of unrest in England in the period from 1485 to 1603.’ How far do you agree?

Response

Religion was only important as a cause of rebellion in the period from the break with Rome in 1536 to the rebellion of the Northern Earls in 1569. However, even within this period it could be argued that it was not the main or only cause of rebellions that had religious elements, such as in Wyatt's rebellion of 1554. In the earlier part of the period both dynastic and factional rebellions, as well as taxation, were important causes of unrest, with Yorkist rebellions under Henry VII and the Cornish and Amicable Grant risings due to taxation. Dynastic and factional causes remained important throughout the period, with them playing at least some role under all of the monarchs, while taxation rebellions died out after 1549. Other issues, such as enclosure, played a role in causing unrest, but their importance was limited to 1549 and 1596. As a result, dynastic and factional issues, rather than religion, were the most important cause of unrest in the period.

Analysis of response

- The opening offers a clear view about the importance of religion as a cause and the period during which it was relatively important.
- It outlines some of the other factors that will be considered and offers a view as to their relative importance.
- It reaches a judgement as to the most important cause – it is this line of argument that should be carried through the rest of the essay.

The focus of this section has been on planning and writing a good opening paragraph. Use the information in this chapter to plan answers and write the opening paragraph to the questions below.

Essay questions

1 How far did the causes of rebellion in England remain the same throughout the period 1485–1603?
2 'Faction was the most important cause of unrest in Tudor England.' How far do you agree?
3 Assess the view that causes of unrest in Ireland were different from those in England.

Study skills: depth study interpretations question

How to plan the essay

The specification identifies the three topics from which the interpretations question will be drawn. In answering this type of question, you have to assess and evaluate the arguments in the passages by applying your own knowledge of the events to reach a supported judgement as to which is the stronger interpretation.

The question will require you to assess the strengths and limitations of the two interpretations of an issue related to one of the specified depth studies. You should be able to place the interpretation within the context of the wider historical debate on the key topic. However, you will not be required to know the names of individual historians associated with the debate or to have studied the specific books of any historians, and it may even be counterproductive to be aware of particular historians' views, as this may lead to your simply describing their view, rather than analysing the given interpretation.

How should the question be approached?

Using the question and the two passages below on the causes of the Western rebellion as an example, it might be helpful for you to think of a four-paragraph structure to your answer:

- In the first paragraph, explain the interpretations in the two passages and place them in the wider debate about the causes of the Western rebellion.
- In the second paragraph, apply your own knowledge of the causes of the Western rebellion to Interpretation A to evaluate the validity of its view about the causes. What knowledge do you have of the causes of the Western rebellion that either supports or challenges the view of Passage A?
- Repeat the second point, but for Interpretation B: what knowledge do you have of the causes of the Western rebellion that either supports or challenges the view of Passage B?
- In the final paragraph, reach a supported and balanced judgement as to which passage you think is more convincing as an explanation for the outbreak of the Western rebellion.

Evaluate the interpretations in both of the passages (on page 55) and explain which you think is more convincing as an explanation of the reasons for the Western rebellion. [30]

PASSAGE A

The response from the parishes to the new Prayer Book was hostile, especially as it was introduced at a time of widespread grievances about taxation and agricultural change. The motives of the western rebels were certainly mixed. There was economic discontent, and a hostility against gentry who had co-operated with government policy. But religion was at least the common grievance which held the rebels together, and the Prayer Book was the issue which turned local disorder into regional rebellion. On June 6 a town meeting at Bodmin agreed to protest against the new services, and on 10 June the parishioners at Sampford Courtenay in Devon forced their priest to say mass, claiming that they 'would keep the old and ancient religion as their forefathers before them had done'. The articles the rebels produced wanted the Latin mass and the old ceremonies restored. Somerset claimed the commons had been tricked by the clergy into supporting a campaign against the Reformation, and the articles were apparently edited by priests. On 11 June Somerset warned that priests were taking advantage of economic discontents to turn people against the new services. But the Catholic cry was not limited to the clergy and rebel leaders would not have agreed to a programme which focused almost entirely on a fringe issue. The western rising was a determined protest against Somerset's policies, especially, but not exclusively, on religion.

(Adapted from C. Haigh, English Reformations: Religion, Politics and Society under the Tudors, *Oxford University Press, 1993, pp. 174–5.)*

PASSAGE B

The rebellions of 1549 occurred in an atmosphere of economic distress, for people of all ranks and degrees suffered from rising prices and a poor harvest. The growing shortage of arable and pastoral lands, caused by an increasing rural population, affected the poor most adversely and set peasants against landlords. Although a generalized description of social conditions does not by itself establish a cause for the Western Rebellion the circumstances of the Western Rebellion and the behavior of the rebels points toward social conflict as the cause. The non-religious leaders of the rising were not among the gentry elected to parliament, had not served at court under Henry VIII or Edward VI and therefore had more in common with the rebels and those from a lower social status. The behavior of the rebels also leaves little doubt that the gentry were their main enemy, for the commons expressed resentment and anger towards the ruling class throughout Devon and Cornwall. While the rebel grievances only touch on the social question in regard to limiting the number of household servants of the gentry and restoring church lands, the rebels' actions are a better guide to their outlook. From the beginning to the end, the Western rebellion found the commons fighting on one side and the leading gentry families on the other. This view is supported by eyewitness observers and commentators who confirm the existence of social conflict.

(Adapted from Barrett L. Beer, Rebellion and Riot, *Kent State University Press, 1982, pp. 68–70.)*

Using this model, a developed plan to the same question might look something like this:

1 The two passages agree that there was more than one cause of the Western rebellion. Passage A stresses the importance of religion, but does not ignore economic factors, whereas B places more emphasis on social and economic issues, particularly noting the attacks by the rebels on the gentry.

2 Passage A notes the economic context of the rebellion, but argues that the main concern of the rebels was religion: they particularly disliked the new prayer book and this was reflected in their demands; even if they were drawn up by clergy they would not focus on a minor issue as it would not attract large-scale support. There is evidence to support Passage A: the timing of the rebellion, which followed the introduction of the new prayer book, the banner of the Five Wounds of Christ, the earlier attack on William Body when he supervised the destruction of images, the traditional religious views in the West Country. However, the passage ignores the actions taken by the rebels, which involved attacks on the gentry, suggesting class conflict was an issue.

3 Passage B focuses on long-term economic and social issues, with the actions of the rebels suggesting class conflict was a cause; the own knowledge that might be applied includes: the attacks on gentry such as Hellyons and the cry at Bodmin of 'Kill the Gentlemen'. However, a challenge to Passage B is that it largely ignores the religious nature of the rebels' demands.

4 Both passages acknowledge that the rebellion was multi-causal; however, Passage B dismisses religion, whereas Passage A accepts that although the rebellion was mostly religious, there were other causes and is therefore stronger.

How to write the opening paragraph

Now look at this possible opening paragraph to the interpretation question on page 54.

Response

The two passages both acknowledge that the rising in the west of England in the summer of 1549 was caused by a variety of reasons. However, they differ in their view as to the most important factor in bringing about the Western rebellion. Passage A argues that 'religion was at least the common grievance which held the rebels together' even if there were other factors, while Passage B puts forward the view that social and economic grievances, but particularly class differences, were important as it states that 'From the beginning to the end, the Western rebellion found the commons fighting on one side and the leading gentry families on the other'.

Analysis of response

- The student is aware that the interpretations both acknowledge that the rising was multi-causal.
- The student is aware that the two interpretations put forward different reasons for the outbreak of the unrest.
- The student is able to identify what Interpretations A and B consider to be the most important reason.

CHAPTER 2

The nature of rebellions

The nature of the rebellions in England and Ireland was varied. This chapter will examine a range of issues which will allow us to reach a judgement as to why some rebellions were more successful than others. In order to do so, the chapter will discuss the objectives, duration and location of the major rebellions. It will analyse the leadership and organisation of the rebellions and consider how they linked to the size, support and frequency. Comparisons will be made between unrest in England and Ireland so that overall patterns can be established.

This chapter examines the frequency and nature of rebellions in Tudor England and Ireland under the following headings:

★ Objectives, duration and location

★ Leadership

★ Strategy and tactics

★ Organisation

★ Size, support and frequency

★ Irish rebellions

★ Conclusion: success or failure?

It also considers the debates surrounding the three in-depth topics:

★ Whose rebellion was the Pilgrimage of Grace?

★ How violent were the Western rebels?

★ Why was Tyrone's rebellion so difficult to suppress?

Key dates

1487	Battle of East Stoke	**1558–9**	Elizabethan Church settlement
1497	Cornish rebels defeated at Blackheath	**1569**	Northern earls entered Durham
1534	Act of Supremacy	**1596**	Oxfordshire rebels planned to assemble at Enslow Hill, as they had in 1549
1536	Pilgrims entered York and Durham		
1549	Exeter resisted the siege of the Western rebels, but Kett's rebels entered Norwich	**1598**	English forces defeated by Tyrone at Yellow Ford
1553	Northumberland abandoned his attempt to overthrow Mary at Cambridge	**1603**	Tyrone's rebellion finally suppressed

Objectives, duration and location

▶ *Did the objectives of a rebellion usually change or remain the same in the course of the uprising?*

Objectives

Tudor rebellions can be divided into three broad categories:

- dynastic rebellions that aimed to overthrow the monarch
- demonstrations against government policies
- Irish rebellions that sought to gain independence from England.

Dynastic rebellions

The desire to remove the monarch was most evident in the disturbances of 1486, 1487 and 1497, when Yorkist claimants, pretenders and sympathisers wanted to overthrow Henry VII and, if the opportunity arose, to assassinate him. Half a century later, Mary Tudor was the target of Northumberland's revolt when he aimed to prevent her from ascending the throne. Subsequent dynastic rebellions, however, were less clear-cut in their objectives, and it seems likely that as the rebellions developed, the leaders changed their objectives or, in some cases, concealed their aim to overthrow the ruler.

Wyatt, for instance, could not have realistically expected Mary Tudor to cancel her marriage to Philip of Spain in 1554 simply on account of his opposition, and in all probability he planned to put Princess Elizabeth on the throne. Similarly, the northern earls in 1569 initially intended releasing Mary Queen of Scots from her house arrest, marrying her to the Duke of Norfolk and forcing Elizabeth either to abdicate (which seems unlikely) or to recognise Mary as her heir presumptive. Once it became clear that the rebels could not get to Mary, the rebellion turned into a demonstration of northern opposition against Elizabeth's religious and political policies. Finally, Essex's rebellion in 1601 had mixed and wavering motives from the outset. The earl may have considered assassinating the queen but it is more likely that his main objective was to overthrow the political regime in power and, by a show of strength, force Elizabeth to appoint him as her principal adviser. In practice, none of these rebellions succeeded; indeed, few came close to realising their goals.

Anti-government demonstrations

A more frequent type of rebellion, and one that occurred throughout the period, was popular demonstrations against government policies and the councillors who were held responsible for them. For example:

- Protests against taxation took place in 1489 (Yorkshire), 1497 (Cornish) and 1525 (Amicable Grant). On each occasion, England was at war or preparing for war, but the objective of rebellion was not to frustrate the government's foreign policy but to get unpopular taxes rescinded.

- Social and economic issues also lay behind many disturbances in 1549. In East Anglia and the south-west of England, people wanted the government to do something about high food prices, recent taxes on sheep and wool, and unregulated enclosures. Oxfordshire was the scene of anti-enclosure riots in both 1549 and 1596, although stopping enclosures was only one of several rebel objectives.
- Perhaps nothing stirred people more to rise up and rebel than the changes to the Catholic Church and faith. The major rebellions that occurred in England in 1536, 1549 and 1569 were primarily a reaction to Protestant reforms implemented by Henry VIII, Edward VI and Elizabeth in the quarter of a century following the **break from Rome**. A common theme runs through each of these rebellions: discontented Catholics believed the only way they could redress their grievances was to take to the roads and lanes, protest in numbers and, if necessary, fight and die for their beliefs.

KEY TERM

Break from Rome
The name given to Henry VIII's separation of England from the Roman Catholic Church by a series of parliamentary Acts culminating in the Act of Supremacy of 1534.

Irish rebellions

The third type of rebellion occurred only in the final decade of the period in Ireland but political matters had been coming to a head for over half a century. Ever since the 1534 Kildare rebellion, when Henry VIII decided to transfer the administration of Ireland to English councillors, resentment had been growing from Anglo-Irish families and Gaelic clans alike. Rebellions in 1558, 1569 and 1579 owed much to opposition to English policies – political, religious, economic and cultural – all of which coalesced in the 1590s into a national uprising. Its overt objective was to expel the English administration from Ireland and preserve the Catholic faith, notionally on behalf of the Irish people, but privately O'Neill, its leader, desired political power for himself. In this respect, his rebellion was similar to that of the English northern earls: they claimed to be defending the true faith from heresy when in reality their main objective was to recover political and social pre-eminence in the northern counties.

Duration

At some stage in the course of the Tudor period, almost every English county and every Irish province experienced a rebellion. At first sight, there does not appear to be a pattern to either their duration or their location. In some cases, most notably in the spring and summer of 1549 when some 27 counties reported major riots, the protests lasted for only a few days and were dealt with before they escalated out of control. On other occasions, rebellions could run for several weeks and in the case of Ireland many years before they were suppressed.

On closer examination, one can note that the greater the distance from the seat of government, the more troublesome the area and the longer a rebellion tended to last.

In Ireland, for example, the Dublin administration invariably had to wait for instructions from London before countermeasures could be put in place, and then the financial and military resources were rarely equal to the task of dealing with a rebellion effectively. Thus, the Munster rebellion in 1569 took four years to suppress and O'Neill's national rising in 1595 was not subdued until 1603.

In England, disturbances in the south-west and northern counties might last for two or three months, on account of the slow and erratic communications which impeded the ability of the government to act decisively, and local magnates failing to deal with a rebellion before it got out of hand. Certainly, some rebellions, such as the Pilgrimage of Grace, Western and Kett's, took a long time to suppress because governments underestimated their seriousness or failed to make them a priority. Rebellions that began in or near to London, on the other hand, lasted but a short period of time. Rebels needed to strike quickly and take control of the government before troops could be raised against them. Thus, Wyatt's rebellion lasted for eighteen days but only one day was spent trying to enter the city; the Earl of Essex, in contrast, was in revolt for less than twelve hours.

Location

In general, most major disturbances and rebellions occurred in the more distant parts of the kingdom:

- the northern and south-western counties
- East Anglia
- the provinces of Ulster and Munster in Ireland.

Wales was exceptional in that it experienced no rebellions in the course of the period (see Chapter 4).

Pro-Yorkist areas

In the early years of Tudor rule, areas that had been popular with the Yorkist kings were likely to present difficulties, and **Lovel** in Yorkshire and the **Stafford** brothers in Worcester in 1486 tried unsuccessfully to rouse these areas against the king. Yorkshire was again the scene of a more serious disturbance in 1489 when the Earl of Northumberland was murdered while supervising a tax commission on behalf of the king (see page 31).

South-west England

The south-western counties, on the other hand, had no dynastic axe to grind – they simply resented government interference in their daily life:

- The county of Somerset was renowned for its truculent attitude. It contributed most of the rebels that marched to Blackheath in 1497 and proved unwilling to supply troops to suppress a rebellion in Devon in 1549.

 **KEY FIGURES**

Francis, Viscount Lovel (1454–c.1488)

Friend of Richard III and chamberlain to him.

Humphrey Stafford (c.1427–86) and Thomas Stafford (?)

Had fought for Richard III at Bosworth but not been captured; having taken sanctuary they then fled to Worcester.

- Cornwall, in particular, had a strong cultural tradition and resisted innovations or intrusions into its political affairs. The Celtic language was widely spoken there by commoners in the sixteenth century and contributed to Cornwall's geographical isolation from much of England. Above all, Cornishmen resented the English. In his *Description of Cornwall*, written in the late sixteenth century, John Norden claimed that the Cornish seemed to 'retain a kind of concealed envy against the English, whom they yet effect with a kind of desire for revenge for their fathers' sakes, by whom their fathers received the repulse'. In 1537, the Dean of Exeter Cathedral, Dr Simon Heynes, remarked that the region was a 'perilous country', an observation confirmed by the outbreak of two rebellions in 1497, disturbances at Helston in 1548 when the Archdeacon of Cornwall was murdered, and the Prayer Book rebellion of 1549, which originated in the south-west.

Customary practice

In some cases, rebel leaders, aware of their heritage, shrewdly selected the same town, even the same meeting place, which had been the site of earlier disturbances. Areas of open land were ideal meeting places for large crowds to gather:

- The Cornish rebels of 1497 chose Blackheath for their encampment just as rebels Wat Tyler and John Ball had done in 1381 and Jack Cade in 1450.
- In Oxfordshire, the 1596 rebels met at Enslow Hill, where anti-enclosure protesters had gathered 50 years before.
- Some rebels congregated outside their local church. The Prayer Book demonstrators of 1549, for instance, assembled outside Bodmin Church, as had their ancestors in 1497 when they protested at Henry VII's war tax.
- The county of Norfolk also had a long tradition of rebellious activity. In 1381, east Norfolk rebels attacked local gentry as part of the Peasants' Revolt, and further riots occurred against enclosures in 1525 and the gentry in 1540. Rebels who camped at seven locations in the county in 1549 were therefore following a well-established pattern of behaviour.

Influence of local magnates

Particular areas of the country were prone to disorder if the relationship between the leading magnate and the people was fraught or unresponsive. If it was mutually beneficial, as in Hampshire where the Earl of Southampton was a prominent landowner, in Lancashire where the pro-Tudor Derby family dominated county politics and in Sussex where the Earl of Arundel kept effective control, few disturbances of any note occurred. But if the magnate was absent, as in the case of John Russell of Devon in 1549, who as Lord Privy Seal spent most of his time in London, or there was a political vacuum due to the demise of a powerful family, such as the Courtenays in Cornwall and the Howards in Norfolk, trouble was likely to take some time to die down. Ireland posed similar difficulties for English governments once the Kildares ceased to hold

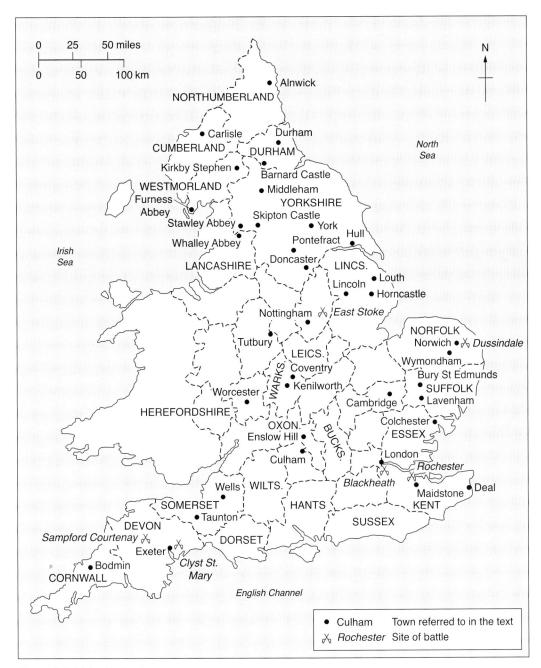

Figure 2.1 Tudor England.

their customary office of deputy lieutenant. The absence of a **paternalistic** administration at county and regional level thus removed a key layer of political cohesion between rulers and subjects and rendered these areas potential flashpoints.

 **KEY TERM**

Paternalistic A policy whereby those in power limit the freedom of others, supposedly in their interests.

London

In the case of politically motivated rebellions such as Simnel, Warbeck, Wyatt, the Northern Earls and Essex, their objective was to reach Whitehall, the seat of central government in London. Most, with the exception of Wyatt and Essex, fell a long way short:

- Warbeck, for example, on landing in Cornwall from Scotland got only as far as Taunton, 160 miles from London.
- Wyatt, who started his rebellion in Kent, came close but was repelled at Ludgate, three miles from the City of London.
- The Earl of Essex, who had the distinct advantage of beginning in the Strand in central London, got as far as Fenchurch Street before retreating by river back to his house.

The capital, in fact, was consistently loyal to the Tudors and never rallied to a pretender, illegitimate claimant or would-be usurper.

Principal towns and cities

In the case of protest marches, rebels targeted county and diocesan towns to stage their demonstration. These objectives entailed far shorter journeys than marching to London, which was a key factor in retaining a large following if harvests were due to be collected, rebels fed and paid, and long distances overcome:

- In 1549, the Cornish rebels, for instance, walked 50 miles to Exeter.
- Kett travelled ten miles from Wymondham to Norwich.

These were far more manageable distances than the 100 or so miles that Aske and his supporters would have covered in 1536 before arriving at Doncaster.

The Cornish tax revolt of 1497 was unusual in that as many as 15,000 rebels decided to take their grievances to London, some 250 miles away. It is hardly surprising that as the march entered its fourth week, thousands of rebels deserted the cause and returned to their farms in time for the June harvest. The Amicable Grant protesters in 1525 similarly intended walking 50 miles from Lavenham to London to confront Wolsey with their complaints, and appear only to have been stopped by someone removing the clapper from the church bell, which would have been the signal to commence the march.

In all other demonstrations against Tudor policies, the county town was the focus of protest. Few welcomed these insurgents. How local authorities reacted to the challenge often determined the length of the rebellion as well as its course. Rebels needed food, supplies, weapons and popular support. If they were denied these, as at Exeter in 1549, their days were numbered; if the city cooperated and even assisted, as at York in 1536 and Norwich in 1549, the rebellion could be sustained until it was resolved by arbitration or force.

Summary diagram: Objectives, duration and location

Objectives	Duration	Location
• Overthrow the government • Remedy grievances • Increase Irish independence	Hours Days Weeks Months Years	Pro-Yorkist areas South-west England Customary practices Local magnates London, towns and cities

 # Leadership

▶ *Did rebel leaders share any common characteristics?*

Royal claimants

Leadership was clearly an important factor in determining how much success a rebellion was going to enjoy. Ideally, dynastic revolts needed to be led by a **prince of the blood** or royal claimant. For example:

- Simnel's rebellion in 1487: he not only claimed to be the Earl of Warwick, Richard III's oldest nephew, but was also supported by the Earl of Lincoln, another of Richard's nephews, and the self-styled 'white rose' of York.
- Similarly, in the 1490s, Warbeck claimed he was the Duke of York.
- Sixty years later, Edward VI and the Duke of Northumberland championed the cause of Lady Jane Grey, the great-granddaughter of Henry VII.

Legitimacy was vitally important, however. If Henry VII had some difficulty dealing with the pretenders Simnel and Warbeck because his own claim to the throne was somewhat shaky, Northumberland was always likely to fail in his bid to topple Mary Tudor, the legitimate daughter of Henry VIII.

Nobility and gentry

The nobility and gentry were the 'natural' leaders in society and played key roles in most Tudor rebellions. In Ireland the leading rebels were earls such as Tyrone, Kildare and Desmond, who used their position as head of a clan to mobilise large numbers of supporters. Some English nobles, like Lovel in 1486, Audley in 1497, Lumley and Latimer in 1536, Dacre in 1570 and Essex in 1601, also put themselves at the head of a revolt or led a company of rebels against the monarch. Others, like **Hussey** and Darcy in 1536 and the earls of Northumberland and Westmorland in 1569, assumed leadership more reluctantly and later claimed (in the cold light of defeat) that their social inferiors had pressed them into action. It should be recognised, however, that it was a convention for nobles and gentry to deny that they had given their support willingly and to claim instead that they and their families had been forced to participate.

 **KEY TERM**

Prince of the blood
A prince who was a blood relation of the monarch.

 **KEY FIGURE**

Lord Hussey (?)
An elderly northern noble who had links to the Aragonese faction, but was reluctant to be involved in rebellion.

Any protest that aspired to authority and legitimacy needed a noble as its leader:

- The Cornish in 1497 looked to Lord Audley, an impoverished Somerset peer, whose father had once been treasurer of England but was dismissed by Richard III and never trusted by Henry VII.
- The Yorkshire rebels in 1536 similarly besieged Lord Darcy in his castle at Pontefract to enlist his support, if not his leadership.

As the period advanced, however, the Tudor nobility became less inclined to indulge in treasonous activities and instead rebel leaders tended to come from the gentry, lawyers and clergy:

- There were no nobles in Norfolk to whom rebels might turn in 1549, and Robert Kett, a minor landowner, assumed command.
- It was a Yorkshire gentleman, Sir John Egremont, who led the anti-tax demonstrations in 1489.
- The revolts in Lincolnshire and the Pilgrimage of Grace were notable for the large number of county gentry who either supported or led rebel groups. The sheriff of Lincoln, for instance, Sir Edward Dymoke, his associate Sir Christopher Willoughby, and Sir Robert Bowes, Sir Ingram Percy and Sir Stephen Hammerton were all gentry captains of their troops.
- The lay leaders of the Western rebellion, Sir Humphrey Arundell, John Winslade and John Bury, were also minor gentry on the fringe of county politics.
- Sir Thomas Wyatt, who led the Kent rebels in 1554, was a courtier and former sheriff.

Clergy

The clergy, on the other hand, rarely led a revolt. Rebellion against a divinely anointed ruler was a sin as well as an act of treason, although rebelling against a usurper could be justified, as several Irish bishops claimed in 1487. Nevertheless, in regions where the Catholic faith was deeply entrenched, such as Cornwall, Lincolnshire, Durham and parts of Lancashire and Yorkshire, the clergy were prepared to stand shoulder to shoulder with their community, and from time to time assume leading roles in a rebellion. For example:

- In 1536, the abbots of Kirkstead, Furness and Barlings, and the vicars of Louth, Brough and Brayton, supported the Lincolnshire and Pilgrimage revolts.
- The vicars of St Clare, St Uny and Poundstock all travelled to Exeter with the Cornish rising of 1549. It is even possible that the vicar of St Thomas, Exeter, was the most significant figure in uniting the Devon and Cornish rebels.

Lawyers

Since the main objective of most rebels was to bring their grievances to the attention of local authorities, it is quite understandable that men with legal experience and social standing in the region emerged as leaders:

- Thomas Flamank from Bodmin (1497)
- Thomas Moigne, the recorder of Lincoln (1536)
- William Stapleton in the East Riding of Yorkshire (1536).

These all took a prominent part in their rebellions, but the most celebrated lawyer to lead a revolt was Robert Aske, who headed the Pilgrimage of Grace. As attorney to the Earl of Northumberland, a cousin of the Earl of Cumberland and a respected lawyer in Yorkshire and London, Aske had all the attributes of an outstanding leader. Not surprisingly, his contemporaries dubbed him the 'Great Captain' and several minor nobles and gentry deferred to his leadership.

Commoners

With the notable exception of the 1549 revolts, few rebellions were led by commoners or could hope to have much success if they were. However, most of the rebel leaders in 1549 came from the ranks of the commons. Kett, for instance, was a tanner by trade and Thomas Underhill, who appears to have started disturbances at Sampford Courtenay in Devon, was a tailor. The Oxfordshire rising of 1596 was organised by local servants and tradesmen – millers, masons, weavers, bakers – and headed by a carpenter, Bartholomew Steer. They failed to attract any substantial support and the rising collapsed

Robert Aske

c.1500	Born
1536	October: recognised as chief captain of the rebels
	November/December: met the Duke of Norfolk and presented the rebel demands
	Agreement reached with the Duke of Norfolk; rebels pardoned and dispersed
1537	Arrested
	July: executed at Clifford's Tower, York

Early life
Robert Aske was born into a gentry family in the East Riding of Yorkshire. As he was not the eldest son he would not inherit the estate and so he trained to be a lawyer in London, becoming the legal adviser to the Earl of Northumberland.

Aske's emergence as a leader
It is difficult to assess Aske's exact role as all of the evidence comes from Aske himself. He claimed he was captured by the Lincolnshire rebels and forced to take their oath. However, it appears at some point he was shown the rebels' demands and persuaded that they agreed with his own views. As a result, he took on a more prominent role, becoming leader of the rising and giving it its name.

Leadership
Aske led the rebels into York and accepted the surrender of Pontefract Castle. His intelligence and legal training made him the ideal spokesman for the rebel force and it was no mean feat to keep together some 40,000 rebels, many with different aims. He was able to prevent unrest and a move south towards London. Following the drawing up of the final rebel demands, Aske met with the Duke of Norfolk, commander of the royal forces. An agreement was reached and a pardon issued to the rebels, who reluctantly accepted the terms. While Aske toured the northern counties trying to persuade the commons to accept the deal, Francis Bigod, unconvinced by the deal, raised a force but was defeated in January 1537 at Carlisle.

Arrest and death
Bigod's rising gave Henry the opportunity to go back on his pardon and promises of reform. Many rebels were arrested and some 170, including Aske, were executed.

within hours of its start. On the other hand, the Amicable Grant revolt of 1525, which was led by husbandmen, urban artisans, weavers and rural peasants, owed its success to its size and to the sympathy it received from members of the king's council.

Leadership qualities

There was no single quality that made a good leader:

- Age was clearly of some importance. Simnel was too young to command respect and the earls in 1569 were too old to lead a rebel army. Warbeck, on the other hand, was 25, Wyatt 33 and Kett 57 years old at the time of their uprisings.
- Legitimacy and social standing were obviously key factors but so too was the capacity to employ the right strategy and tactics, and demonstrate good organisational skills.

Leading a rebellion was an enormous responsibility: the consequences were usually fatal and the larger the host and longer the revolt, the more the qualities

Robert Kett

1492	Born at Wymondham, Norfolk
c.1515	Married Alice Appleyard
1549	10 July: led rebels to Norwich
	12 July: established camp on Mousehold Heath
	22 July: rebels took Norwich
	30 July: rebels retook Norwich
	27 August: defeated
	26 November: hanged

Background

Robert Kett was a tanner and landowner or yeoman, while his brother, William, was a butcher and landowner. Kett had enclosed some common land near the abbey church in the market town of Wymondham in Norfolk. John Flowerdew, an unpopular lawyer, who had seen some of his own hedges destroyed, attempted to get the crowd to turn on Kett and attack his land as he was in dispute with the family over the abbey church, which Flowerdew had looted.

Into rebellion

Kett agreed to take down the hedges round the common land and said he would support the rioters

until their grievances were met. His leadership skills soon emerged and he decided to lead the rioters to Norwich, gaining support *en route*.

Rebellion and Kett's motives

It is unclear why he decided to join the rebels. It might have been the opportunity for him to vent his feelings about being just below the class of gentry.

By 10 July they had reached Norwich and by 12 July they had set up camp with some 16,000 men on Mousehold Heath, where grievances were drawn up. From the camp, Kett issued warrants for food and dispensed justice. Kett rejected the offer of pardon and his forces entered Norwich on 22 July. A royal force under the Marquis of Northampton was defeated, having first taken Norwich, and Kett re-entered the city. An army under John Dudley, Earl of Northumberland, was now sent.

Defeat

Kett made an error in moving the rebel camp from the fortified position on top of Mousehold Heath to the Vale of Dussindale. By this time, Northumberland had assembled a large force which attacked the rebels, killing over 3000. Kett was arrested, tried for treason and hanged.

of the leader were tested. It is for these reasons that historians have generally regarded Aske and Kett as the outstanding English rebel leaders and Hugh O'Neill the most effective Irish leader during this period. These men were able to unite disparate factions, command thousands of troops in a disciplined manner and keep Tudor authorities on tenterhooks for a considerable period of time.

All rebellions needed men who were physically strong and intimidating, and some craftsmen and labourers figured among the leaders:

- Michael Joseph, who led the Cornish rebels into battle at Blackheath in 1497, was a blacksmith.
- Nicholas Melton, the captain of the Louth rebels in 1536, was a cobbler.
- Robert Welsh, vicar of St Thomas's, who led the rebel host at the siege of Exeter in 1549, was a well-known wrestler.

These were charismatic figures in their communities and must have been an inspiration to others. Similarly, a man with military experience was always an asset in times of crisis:

- Arundell, who became the Cornish leader in the Western rebellion of 1549, had fought for Henry VIII in France.
- Wyatt, who had been a military strategist to the king, put his theories into practice against Mary Tudor in 1554.

These men were used to commanding troops and leadership came naturally to them. What seems apparent therefore is that some men were born leaders and some had leadership thrust on them. At first, most disturbances started with the lower ranks of society – craftsmen, artisans, labourers and peasants – who looked to their superiors, often men with legal and clerical backgrounds, to lead them and articulate their complaints. Before long, in most cases, the gentry assumed control, either willingly or under duress (as many claimed). Only occasionally, and usually for selfish and feckless reasons, lesser nobles got involved, but the heads of noble families and the aristocracy remained steadfast in their loyalty to the Tudors.

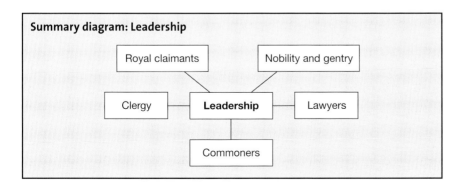

Summary diagram: Leadership

Strategy and tactics

▶ *How did Tudor rebellions compare in respect of their strategies and tactics?*

🔑 **KEY TERM**

Strategy and tactics
Strategy is an overall plan and the management of troops designed to achieve an objective; tactics are the means by which the plan is carried out.

Dynastic rebellions

The **strategy and tactics** deployed by rebel leaders varied from rebellion to rebellion. If the prime objective was to overthrow the monarch, first he or she had to be drawn out of the capital and either forced to abdicate or be killed on the battlefield. Until London had been seized, no rebel leader could claim victory and, as Londoners tended to stand by legitimate rulers, the odds in favour of a successful coup were not good. To achieve their ends, dynastic rebellions therefore needed to have an alternative and *bona fide* claimant ready to rule:

- The Yorkists had pretenders as well as genuine claimants.
- Northumberland championed Lady Jane Grey.
- Wyatt favoured Princess Elizabeth.
- The Northern Earls wanted Mary Stuart.

In each case, their tactics entailed raising noble and gentry support, enlisting foreign diplomatic and military aid, and putting pressure on the incumbent ruler to yield:

- Simnel (1486–7) and Warbeck (1497) landed in Lancashire and Cornwall, respectively, with the expectation of raising troops from disaffected counties before marching on London. In practice, they each raised only 4000–5000 troops and failed to advance beyond Nottinghamshire and Somerset, some 150 miles from the capital.
- Wyatt (1554) and Essex (1601) had the advantage of starting in or near to London. Wyatt was a good strategist but a poor tactician. He understood the need to have nation-wide support but delayed his entry into London when time was of the essence. Essex, in contrast, had an uncertain strategy and no clear tactics. Disorganised from the start, his revolt quickly disintegrated into chaos.

Protests against government policies

Demonstrators against government policies and ministers adopted a different strategy. These protests were essentially peaceful and, in the opinion of the participants, justified. Their strategy was:

- to raise as much popular support as possible
- to acquire the backing of gentry, clergy and nobles
- to pressurise the authorities to respond to their requests (or, in the case of the Western rebels, their demands)

- to present grievances as articles to the Crown's representatives; once these had been submitted, there was little more that a rebel host could do but wait for a reply.

All demonstrations claimed to be peace-loving and few rebel leaders relished the prospect of military confrontation, but beneath the surface of most revolts was the implicit threat of social violence.

Fear and intimidation

If the revolts of 1536–7 are taken as an example, hundreds of gentry and lesser nobles appear to have been intimidated by the commons and forced to participate:

- The Abbot of Jervaulx recounted that he was threatened with beheading if he did not surrender his abbey.
- Marmaduke Neville claimed that his wife and goods were at risk if he refused to join in.
- Sir Roger Cholmeley was told his house would be looted there and then.
- At Horncastle, in the Lincolnshire Rising, William Leach informed the sheriff of Lincoln that he must 'be sworn to do as we do, or else it shall cost you your life'. Outside, a mob of 100 men waited for his answer.

Fear clearly induced many men to enlist. Aske claimed that he was 'persuaded' and Lord Darcy yielded Pontefract Castle when 3000 rebels approached. Barnard Castle similarly fell, as did the towns of Lincoln, Hull, York, Lancaster and Durham, ostensibly to save the citizens from unnecessary bloodshed. According to Thomas Moigne, the main reason why he and other Lincoln gentry agreed to become captains was to enable him to 'do the most good amongst his own neighbours in the staying of them [the commons]'. This may well have been true, although Henry VIII did not believe him and Moigne paid for his involvement with his life.

The Lincolnshire rising and the Pilgrimage of Grace may have been exceptional cases on account of the scale and duration of the disturbances, but the tactic of intimidation can also be found in the 1549 rebellions in both the West Country and East Anglia:

- The Western rebels kidnapped local gentry, detained passing merchants and put the sheriff of Devon under house arrest.
- In Suffolk, four magistrates were imprisoned at Melton.
- In Norfolk, Kett's captains held and humiliated any gentry who would not cooperate. Sir Roger Wodehouse tried to persuade rebels on Mousehold Heath to disperse by bribing them with three carts of food and drink, only to be chased, imprisoned and have his provisions seized. Thomas Gawdy MP, Richard Catlyn and other gentry were chained and fettered and placed in the front line as battle-shields at Dussindale.

Violence against the upper classes was, however, a rarity. It is hard to judge whether the Oxfordshire rebels of 1596 were serious when they spoke about murdering seven local landlords who had enclosed nearby fields, but it could explain the reluctance of serving men to join them.

When violence did occur, the victim was usually a figure of hatred and the source of local anger:

- In 1489, it was the Earl of Northumberland, Henry VII's sheriff of Yorkshire, who was responsible for collecting an unpopular war tax.
- In 1497, the target was the Provost of Penryn, the collector of a war tax in Cornwall, who escaped to Taunton before being murdered in the marketplace.
- In 1536, during the Pilgrimage of Grace, Dr John Raynes was hacked to pieces by an angry mob and another innocent man was hanged.
- In 1549, at the start of the Western rebellion, William Hellyons was cut down at Sampford Courtenay when he tried to buy off the rebel host with a cartload of provisions and, in the same year in Norwich, Kett's rebels captured an Italian mercenary and hanged him from the city walls.

Nevertheless, apart from these isolated incidents and the fatalities of armed conflicts, we can believe the peaceful intentions of most rebels. The Cornishmen in 1497 wished 'to do no creature hurt'; the Lincolnshire rebels claimed they were 'true and faithful subjects' and the Western protesters declared 'God save king Edward, for we be his, both body and soul'. Pulling down a hedge, pillaging a deer park, or destroying Protestant bibles and ransacking a bishop's library were physical, even symbolic gestures of righting a wrong, while disrupting local communications and stealing supplies from the gentry were considered to be valid tactics in achieving the rebels' goal.

Sieges of county towns

Laying siege to county towns was a standard tactic in most uprisings. Apart from securing the support of several thousand citizens, a successful rebellion looked to win over the mayor, aldermen and sheriff whenever possible. Their involvement also gave the protest added strength and respectability and increased the rebels' bargaining power when dealing with the government. Camps of rebels became a common sight in 1549, the 'year of commotions', when thousands of demonstrators encamped on open fields and heaths outside city walls:

- Exeter on three occasions – twice in 1497 and again in 1549 – repelled rebel sieges.
- Carlisle in 1537 and 1570 refused to submit to rebel leaders.

However, some county officials cracked under the strain and opened their gates:

- Taunton (1497)
- York (1536)

- Lancaster (1536)
- Norwich (1549)
- Durham (1536 and 1569)

all yielded to violent threats.

Only a minority of mayors, for example:

- Wells (1497)
- Lincoln (1536)
- Torrington (1549)
- Bodmin (1549)

openly supported the protesters.

Thomas Codd, Mayor of Norwich, fraternised rather too readily with Kett's rebels on Mousehold Heath for his later claim to be believable, that he did it to protect the welfare of his fellow citizens.

Raising rebel support

A common way of alerting people that something important was going to happen was to ring the church bells, light beacons and post notices on village halls and church doors. Such tactics kept people informed and maintained the unity among rebel groups. Robert Kett held daily council meetings at his camp. Robert Aske issued badges to the pilgrims who adopted the Five Wounds of Christ as their banner. It was the traditional cry of religious conformity in the face of heresy and chosen by rebels in 1549 and 1569, and all pilgrims swore an oath of allegiance 'to be true to God, the king and the commons'. This novelty bound the rebel host together and most of the rebels in 1536 took it. Swearing an oath was an important element of rebel propaganda; so too was utilising the printing press. Ballads and seditious rhymes were composed, letters and circulars published, and posters nailed to church doors claiming that the Catholic faith was 'piteously and abominably confounded'.

Irish rebellions

The strategy and tactics of Irish rebellions were not dissimilar from those found in modern guerrilla warfare. English landowners and Anglo-Irish government officials were prime targets of attack, and the inhospitable terrain, particularly in Ulster and lands to the west and south of the Pale around Dublin, made combating rebel troops very hard. The Irish wisely avoided military confrontations unless an English army was outnumbered or caught isolated, as occurred at Yellow Ford in 1598, during Tyrone's rebellion, when English troops suffered heavy losses. If the Irish rebels faced defeat or capture, the leaders 'disappeared' into the more remote regions of Ireland where few Englishmen dared to venture. Of course, English rebels similarly escaped to the mountains of Wales, the Lake District and Scotland or to the moors of south-west England, but in Ireland rebels often survived to continue their fight several months later. James Fitzgerald, for instance, evaded capture in 1573 after four years of intermittent hostilities, only to resurface in 1579 and renew his rebellion in concert with his cousin, the Earl of Desmond. Such tactics proved very frustrating for loyalist commanders who might win a skirmish but rarely won a battle. And unlike English rebellions, Irish revolts were altogether more violent, brutal and protracted.

Summary diagram: Strategy and tactics

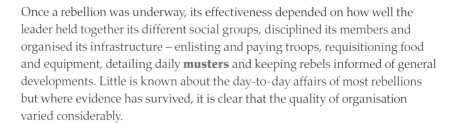

Type of rebellion	Strategy	Tactics
Dynastic rebellions	Raise an army and overthrow the ruler	Gather widespread support prior to fighting a battle
Anti-government protests in England	Pressurise the authorities into remedying grievances	Popular demonstrations and intimidation of officials and local leaders
Irish rebellions	Disrupt the Dublin administration	Attack English landowners and officials through the use of violence and guerrilla warfare

 # Organisation

▶ *What organisational difficulties were the rebel leaders faced with?*

Once a rebellion was underway, its effectiveness depended on how well the leader held together its different social groups, disciplined its members and organised its infrastructure – enlisting and paying troops, requisitioning food and equipment, detailing daily **musters** and keeping rebels informed of general developments. Little is known about the day-to-day affairs of most rebellions but where evidence has survived, it is clear that the quality of organisation varied considerably.

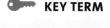 **KEY TERM**

Musters Summoning soldiers for inspection.

Poorly organised rebellions

Rebellion of the Northern Earls 1569–70

Some rebellions were poorly planned from the start and got progressively worse. In 1569, the Earl of Northumberland left himself insufficient time to call on his own tenants in Yorkshire to rise and failed to appreciate how long it would take to march from Durham to Tutbury in Staffordshire in order to release Mary Stuart from captivity, or indeed realise that she had been moved 30 miles further south to Coventry. Moreover, when he and the Earl of Westmorland came to pay 1000 footmen at North Allerton, they could raise only £20 between them. Six hundred potential troops deserted there and then.

The Simnel rebellion 1486–7

The Simnel rebellion was another badly organised uprising. The presence of 2000 German mercenaries and 40 Irish nobles with their 'wild' tenants deterred many English from joining the rebel army as it progressed south from Lancashire.

The Western rebellion 1549

The Western rising had problems of a different kind among its ranks. Not only was there animosity between the Cornishmen and Devonians, there was tension between the peasantry, clergy and gentry. Hints of social radicalism were apparent when some of those in the Clyst camp outside Exeter wanted to 'kill all the gentlemen', but nothing further transpired. Significantly, the nine captains who commanded the siege comprised three Devon gentry, three Cornish gentry and three commoners. However, when the rebels' final petition was presented to the Crown, it contained no reference to any economic grievances, and it was these that really mattered to the peasants.

The Oxfordshire rising 1596

On the face of it, there seemed to be little wrong with the organisation of the Oxfordshire rising in 1596: the ringleaders spent a great deal of time planning their moves and determining when and where it would take place. Unfortunately, secrecy was not high on their agenda and a fair-weather colleague alerted his lord of the intended rising. The rebels' choice of Enslow Hill, which was where a revolt had been staged in 1549, made their arrest fairly predictable and the attempted rebellion was defeated before it could start.

Essex's rebellion 1601

Essex's rebellion fared little better. He too had advertised that he was going to do something dramatic – he even hired a troupe of actors to perform Shakespeare's **Richard II** on the eve of the rebellion – and when it began, he expected Londoners to rally to his cause. Instead, most stood and watched his assembly pass by in bemusement. Once he had failed to enlist the support of the mayor and sheriff of London, whom he mistakenly thought would back him, he decided to retreat. Unfortunately, he had no exit strategy and, finding Ludgate blocked, was forced to withdraw in total disarray.

Well-organised rebellions: 1536 and 1549

The Pilgrimage of Grace 1536–7

Not all rebellions were disorganised affairs. Indeed, those led by Aske and Kett are noteworthy precisely because of their excellent organisation.

Aske had the unenviable task of trying to manage more than 30,000 followers from a variety of social backgrounds and geographical regions who were pursuing different objectives. Recruits were mustered into companies according

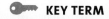 **KEY TERM**

Richard II In 1399, Henry Bolingbroke had seized the Crown from Richard II. The re-enactment of Shakespeare's play (written in 1595) reminded Londoners that the deposition of Elizabeth I would not be unprecedented.

to their district, town or village, which meant that most men knew each other at least by sight and were able to elect a captain to represent and lead them. The captains met each day, received instructions from Aske as to where they would be going and attended regular council meetings with other captains. Villages usually elected one captain, towns as many as four. Each recruit was given a badge and a supply of food and wages, and took the pilgrim oath of good behaviour. While some companies raided churches and abbeys, most appear to have been well disciplined. For instance, when 8000 rebels approached York, Aske arranged that half would camp outside the city while the rest would accompany him, and all paid for their board and lodging.

Aske kept firm control of the majority of the pilgrims but those rebels who came from regions to the west of the Pennines proved more difficult to manage. There was, moreover, as in other disturbances, tension between the gentry leaders and the commoners. For instance, 300 representatives from all counties north of the River Don assembled near Doncaster in November 1536, while the rest of the host waited at Pontefract. Forty pilgrims were selected to parley with the Duke of Norfolk, and Aske then returned to the main body of rebels to explain what had been discussed. Most of the commons feared that the gentry were going to betray them, as had happened at Lincoln earlier in October. Although they were given assurances to the contrary, later events proved their suspicion was not misplaced.

Kett's rebellion, 1549

Robert Kett was the undisputed leader of his rebellion in Norfolk and demonstrated how to marshal a peaceful protest of at least 16,000 rebels for nearly seven weeks. Camps of protesting rebels were set up in many English counties in the summer of 1549 but we know most about the one that Kett organised on Mousehold Heath, outside Norwich. The community occupied Surrey Place, a mansion on the heath, and he ran the camp like a model local government. One of his objectives was to show that he and his colleagues could manage business affairs as well as the gentry or government officials. Each of the 24 **hundreds** in the county that contributed rebels elected two governors to sit on an advisory council, courts of justice imposed disciplinary fines and punishments, and proclamations and warrants were issued. For instance, when seeking supplies, a warrant undertook that 'no violence or injury be done to any honest or poor man', and this promise of decent behaviour appears to have been upheld.

Kett sent out search parties to keep the camp supplied with food and beer, negotiated with the Mayor of Norwich to purchase general provisions and gunpowder, and arranged for artillery to be brought from the coast. Twice-a-day prayers were taken by a minister, Thomas Conyers, under the **Oak of Reformation**. Even when the rebels attacked the city and held it for a week before retiring to their encampment, discipline was maintained. A garrison

 **KEY TERMS**

Hundreds Norfolk, like most counties, was divided administratively into hundreds.

Oak of Reformation An old oak tree on Mousehold Heath outside Norwich, so called because it was where the rebels held Protestant or reformed services.

was established in the cathedral grounds, aldermen and constables were appointed, citizens conscripted as night watchmen, and the city gates, castle and guildhall guarded. Significantly, no one was killed until royal troops and foreign mercenaries arrived to recover control of the city.

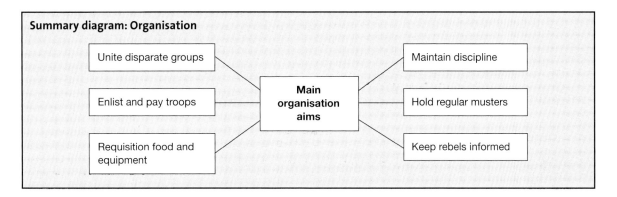

Summary diagram: Organisation

Unite disparate groups

Enlist and pay troops

Requisition food and equipment

Main organisation aims

Maintain discipline

Hold regular musters

Keep rebels informed

 # Size, support and frequency

▶ *Why were some rebellions larger than others?*

Size

Rebellions came in all shapes and sizes. Although it is impossible to be certain of exact numbers, Tudor rebellions seem to have ranged from as small as four rebels in the 1596 Oxfordshire rising to as many as 40,000 in the 1536 Pilgrimage of Grace. Most disturbances gathered a few thousand supporters; some saw their numbers increase as the rebellion progressed, while the majority fluctuated as circumstances changed:

- The Cornish rebels of 1497, for example, may have grown in size from a few thousand to 15,000 as they travelled east through Devon, Somerset, Wiltshire, Hampshire, Surrey to Kent, but by the time they reached Blackheath an estimated 5000 rebels had deserted.
- The Pilgrimage of Grace was another rebellion in which numbers varied in the course of two months. Some of the 30,000 rebels who occupied Lincoln in October 1536 left to join the Yorkshire movement, but as different groups targeted particular towns, the numbers in individual rebel parties ranged from 3000 at Hull to some 20,000 at York. By the time various dissident groups had converged on Pontefract under the leadership of Aske, there may have been as many as 40,000 rebels.

After 1536, rebellions in both England and Ireland were smaller affairs:

- Perhaps as many as 16,000 protesters descended on Norwich in 1549.
- Wyatt had around 3000 supporters in Kent.

- Some 6000 followed the northern earls.
- Essex mustered no more than 300 men.
- Irish rebellions generally comprised a few hundred men at most and O'Neill's national uprising of 1595 was exceptional in that he was able to rally more than 6000 troops.

Support

Noble and foreign support

Although the size of a rebel host was clearly a problem for the authorities, not least because royal armies took a while to assemble, and even then they might be smaller, of far greater concern was the nature of the support a rebellion might receive.

The most serious revolts were those that attracted noble and foreign interest:

- Nobles were the natural leaders in society; they could call on their own servants and tenants to fight for them, they had the finances to fund an army and they had access to military equipment.
- Foreign-sponsored rebellions presented a different kind of threat. Troops were often battle-hardened mercenaries and the English authorities could not be sure when and where they might strike. Fortunately, in most cases, promises of foreign assistance failed to materialise but the prospect of foreign troops landing in England gave a rebellion added potency.

Rebellions of this nature mostly occurred at the beginning and end of the Tudor period, and sought to overthrow the monarch or alter the line of succession. Henry VII faced four rebellions involving English nobles, two of which were backed by foreign powers:

- In the 1486 rebellions, Lovel and the Stafford brothers were unable to get enough support from their **retainers** before Henry suppressed their conspiracies.
- The rebellions of Simnel (1486–7) and Warbeck (1497) each attracted Irish interest and a small number of English nobles intent on dethroning the king. Simnel had the greater support, which ranged from Irish nobles and bishops to English nobles and clerics and German mercenaries, who were funded by Margaret of Burgundy. Warbeck's support came from disaffected Yorkists keen to remove Henry, from merchants unhappy at trade **embargoes** with **Flanders**, and from renegade Scottish, Irish and Flemish adventurers. Also caught up in the conspiracy were two powerful English nobles, Lord Fitzwater, steward of the royal household, and Sir William Stanley, Henry's step-uncle and lord chamberlain. Significantly, Henry appears to have nipped noble treason in the bud: when Warbeck finally landed in Cornwall, he gathered mainly 6000 Cornish miners, artisans and farmers – none was a noble or gentleman.

 **KEY TERMS**

Retainers Nobles retained servants in their households who might be used as private armies.

Embargoes Trade restrictions such as those imposed on Burgundy in 1493.

Flanders Part of modern-day Belgium and the centre of the cloth trade.

Each of the dynastic rebellions that occurred in the second half of the period had noble involvement and several hoped for some degree of foreign commitment:

- The Duke of Northumberland, in 1553, had the support of aristocrats like the earls of Oxford and Huntingdon, and lords **Grey** and Clinton in his attempt to overthrow Mary, but significantly more nobles rallied to her defence and most of Northumberland's army of 2000 deserted when a confrontation seemed likely.
- Wyatt, in the following year, had expected the Duke of Suffolk and his brothers in Leicestershire, **Sir James Croft** in Herefordshire and **Sir Peter Carew** in Devon, as well as French troops, to support his uprising in Kent but none transpired. Instead, Wyatt had to rely on the county militia and gentry like Sir Henry Isley, Sir George Harper and Thomas Culpepper, all former sheriffs, and a host of minor gentry and their tenants. Significantly, only two leading Kentishmen, Lord Abergavenny and Sir Robert Southwell, were openly loyal to the government.
- Thomas Percy and Charles Neville, the earls of Northumberland and Westmorland, also failed to attract any major noble family to their cause in 1569. None rose in Lancashire, Cheshire or Cumberland, and even some of Neville's tenants were reluctant to get involved. Again, the rebellion rested on mainly disaffected Catholic gentry but the belief that a Spanish army under Alva was preparing to give them military support remained wishful thinking.
- Essex, in 1601, had more noble support than any other rebellion. The earls of Southampton, **Sussex** and Rutland, lords Cromwell, Mounteagle and Sandes, and twelve deputy lieutenants of their counties gathered in London with their servants and retainers. Nevertheless, in spite of soliciting Scottish and Irish aid, Essex received no external help, nor did he get any support from the mayor, sheriff and City of London.
- An Irish earl or clan claimant eager to acquire an earldom always led rebellions in Ireland but most of their support came from their tenants and Catholic clergy, who were loyal to their landlord and faith and opposed to all things English. It was a situation that Spain tried to exploit in 1580 and 1601 when it sent troops to assist revolts in Munster.

Commoners

Revolts that were demonstrations against government policies often attracted support from a range of lower social groups. Few attracted noble or gentry interest and some, like the Amicable Grant and Oxfordshire rising, solely consisted of commoners. In 1525, as many as 4000 rural peasants, urban artisans and unemployed people gathered in Sudbury and Lavenham, Suffolk. It is important to realise, however, that although no nobles or gentry led the revolt, royal councillors and the Archbishop of Canterbury sympathised with the complaints and similar anti-tax protests were voiced in other parts of the country. The Oxfordshire rising, in contrast, had neither sympathy nor support from the landed gentry and nobility, and without their financial backing and

KEY FIGURES

Henry Grey, Duke of Suffolk (1517–54)

The father of Lady Jane Grey and a strong Protestant. He had been pardoned by Mary, but although he played only a minor role in Wyatt's rebellion was executed.

Sir James Croft (c.1518–90)

A knight from Herefordshire, his part of the rising never got off the ground and he escaped punishment, becoming prominent in government under Elizabeth.

Sir Peter Carew (c.1514–75)

Acted for Edward VI to put down unrest in Devon and was an MP for Devon in 1553.

Earl of Sussex (c.1525–83)

President of the Council of the North. He had questioned the northern earls in October 1569 and been assured of their loyalty.

involvement, the rebellion had no hope of success. In fact, even most of the servants of the gentry who had considered giving support to the rebels lost their nerve when the uprising began. Some 30 men were rounded up and all were found to be local workers and tradesmen.

Other social groups

Other large-scale demonstrations of the period were able to attract support from a wide range of social groups and not just from the commons:

- The Cornish rebellion of 1497 not only had a peer, a lawyer and a blacksmith at the helm, it was backed by 44 parish priests, several abbots, monks and local gentry. As such it was a formidable assembly. When it reached Somerset, 22 gentry, four sheriffs, three members of parliament (MPs) and four abbots were among the 4000 rebels who enlisted, although the majority who joined were urban artisans and peasant farmers.
- In 1549, a similar protest was launched in Cornwall against a new English prayer book; it too had the same broad cross-section of support that included at least eight priests, several justices of the peace (JPs), two mayors, gentry such as Arundell and Winslade, and a large number of farmers, labourers, artisans and itinerant unemployed. Significantly, it attracted no noble support.
- Kett's rebellion (1549) also had no major landowner in its ranks. Its support came from small tenant farmers, lesser gentry, rural workers and unemployed craftsmen, many of whom joined the revolt once the city of Norwich had fallen.

The Pilgrimage of Grace 1536–7

The rebellion that reflected the greatest degree of social variety was the Pilgrimage of Grace. Among the leading nobles were younger sons and relatives of the four major northern houses – Stanley, Neville, Percy and Clifford – including Sir Ingram and Sir Thomas Percy, Lords Darcy and Hussey, George Lumley, son of Lord Lumley, and John Neville, Lord Latimer, and his younger brother Marmaduke. Although several revolts against religious reforms and economic and social conditions were started in 1536 by lower orders and parish clergy, leadership and control soon passed to the gentry and the more politically important families. The Dymokes and Willoughbys, for example, ultimately led the Lincolnshire rising but it began in Louth at the hands of 'Captain Cobbler' and the local clergy.

What made the Pilgrimage of Grace unique, however, was the high-profile involvement of the commons, clergy, gentry and lesser nobles at every stage of the revolt. Many became captains of the nine host armies under the overall leadership of Aske. Of course, it is impossible to say who enlisted voluntarily and who was forced to join and lead the rebel hosts. Many gentry, like Sir Christopher Hilyard, John Hallam and Robert Bowes in Yorkshire, later claimed they were threatened, but most had ulterior motives in accounting for their involvement. The Willoughbys in Lincolnshire, for instance, resented the Duke of Suffolk's acquisition of family lands, Sir Ingram Percy of Alnwick had been disinherited, and Lord Darcy of Pontefract was out of favour with the king. All claimed they supported the pilgrims under duress but it was widely reported that once the rebellion had begun, the gentry were 'first harnessed of all others'.

Frequency

Most English rebellions occurred at the beginning of the period, when the Tudor dynasty was very vulnerable. Henry VII faced five serious revolts, three of which aimed to overthrow him. The summer of 1497 was a particularly critical time. England was at war with Scotland, Henry had to fight the Battle of Blackheath to suppress the Cornish rebellion and Warbeck was laying claim to the throne. The Spanish ambassador to the imperial court may have been exaggerating when he wrote that 'the whole kingdom was against the King', but he was closer to the mark when he claimed that 'had the king lost the battle he would have been finished off and beheaded'.

As the Tudors became more secure, alternative claimants died out and people grew accustomed to their rule. At the same time, the politically important groups, the nobility, gentry and yeomen, saw the benefits of allying with the ruling family and turned away from rebellion as a means of solving their problems. Instead, issues of major concern came to be aired and often resolved at court, in council and in parliament. Thus, after 1570, Elizabeth faced only one rebellion of note, and this lasted for less than twelve hours. Of course, she did have to contend with numerous plots on her life, notably **Ridolfi**, **Babington** and **Throckmorton**, but none grew into a rebellion. Ireland, on the other hand, gave Elizabeth a lot of trouble. There she had to deal with more rebellions than any of her predecessors due to a combination of factors that are considered below (see pages 83–4).

In contrast, most of the disturbances that faced Henry VIII, Edward VI and Mary I between 1536 and 1554 were principally a reaction to their religious and economic policies. Undoubtedly, 1549 was the worst year, when between June and August some 27 English counties experienced revolts or longer periods of rebellion. Riots and disturbances continued to be reported in the early 1550s but the frequency had peaked in terms of both size and extent. Mary Tudor, for example, faced only two serious revolts, one of which enabled her to secure the throne from Lady Jane Grey, while Elizabeth was confronted with just one serious rebellion in the north of England in 1569.

Reasons for the decline in the frequency of rebellions

A number of reasons, some of which are developed more fully in Chapter 4, may be offered to explain this decline in the frequency of rebellions:

- *The decline in dynastic unrest*: most of the dynastic and political factors that had underpinned Yorkist rebellions began to lose their impetus as the Tudors

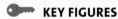
KEY FIGURES

Roberto di Ridolfi (1531–1612)

An Italian merchant who had European connections and persuaded the Duke of Norfolk to become involved in a plot to help put Mary Stuart on the throne.

Anthony Babington (1561–86)

A fervent Catholic and supporter of the Jesuits who was in contact with Mary Stuart. In 1586, he offered to release her from jail and murder Elizabeth. His letters were intercepted and he confessed.

Francis Throckmorton (1554–85)

A Catholic, who on his travels in Europe met some of Mary Stuart's agents. He became involved in a plot to overthrow Elizabeth with the help of French forces.

systematically removed pretenders and claimants. As late as 1541, Henry VIII was still eliminating members of the Pole family, who were descended from the royal house of Plantagenet, but thereafter there were no more scions of the House of York lurking in the political woodwork.

- *The decline in religious unrest*: the Reformation was a source of provocation to many Englishmen, and religious issues in 1536 and 1549, and to a lesser extent in 1569, lay behind armed rebellions. The Elizabethan Church settlement of 1559, however, was a moderate policy that satisfied most religious groups. Moreover, the government and the Church wisely held back from strictly enforcing its terms. If no offence was given, then it was hoped that none would be taken, and so it proved. After 1549, religion ceased to be a major issue worthy of a rebellion.

- *The decline in social and economic unrest*: social and economic problems, which could be a frequent source of discontent, peaked in the 1540s. Although difficulties remained for the rest of the period, issues such as enclosures, engrossments, excessive taxation, hyperinflation and poor tenant–landlord relations all abated.

- *Government action and the decline in unrest*: a major factor that prevented the outbreak of disturbances in the second half of the sixteenth century was the measures taken by Mary and Elizabeth. In particular, the poor and unemployed were helped rather than punished, JPs and lords lieutenant kept a closer eye on local tensions and endeavoured to overcome potential difficulties before they got out of hand, and people were encouraged to resolve their problems by peaceful means such as arbitration, litigation and parliamentary bills rather than by acts of lawlessness and violence.

As a result of these developments, many of which did not operate in Ireland, rebellions in England became less frequent in the course of the period.

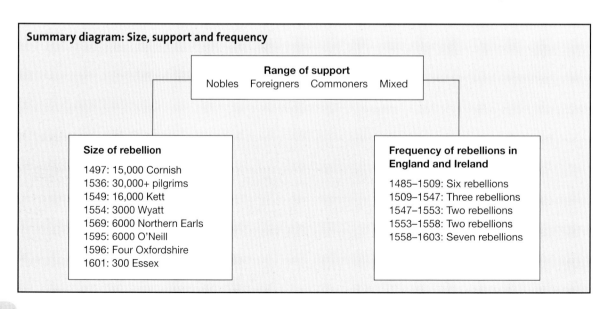

Summary diagram: Size, support and frequency

Range of support
Nobles   Foreigners   Commoners   Mixed

Size of rebellion

1497: 15,000 Cornish
1536: 30,000+ pilgrims
1549: 16,000 Kett
1554: 3000 Wyatt
1569: 6000 Northern Earls
1595: 6000 O'Neill
1596: Four Oxfordshire
1601: 300 Essex

Frequency of rebellions in England and Ireland

1485–1509: Six rebellions
1509–1547: Three rebellions
1547–1553: Two rebellions
1553–1558: Two rebellions
1558–1603: Seven rebellions

Irish rebellions

▶ *In what ways were Irish rebellions different from those in England?*

It has often been claimed that during this period rebellions in Ireland were quite different from those that occurred in England:

- There were differences in scale and duration. Most Irish disturbances lasted for several years and, like bushfires, no sooner had one been put out than another started up. The scale of fighting also increased in the course of the period. Sir Edward Poynings, Henry VII's Lord Deputy of Ireland in the 1490s, tried to defend English interests in the Pale with some 400 troops; a century later, the Earl of Essex took 17,000 men and Lord Mountjoy 13,000 troops to combat O'Neill's rebellion. English soldiers were usually better trained and equipped but, until the 1590s, the Tudors consistently underestimated the nature of the problem confronting local garrisons and the amount of money needed to keep effective control. In practice, if an Irish chieftain was determined to resist English rule, there was little that could be done to stop him.

- Although all Irish leaders pledged their loyalty to the English monarch, they were not averse to acting dishonourably when it suited them. The Earl of Kildare, for instance, backed the pretender Simnel before swearing allegiance to Henry VII, and made little attempt to apprehend Warbeck when he landed in Ireland. Similarly, the Earl of Desmond spent five years in the Tower of London but it still did not prevent him from taking part in the Geraldine rebellion of 1579. And if a truce was signed between leaders, as O'Neill and English commanders agreed in 1596 and 1599, it was simply regarded as a device to buy more time. In effect, Irish rebellions were most likely to end when the clan leader was killed, and even this could not be guaranteed. As Lord Grey discovered in 1579, no sooner was Fitzgerald killed than Desmond took his place and prolonged the rebellion for another four years.

After 1534, three factors affected Anglo-Irish relations and influenced the nature and course of rebellions in Ireland:

- Henry VIII ended generations of Irish aristocratic rule and seriously destabilised relations between English governments and Irish subjects and between Irish and **Gaelic clans**. This was because for the first time English-born officials were appointed to key administrative posts as lord deputies, lieutenants, treasurers and chancellors. The Crown no longer had an Irish family, such as the Kildares, to safeguard its interest, and rival clans, like the Butlers, O'Neills, O'Mores, O'Connors and O'Donnells, felt less intimidated and more willing to break the law.

- Once Henry became King of Ireland in 1541 rather than 'Lord of Ireland', his relationship with Gaelic chiefs changed. They were now obliged to 'surrender'

 **KEY TERM**

Gaelic clans Some native and older Irish families spoke Gaelic, and were distinguished from the families of Norman descent and more recent immigrants who spoke English.

Figure 2.2 Tudor Ireland.

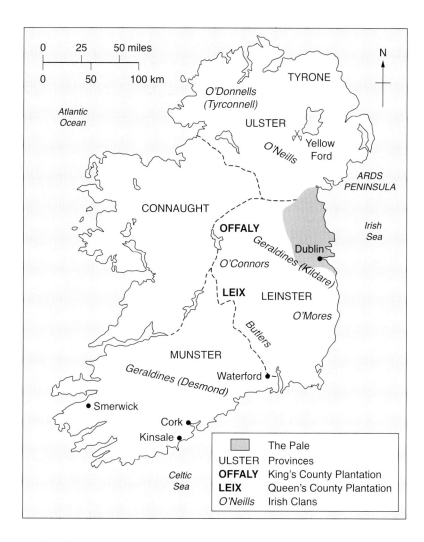

 **KEY TERMS**

Anglicise To make English.

Firebrands People who cause unrest.

their lands, renounce their traditional customs and have their lands 'regranted' according to English usage. Attempts by Henry and later Tudors to **Anglicise** the Irish led to fierce resistance that soon developed into a more general and national resentment. Gaelic tribes defended their language, laws and customs, and resented attacks on their culture as much as incursions on their lands by 'new' English colonists and absentee landlords.

- Many 'old' English families resented attempts by the Tudors to introduce a Protestant reformation. Although Elizabeth had no desire to provoke the Irish over religious matters and deliberately discouraged her bishops from sending over Protestant evangelists, after her excommunication in 1570 Roman Catholic missionaries arrived in Ireland from the continent intent on whipping up anti-English sentiment. This religious zeal was indeed a feature of the Geraldine and O'Neill rebellions, and reminiscent of Catholic **firebrands** operating in the Northern Earls' revolt in England in 1569.

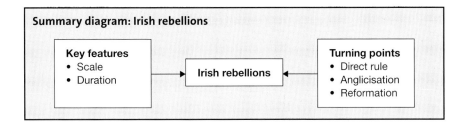

Summary diagram: Irish rebellions

Key features
• Scale
• Duration

→ **Irish rebellions** ←

Turning points
• Direct rule
• Anglicisation
• Reformation

7 Conclusion: success or failure?

▶ *Why were some rebellions more successful than others at achieving their objectives?*

How can success or failure be measured? It is not enough to say that a rebellion was a success if particular grievances were brought to the government's attention, unless those grievances were redressed. Nor is it acceptable to claim that a rebellion was successful if some of its lesser grievances were corrected but the more important issues were ignored or left unresolved. For a rebellion to succeed, it had to fulfil its principal objectives. In this respect:

• None of the dynastic rebellions achieved their goal and only Mary succeeded in removing the government *in situ*, namely Northumberland and Lady Jane Grey. Indeed, rebellions were always going to fail as long as the government held its nerve.
• Only one rebellion that involved the commons achieved its objective – the withdrawal of the Amicable Grant – and this was precisely because several councillors alerted the king to the likely consequences if he did not comply. Apart from the wide geographical spread of opposition, resistance in London was too close to the government for comfort. Of course, Henry VIII had the neat let-out of being able to blame Wolsey for the problems that precipitated the revolt and so the government emerged with credit and the king enhanced his undeserved reputation for generosity.
• Other demonstrations resulted in some satisfactory resolutions (see Chapter 3, pages 125–7). The Yorkshire and Cornish tax rebellions of 1489 and 1497 discouraged Henry VII from making any further novel demands.
• Protests against religious changes in 1536 (Pilgrimage of Grace) may have deterred Henry VIII from implementing further Protestant reforms, and the repeal of the Statute of Uses, which was one of the pilgrims' requests, occurred in 1540.
• The Edwardian government also made concessions. It responded to the 1549 Western and Kett rebellions by repealing the Subsidy Act, passing Enclosure and Tillage Acts, and enacting poor law legislation, all of which was designed to assist the commons in a constructive and benevolent manner.

- Complaints by northern rebels in 1536 (Pilgrimage of Grace) and 1569 (Northern Earls' rebellion) led to changes in the composition of the Council of the North (see pages 128–9), and concern raised by the Oxford rebels in 1596 saw the Privy Council restore land under tillage and initiate prosecutions against illegal enclosures.
- Only one rebellion resulted in the overthrow of a leading politician. Ironically, it was the Duke of Somerset who, of all Tudor ministers, wanted so desperately to help the rank and file in times of economic and social crisis. Yet his overthrow was less the objective of any rebellion but more the result of gentry and privy councillors reacting to his inept policies and failure to suppress widespread revolts. This occurrence was exceptional.

In general, rebellions failed to achieve their main objectives.

Reasons for success or failure of rebellions

There are several explanations why most rebellions failed:

- *Leadership*: successful rebellions needed strong and effective leadership, and this feature was not always present. Often the best leaders were the gentry, lawyers and yeomen rather than their social superiors, the nobility and clergy, and the lack of support from these two groups largely explains why rebellions failed.
- *Government action*: the government deployed a strategy of playing for time, offering pardons to all but the ringleaders, and agreeing to discuss grievances on condition that the rebels dispersed (see Chapter 3, pages 107–10). Once this occurred, no matter what government promises were made, the likelihood that the rebels' complaints would be addressed was slim. Tudor rebellions are littered with examples of betrayal by the authorities:
  - The Lincolnshire rebels implored Aske in Yorkshire not to bargain with the Duke of Norfolk, as earlier the Duke of Suffolk had duped them and their rising had accomplished nothing.
  - The Western rebels likewise suspected a deal was going to be done when gentry leaders met Devon JPs outside Exeter in 1549.
  - Similarly, Kett was discouraged from holding private talks with the Earl of Warwick as his supporters feared he might be tempted to make a deal.
  The authorities knew that the longer a rebellion continued, the more likely it would end in failure. The possibility that rebels would quarrel, desert or betray their cause increased as food supplies ran out and living conditions deteriorated. Rebels also needed to consider the welfare of their families who they had left behind, farmers had to harvest their crops and, if a royal army was known to be approaching, the possibility of death on the battlefield was not a welcome proposition.
- *Military action*: unlike political rebellions, which could only be successful if the monarch was defeated or killed in battle, and at Stoke (1487), Blackheath

(1497) and Cambridge (1553) when the thrones of Henry VII and Mary were at risk, most protesters tried to avoid a military confrontation:

- Aske, in 1536, wrote to rebels at Clitheroe Moor ordering them not to fight the Earl of Derby's troops.
- Aske had a following of some 40,000 at Pontefract, but had no wish to do battle with the Duke of Norfolk's troops assembled nearby.
- Both Arundell at Exeter and Kett at Norwich felt the same way, but once a royal army had gathered enough men, such that its commander believed victory was certain, there was only going to be one winner. Lack of funding for rebels resulted in inadequate cavalry, weapons, ammunition and supplies, whereas government troops could bide their time until they were ready to attack. If foreign mercenaries supplemented the latter, as occurred at Clyst and Dussindale in 1549, the more hardened professional army was likely to prove victorious.

- *Provincialism*: rebellions failed on account of their provincialism. Most aimed to resolve local grievances and had no desire to link up with other disaffected areas or to broaden their appeal. Only on one occasion were rebels known to have made contact with protesters some distance away, when the Exeter rebels made overtures to demonstrators in Winchester, Hampshire, in July 1549, but the latter was discouraged from marching to their assistance. Understandably, the government felt more anxiety the nearer a rebellion got to London, and this increased the rebels' chances of success. In practice, however, only the Cornish revolt in 1497, Wyatt's rebellion in 1554 and Essex in 1601 came within striking distance of Whitehall. In each case, the government withstood the challenge, loyal troops dispersed the insurgents and the insurrections ended in failure.

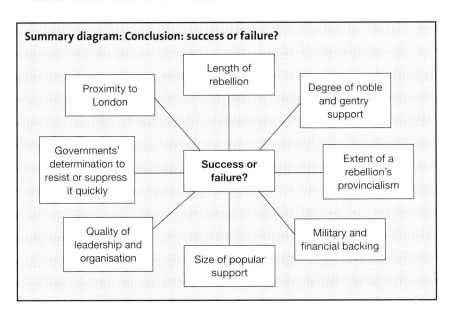

Summary diagram: Conclusion: success or failure?

Chapter summary

There are a number of factors that need to be examined when analysing the nature of Tudor rebellions. These include their objectives, the duration, location, leadership, tactics, organisation and support. It is these factors that help to explain why most Tudor rebellions failed to achieve their primary goal. However, as this chapter has shown, their importance varied from rebellion to rebellion, although a few themes, such as the failure of dynastic unrest and attempts to change government religious policy, do emerge, while those that were primarily taxation rebellions did achieve some success. Many rebellions lacked both the organisation and tactics to successfully challenge the state, even though it did not have a standing army, as for most of the period the nobility remained loyal and acted to put down unrest. The frequent rebel failures discouraged other would-be rebels, particularly in the latter part of the period, and would lead to many seeking other ways to resolve their grievances. This pattern did not occur in Ireland, where rebellion became more frequent and longer lasting in the second half of the sixteenth century.

 Refresher questions

Use these questions to remind yourself of the key material covered in this chapter.

1 What were the objectives of Tudor rebellions?

2 Why did some rebellions last longer than others?

3 Which areas of England and Ireland were more prone to rebellions than others?

4 Why did rebels want to take control of county towns?

5 What strategies did the organisers of Tudor rebellions follow?

6 What were the most frequent tactics of rebels?

7 Why were the nobility and gentry the best leaders of a rebellion?

8 Why did some rebellions attract only limited support?

9 Why did the leaders of rebellions encourage foreign support?

10 Why were there so many rebellions in the period up to 1554?

11 Why were Irish rebellions more difficult to put down?

In-depth studies and debates

The examination requires you to study three topics in depth and for this unit they are:

- The Pilgrimage of Grace
- The Western rebellion
- Tyrone's rebellion.

This section will go into more detail about the three topics and introduce you to some of the key debates about them, so that you will have enough depth of knowledge to be able to evaluate passages that are set on any of these three rebellions.

Key debate 1: whose rebellion was the Pilgrimage of Grace?

There has been much debate as to who actually led the Lincolnshire rising and the Pilgrimage of Grace. Some historians, such as G.R. Elton, argued that it was organised by an out-of-favour court faction, led by men such as Lord Hussey, while Steve Gunn (1989) has argued that, at least in Lincolnshire, it was the work of the parish clergy, but more importantly the leaders of society in the villages and small towns, the richer yeomen and tradesmen. These men were often local officers, such as churchwardens and parish constables. Michael Bush, in his detailed study of the rebel armies, *The Pilgrimage of Grace: A Study of Rebel Armies of 1536*, published in 1996, has shown that the Pilgrimage was primarily a 'movement of the commons', with the armies representing a protest of the people. Such accounts argue that the gentry were put under pressure to take part and lead the host armies that were assembled, as they would give the movement greater legitimacy and because these people were seen as the natural leaders of society.

There is some evidence to suggest that it was a rebellion of the gentry:

- The organisation of the rebellion suggests that it was not spontaneous and only the gentry would have the ability or connections to organise such a large-scale rising.
- Some of the rebel demands (see Chapter 1), such as the complaint about the Statute of Uses, appealed only to the gentry.
- The gentry were those most affected by changes in royal policy and the increased influence of the Duke of Suffolk in Lincolnshire.
- Men such as Hussey and Darcy had court connections, and played key roles in the rebellion.
- The nobility and gentry involved certainly had the motives to lead a rising as they had lost their position at court and resented the influence of Thomas Cromwell and Anne Boleyn.
- The rebel demands also attacked Cromwell, Richard Rich and Thomas Audley; all men to whom the gentry had lost out and who they viewed as upstarts.

- The names of heretics who were attacked would not have been familiar to the commons.
- Although the gentry argued that they were coerced into joining, this was a useful way to excuse their behaviour once the rising had failed.

In arguing that it was a popular rebellion in which the gentry were coerced into joining:

- The nine host armies began as a protest of the people.
- It was the belief in the 'society of orders' that led the commons to insist on the gentry and noble families leading the armies; the commons also believed that the gentry would best articulate their views.
- The original name of the movement was the 'pilgrimage for grace for the commonwealth'.
- The aims of the rebels were to protect the commonwealth, hence the demands on taxation, tenants' rights and the wealth of local churches.
- The gentry, such as Hussey, did not have the influence in local society to raise such numbers.
- Once the gentry were forced into joining they tried to control the rebellion and prevent it from becoming violent.
- The clergy and monks played a significant role in the rising; this might be expected as they were the ones whose lives had been most dramatically hit by the religious changes.
- The clergy supplied money for the rising: in Lincolnshire they provided the rebels at Louth with funds. Some monks joined the rising, armed and horsed.
- In Louth it was the priest who encouraged the rising and it was the cobbler Nicholas Melton who originally led it.

There is little doubt that the rising was the result of a complex range of causes, as was seen in Chapter 1. It also involved a wide range of social groups – across classes – and each with their own grievances, which was reflected in the demands. It should also be remembered that the rising was actually a series of regional revolts, each with its own peculiar characteristics. In order to try and work out the main causes of the rising, historians have asked whose revolt it was. However, as we have seen, this has failed to produce a consensus as to whether it was a rising of the commons aided by the gentry, or of the gentry assisted by the lower orders. Perhaps the best conclusion that can be reached is that the whole of northern society was out of joint.

Key debate 2: how violent were the Western rebels?

The Western rebellion has been characterised as one of the more violent Tudor rebellions, from the inflammatory nature of the rebels' demands, 'We will have', to the murder of members of the gentry. The rebels also put up strong resistance to government forces, with evidence of five battles or significant skirmishes before they were finally defeated. However, it can also be argued that the rebel behaviour was encouraged by the hostility of the government forces they faced and that, unlike Kett's rebels, they did not force their way into the regional capital and fire the city.

In arguing that the rebels were violent:

- The Cornish rebels had started by attacking and robbing the gentry who had retreated to St Michael's Mount.
- At Bodmin, the rebels had shouted 'Kill the Gentlemen'.
- In Devon, the rebels murdered William Hellyons, who was the only member of the gentry who resisted them.
- They attacked Trematon Castle, plundered it and put its owner in jail.
- The rebels refused to negotiate with the gentry, even though there was some evidence that they had sympathy with the rebels' religious grievance that religion should remain as Henry VIII had left it until Edward came of age.
- There were clashes between the city of Exeter and the rebels. The rebels attempted to set fire to the city gates. The rebels also attempted to mine the walls.
- There were a number of engagements between the rebels and the government forces, with significant encounters at Fenny Bridges, Clyst St Mary, Clyst Heath and Sampford Courtenay.

In arguing that the rebels were not violent or were provoked into violence by the action of government forces:

- It was government forces who set fire to the rebel defences at Crediton, which caused barns and houses to be set alight.
- The view of the rebels as violent and 'refuse, scum of the whole county' is from a member of the gentry and should therefore be treated with caution.
- Sir Peter Carew, a leading Protestant sympathiser, attempted to meet the rebels near Crediton, but his attitude only made the situation more tense. He was later reprimanded by the government for his actions.
- The only contemporary writer of the rebellion, John Hooker, commented, 'the common people noised and spread it abroad that the gentlemen were altogether bent to overrun, spoil and destroy them', which only encouraged further resistance.
- Divisions within the gentry over tactics encouraged the rebels to be more aggressive.
- The rebels did not launch an attack on Exeter but wanted to show that they were serious by controlling the area. When they did advance towards Exeter they carried the banner of the Five Wounds of Christ, as had the peaceful Pilgrimage of Grace.

The Western rebels certainly resisted strongly, but how much of this was due to fears of government retribution is a matter of debate. Certainly, the brutal treatment that followed the suppression suggests that the rebels were right to be fearful of the government. This may explain why even after defeat on the battlefield there was rearguard action and pockets of resistance. The government may also have felt justified in its action, given the strength of resistance. There is little doubt that the government acted illegally, executed without trials and confiscated property. Some of the violence was also provoked by personality clashes, particularly with Carew, and it can be argued that government operations further deepened the already existent hostility.

Key debate 3: why was Tyrone's rebellion so difficult to suppress?

Tyrone's rebellion was serious; it was the longest lasting Tudor rebellion, taking place from 1595 to 1603, and being pacified only after Elizabeth's death. There were constant concerns that discontented Irishmen would allow Spanish troops to land and therefore pave the way for an invasion of England. The situation was made worse by Tyrone's capture of a key fort on the River Blackwater, which guarded one of the main entries to Ulster. He also defeated the English at Yellow Ford in 1598. As a result, he was able to seize Munster and take control of much of Ireland.

It is important to have a clear understanding of the events in order to assess why it was difficult to put down the rising. The debate centres around the extent to which the longevity of the rebellion was due to the strength of Tyrone and his forces or to the weakness of the English response.

In arguing that the strength of Tyrone's rebellion was the main factor behind the difficulty in putting it down, the following could be considered:

- It was the first national rebellion in Ireland and this gave Tyrone widespread support.
- As Tyrone had control over Ulster he had a good supply of resources for his troops.
- Tyrone's forces were well trained and were often led by men who had been trained and served in Elizabeth's armies.
- Tyrone had reinforcements from mercenaries from Scotland.
- Tyrone was a competent leader and was well trained in the art of ambush and, as with other Irish rebels, he had a good knowledge of the countryside so could conduct a guerrilla-based campaign when it suited him.

However, it can be argued that it was Elizabeth's actions and policies that were the main reason why the rebellion was so difficult to suppress:

- War with Spain meant that expenditure on Ireland had to be kept low, but the area needed to be secured so that it could not be used as a base by Spain to invade England.
- Ireland had been increasingly neglected by Elizabeth and her council, so many in Ireland felt alienated.
- The Lord Deputy, Fitzwilliam, was old and unable to control the factional disputes.

- The council was divided over strategy, with Elizabeth wanting peace and other advisors arguing for a more aggressive policy to deal with the threat.
- The appointment of Essex was a mistake; he had argued for the job as her most experienced captain, but he was ill-suited and wasted time and troops in needless manoeuvres.
- Essex dared not risk giving battle with Tyrone as he took only 4000 men with him.
- Essex did not make good use of the vast amount of resources given to him; this is seen by how quickly Mountjoy, his replacement, was able to resolve the issue.
- Essex may have entered into secret negotiations with Tyrone.

There is certainly some justification to the argument that the rebellion was difficult to suppress because of English mistakes, particularly the appointment and behaviour of Essex. This is confirmed by the speed with which the rebellion was ended by Mountjoy. He had an army much the same size as Essex, but was also better at conciliating the native Irish. It can be argued that he was fortunate in capturing some of their leaders, but it should also be remembered that he was able to overcome some Spanish forces who landed in 1601.

Study skills: thematic essay question

How to develop analysis and write a paragraph that shows synthesis

If you have already studied units 1 and 2 of the OCR course, the essay-writing skills that you have developed are similar to those needed for unit 3. However, there are two key differences. On page 51 we stressed that the title of the unit, thematic study, makes it clear that the essay section should be approached thematically rather than chronologically, particularly if you want to reach the higher mark range. In addition, in this unit there is a significant emphasis on synthesis.

In answering essay questions you are required to make connections, comparisons and links between different elements of the period and aspects of the topic; this is that crucial element of synthesis – the comparison between different parts of the period – to show similarities and differences between events or people. It is not simply enough to list examples from across the period in each paragraph; you must make direct comparisons between them. You do not need to make comparisons across the whole period in every paragraph, but the whole period needs to be covered in the essay.

As with essays in units 1 and 2, you should aim to write analytically. This is perhaps the hardest, but most important skill you need to develop. An analytical approach can be helped by ensuring that the opening sentence of each paragraph introduces an idea, which directly answers the question and is not just a piece of factual information. In a very strong answer it should be possible to simply read the opening sentences of all the paragraphs and know what argument is being put forward.

Consider the following question:

How far did ineffective leadership explain the failure of Tudor rebellions?

Possible opening sentences for an answer in response to this question could be as follows:

- Not all rebellions were led by ineffective leaders; both Kett and Aske were competent and therefore there were other causes in these rebellions which explain their failure.
- In some instances, such as Warbeck's and Wyatt's rebellions, ineffective leadership was certainly a factor in the failure of the rebellion.
- Government measures, such as the raising of forces, were more important in defeating rebellion.
- A significant number of rebellions failed because they were unable to attract support from either the nobility or the clergy.
- It was much harder for rebellions to achieve their aims if they were a long way from London.
- As the period progressed, many who were disaffected were reluctant to join rebellions because they had seen what had happened at places such as Dussindale or in the aftermath of the Western rebellion and were unwilling to risk their lives, and this limited the numbers involved.

You would then go on to discuss both sides of the argument raised by the opening sentence, using relevant knowledge about the issue to support each side of the argument. The final sentence of the paragraph would reach a judgement on the role played by the factor you are discussing in the failure of the rebellions. This approach would ensure that the final sentence of each paragraph links back to the actual question you are answering. If you can do this for each paragraph you will have a series of mini-essays, which discuss a factor and reach a conclusion or judgement about the importance of that factor or issue.

Developing synthesis

Some of the opening sentences have already hinted at comparisons between different rebellions across the period, but this comparison would need to be developed and more of the period covered if an answer was to reach the highest level. The two responses below illustrate a weak approach (Response A), which does not really illustrate synthesis, and a strong approach (Response B), which shows a high level of synthesis.

Response A

One of the reasons for the failure of the rising of the northern earls was certainly weak leadership. The earls had to be pressured by their wives into undertaking the rising and were therefore reluctant leaders, which would not have given potential supporters much confidence to join the rising and may explain the small numbers the rebellion attracted. The earls had been driven into rebellion out of despair and financial hardship and they had not developed a coherent plan for the rising, which was another reason for its failure. The leadership of Thomas Wyatt was a factor in the failure of the 1554 rising. His failure to advance rapidly on London and instead seize Cooling Castle allowed Mary to prepare and fortify London Bridge. Wyatt's delay also had an impact on his forces and lowered their morale, which may also have been a factor in their failure. The leadership of Warbeck was also a factor in the failure of the rebellion. Although he claimed to be the Earl of Warwick, he was too young to lead a rebellion or inspire people to follow him and this may explain why the rebellion attracted limited support. He was not physically strong or intimidating and lacked the charisma needed to inspire others.

Response B

Leading a rebellion was a great responsibility, particularly when the numbers involved were large or the longer a revolt lasted. Ineffective leadership was a factor in the failure of a number of rebellions. There is little doubt that age was a factor in the qualities of a leader; while Simnel was too young, Northumberland and Westmorland were too old and this would have done little to inspire loyalty or provide the charisma needed to lead a major rebellion. Leaders who were indecisive or lacked strategy were also less likely to be effective. Wyatt was indecisive and failed to advance quickly on London when he might have succeeded; similarly, the northern earls had no clear plan and not only failed to realise how long it would take to march to Tutbury to free Mary Queen of Scots, but also were unaware that she had been moved. Ineffective leaders were also more likely to fail as they could attract little support or the wrong type of support. The northern earls and Simnel were unable to attract support because of their poor organisation. While the northern earls lacked funds to pay supporters, with the result that 600 promptly deserted, Simnel failed to realise that the presence of Irish nobles and their 'wild tenants' would discourage many English from joining as his force made its way south from Lancashire.

Analysis of the responses

Response B is the stronger answer and displays high-level synthesis:

- Response A simply lists and explains three ineffectual leaders – the northern earls, Thomas Wyatt and Lambert Simnel – but there is no link or comparison between those leaders in terms of their significance in the failure of the risings.

- There is sound detail in Response A, and there is some argument and analysis about the importance of each leader in the failure, but there is no judgement about leadership or comparison with other factors.
- Response B compares the leadership of different rebellions and shows synthesis across most of the period, with examples from the early, middle and later periods.
- There is sound factual detail in Response B, which is sufficient to support the argument, and own knowledge is being 'used' and not simply imparted.
- The strongest answers will compare the role of ineffectual leadership with other factors to reach a judgement as to the most important reason for the failure of unrest.

Activities

- Write paragraphs similar to Response B for the other themes that were considered in the opening sentences above (see page 94).
- Try writing paragraphs for essays from the essay questions below.
- In order to ensure that you have demonstrated synthesis across the period, highlight the examples of synthesis in your paragraphs and make a checklist to ensure that, over the course of the essay, your paragraphs cover all of the period from 1485 to 1603.

The focus of this section has been on planning and writing analytically and developing synthesis. Use the information in this chapter to plan answers and write a paragraph to answer each of the questions below which shows a high level of analysis and synthesis.

Essay questions

1 'Poor organisation was the most important reason for the failure of rebellions in the period from 1485 to 1603.' How far do you agree with this view of rebellion in England?
2 To what extent were some regions of England and Ireland more prone to unrest than others?
3 Assess the reasons why some rebellions in England and Ireland attracted more support than others.

Study skills: depth study interpretations question

How to evaluate the interpretations

On page 54 we considered how to structure and plan an answer to the depth study interpretations question. This chapter looks at how to evaluate, or apply own knowledge to, one of the interpretations to judge its strengths and weaknesses. After you have started your essay by explaining the two interpretations and placing them in the context of the wider historical debate about the issue, you need to go on to looking at each interpretation in turn, to judge their strengths and weaknesses.

A good paragraph will:

- remain focused on the question
- directly link own knowledge to the view offered in the passage about the issue in the question in order to explain whether the view in the passage is valid or not
- use relevant and accurate knowledge to evaluate the view
- evaluate a range of issues mentioned in the passage.

Read the question and the two interpretations below (on pages 97–8) about the nature of the Pilgrimage of Grace. Then look at the response, which gives a strong evaluation of the strengths and weaknesses of Interpretation A.

> Evaluate the interpretations in both of the passages and explain which you think is more convincing as an explanation of the nature of those involved in the Pilgrimage of Grace.

PASSAGE A

The armies of October 1536 were undoubtedly part of a long tradition. As the product of the so-called risings of the commons, which aimed to put the government right, they belonged to a genre of protest that had its beginnings in 1381 (the Peasants' revolt) and that came to spectacular fruition between 1489 and 1549. In these rebellions the armies acted in the name and interest of the commons. Each of the armies in 1536 was several thousand strong; each professed to be a rising of the commons; each was similarly moved by a concern for both the faith of Christ and the commonwealth; each hated the government for being extortionate and heretical. Within this tradition of revolt, the northern rising was distinctive. It recruited from the whole range of society, their supporters including gentlemen and clerics as well as townsmen and peasants. Some of the participants claimed they were forced to join, but clearly evident was not only a fury of all three orders but also their ability to find common accord. None of these armies or hosts was the work of one particular social group. Moreover, in each case gentlemen and clerics sought to manipulate the people. But from the latter came a strong drive of protest and rage which rendered the uprisings, in initiative and impetus, popular movements.

(Adapted from Michael Bush, The Pilgrimage of Grace: A Study of the Rebel Armies of October 1536, *Manchester University Press, 1996, pp. 7–8.)*

PASSAGE B

In short, the Pilgrimage, though it had its spontaneous moments, was in itself no spontaneous event but in great measure a planned rising. The point is proved by a look at the real leaders who did not come from either the commons or the great northern families. The three chiefs were Darcy, Constable and Hussey, with Aske providing a cover for them. These were the men who really organised the rising – the remnant of the Aragonese party. The idea of a spontaneous combustion which then brought in the existing inflammatory material to set the whole north ablaze is not in accord with the facts; it is necessary to regard the evidence of manifest advance planning. Was it pure coincidence that Aske crossed the River Humber three days after the Lincolnshire rising had begun, that he should be taken by the rebels, that he should have returned to Yorkshire rather than continued his alleged intention of making for London for the beginning of the law term? Cromwell also had a very good point when he asked Darcy how it had been possible to produce thousands of badges of the five wounds virtually at a moment's notice. Even in Lincolnshire, there is evidence of rioters being paid for their work – and that money must have come from somewhere. The Pilgrimage also collapsed really too quickly to justify the common view of it as a genuine mass movement.

(Adapted from G.R. Elton, Reform and Reformation: England 1509–1558, *Harvard University Press, 1977, pp. 266–7.)*

Response

There is certainly some credibility in Interpretation A's view that the Pilgrimage of Grace was part of the tradition of the rising of the commons[1]. The passage makes reference to the size of the rebel armies, which could only have been achieved if there was genuine popular support, and also comments on the claims of the armies that they were a rising of the commons[2]. This view is supported by the very title given to the movement, which was the 'pilgrimage for grace for the commonwealth'. Such a view is given further support as the rebels' aim was to protect the commonwealth, or commons, from unfair and heavy taxation, and agrarian threats, such as attacks on tenants' rights, and also to stop the government's attack on the wealth of parish churches[3]. Moreover, the claim that the rebellion recruited from all elements of society, including the clergy, is correct when one examines those who led the Lincolnshire rising, such as the Vicar of Louth, but also the commons, as the rising was originally led by Nicholas Melton, a cobbler[4]. The passage is also correct to stress that some gentry claimed they were coerced into joining, as Robert Bowes did in Yorkshire, although we should treat their claims with caution as they were attempting to avoid prosecution[5]. The interpretation is also valid in claiming that the initial drive for the rebellion came from the commons as the majority of the host armies were initially mustered by the commons and only later did the gentry assume the leadership[6].

Analysis of the response

1 Starts to evaluate the view of the interpretation about the nature of the rising.
2 Evidence from the interpretation is used to support the claim that it is a valid view.
3 Detailed own knowledge is then applied to reinforce and support the evidence in the interpretation.
4 A precise example of the range of support is supplied.
5 There is further evaluation using the example of gentry who were coerced.
6 The evaluation continues with a comment about the initial mustering of the armies.

The paragraph should continue by evaluating the issues raised in the second paragraph of Interpretation A before a judgement is reached about the overall validity of the view of Passage A. Advice about reaching a judgement is given on page 191.

Activities

- Use information from this chapter to evaluate the second paragraph of Interpretation A.
- Use information from this chapter to evaluate Interpretation B.

It might be helpful to consider the following questions to help you structure your answer:

- What is the view of Interpretation B about the nature of the Pilgrimage of Grace?
- What evidence is there in the interpretation to support this view?
- What knowledge do you have that supports this view?
- What knowledge do you have that challenges this view?
- Check your work and highlight the evaluative words that you have used.

CHAPTER 3

The impact of disturbances on Tudor governments

Although nearly all Tudor rebellions failed to achieve their aims, it does not mean that the rebellions did not have any impact. The threat of rebellion was a serious challenge to a government that did not have a police force or a standing army. This chapter will consider the different ways in which the government responded to the threat by considering the strategy, tactics and fate of the rebels. It will also consider the impact of the rebellions on both the government and society and assess the extent to which they resulted in changes in either personnel or policy. The chapter will also assess the extent to which rebellions were a threat to the government.

This chapter looks at the impact of disturbances under the following headings:

★ How did Tudor governments deal with rebellions?

★ The effects of rebellions on government and society

★ Conclusion: were Tudor governments ever seriously threatened by rebellion and unrest?

It also considers the debates surrounding the three in-depth topics:

★ Did the Pilgrimage of Grace slow down the pace of religious change?

★ Was the Western rebellion a serious threat to the government?

★ How serious a threat to Elizabeth was Tyrone's rebellion?

Key dates

1487	Real Earl of Warwick paraded at St Paul's Cathedral in London	1538	Cromwell's Injunctions
		1540	Statute of Wills
1495	Arrest of Sir William Stanley before he could join Warbeck	1549	John Cheke published *The Hurt of Sedition*
		1550	Execution of Arundell, Winslade, Bury and Holmes for involvement in Western rising
1500	People of Somerset fined for involvement in Cornish rising		
1536	Richard Morrison published *A Lamentation in Which is Showed What Ruin and Destruction Cometh of Seditious Rebellion*	1570	500 of Lord Dacre's army killed or captured near Carlisle
1536	Statute of Uses	1597	Acts to maintain tillage and to prevent the decay of towns and husbandry
1537	Sir Francis Bigod's men killed when they attempted to storm Carlisle	1601	Defeat of Spanish troops at Kinsale

At first sight, we might expect the disturbances to have had little impact on government and society. Few administrations were likely to make concessions to rebels, and so appear vulnerable to further demands, and almost all rebellions ended in failure. Yet on examination, it is evident that changes did take place. Sometimes they happened immediately; more often they occurred over a period of time but nevertheless owed their origin to a rebellion. Governments understood that if they were to reduce the likelihood of future disturbances, then it was sensible to consider why a rebellion had occurred and whether policy changes were needed.

 # How did Tudor governments deal with rebellions?

▶ *How did rulers find out about and act on information concerning rebellions?*

Strategy

Consulting advisers

As soon as the government discovered there was trouble in the kingdom, talks were held between the monarch and a select group of councillors to decide on the best course of action: Henry VII consulted one or more of his most trusted household servants, and occasionally convened a meeting of nobles in a Great Council. This is what occurred in February 1487, when the king first heard that Simnel was planning to invade England. Henry VIII, on the other hand, left the strategy of combating rebellion to his council and principal ministers – Wolsey in the 1520s and Cromwell in the 1530s – but insisted on being kept informed. A major criticism that was levelled against the Duke of Somerset in 1549 was that he did not regularly consult or heed the advice of the Privy Council on how to deal with rebellion. Both Mary and Elizabeth, on the other hand, relied on their secretaries and councillors to determine the strategy and suppression of rebellions: Elizabeth was well served and all disturbances in England were effectively handled, but Mary received conflicting advice during Wyatt's revolt. When London seemed open to attack in January 1554, the council began to panic. According to Renard, the imperial ambassador and Mary's confidant, the council was 'quarrelling, taking sides and blaming one another'. Some suggested that they should enlist the help of imperial troops, while others, notably Gardiner, urged the queen to leave the city. Her decision to stay saved her throne and almost certainly her life.

Information gathering

When a rebellion broke out, governments needed to find out as much as possible about its size, location and nature. Did it threaten the life of the monarch or was it a protest against government policies, and were any nobles or gentry involved? Getting reliable information was never easy, and delays in communication sometimes explained apparent inactivity and unwise decisions by councillors as they waited on the latest news:

- *Pilgrimage of Grace*. When Henry VIII heard that Sawley Abbey had been reoccupied by monks in 1536, he wrote to the Earl of Derby ordering him to execute the abbot, monks and rebel captains, without appreciating that the earl, who was heavily outnumbered and some distance from the abbey, was in no position to carry out the order.
- *Western rebellion*. The Duke of Somerset faced a similar communication problem in 1549. In trying to decide the right strategy to deal with the Western rebellion that was occurring some 200 miles away, he had to rely on out-of-date reports. Thus, on 26 June he wrote to the Devon justices of the peace (JPs) that they should try to persuade the ringleaders to return home and use as an argument the rebels' unnatural behaviour, the dangers they were causing to national security and the need to adopt lawful remedies for their grievances. If the JPs failed (which was a near certainty), they were to try to prevent a large assembly from gathering, to raise troops from local gentry and to await reinforcements in the shape of Lord Russell. What Somerset did not know was that by this stage, three JPs had already tried and failed to reason with the rebels, most local gentry had either joined the rebellion or gone into hiding, the combined size of the rebellion exceeded 6000, the Cornish and Devon protesters had joined forces and they were already camped outside Exeter.

Most of the Tudors employed spies, secret agents and informers to find out what was happening and to forward intelligence reports, sometimes from inside rebel camps or within the conspirators' circle.

Henry VII's agents tracked rebels who had escaped from the Battle of Bosworth, such as the Stafford brothers and Lord Lovel. These rebels had first taken sanctuary in Colchester Abbey before fleeing west to Worcester and Yorkshire, respectively, but Henry's agents followed them. The Staffords were tracked down to Culham Church near Oxford, where they were arrested, while Lovel was forced to leave the country after his abortive uprising in Yorkshire. Elizabeth came to rely heavily on **Sir Francis Walsingham**'s gathering of intelligence. He employed over 50 agents at home and overseas who enabled him to detect conspiracies, identify and arrest suspects, and reduce the likelihood of rebellions occurring. The ineffectiveness of continental schemes to stir up domestic rebellions after 1572 owed a great deal to his vigilance.

 **KEY FIGURE**

Sir Francis Walsingham (1532–90)

Known as Elizabeth's spymaster, he organised a secret service that uncovered plots and targeted Catholic priests who had come to England.

Henry VII also had an extensive network of spies in various European courts who kept him informed of the pretenders' whereabouts and who their supporters were. For instance, men like Sir Edward Brampton in Flanders and Sir Robert Clifford, who infiltrated Yorkist circles in England, supplied the king with vital information about Warbeck. It was principally due to secret intelligence that Henry discovered the treason of **Sir William Stanley** and arrested him in 1495 before he could join up with the pretender. Attached to many **bonds of allegiance** that Henry imposed on suspected rebels were conditions that obliged them to inform the council if they heard any seditious information, and this requirement may well have deterred individuals from further involvement and enabled the king to gather useful intelligence.

Role of the nobility

Amicable Grant rising

Once news was confirmed that a rebellion had broken out, letters were written to JPs and sheriffs of a disturbed region ordering them to deal with the problem. Nobles and councillors who held estates or lived in the vicinity of the disturbance were only called on to restore order if the JPs proved to be ineffectual. This is what occurred in Suffolk in 1525, when the Amicable Grant protesters threatened to march on London. The dukes of Norfolk and Suffolk assumed command and successfully dealt with the rebellion. It was in the nobles' interests to contain the unrest, and the government certainly did not expect the disturbances to spread to neighbouring areas or to get out of hand.

Lincolnshire rising

Ten years later, a more serious uprising occurred in Lincolnshire. On 5 October 1536, the Privy Council first learned that 20,000 rebels were preparing to converge on the county town of Lincoln. Worse, the sheriff, Sir Edward Dymoke, the mayor, Robert Sutton, several leading gentry like William Willoughby, and a member of parliament (MP), Vincent Grantham, had, out of sympathy or fear, also joined the rebels. Henry VIII's response was to command Lord Hussey, the most senior peer in the county, to raise his tenants and deal with the rising. The king was naturally alarmed to discover that the elderly lord had first considered mediating with the rebels and then, on failing to raise enough loyal men, had fled to the safety of Nottingham. Again, it fell to the dukes of Suffolk and Norfolk to suppress the rising but, because of the number of rebels involved, the Earl of Huntingdon in Leicestershire and the Earl of Shrewsbury at Sheffield were also requested to stand by.

Duke of Somerset's handling of rebellions

A similar situation occurred in 1549. The Duke of Somerset first heard that there were disturbances in Devon and Cornwall in June but he considered the problem to be an isolated incident that could be dealt with locally. Unfortunately, the absence of a powerful privy councillor and major landowner in the south-west

KEY FIGURE

Sir William Stanley (c.1435–95)
Supported Henry VII at Bosworth and was appointed Lord Chamberlain but then plotted against Henry.

KEY TERM

Bonds of allegiance
Financial and legal penalties were imposed on rebels and on anyone of doubtful allegiance.

Edward Seymour, Duke of Somerset

c.1506	Born
1537	Became a member of the Privy Council
1540s	Experienced wars against France and Scotland as both a diplomat and a soldier
1541	Created Earl of Hertford
1547	Elected by the Privy Council as Protector
	Became Duke of Somerset
1549	Dismissed from office and imprisoned
1550	Released and rejoined the Privy Council
1552	Tried and executed

Early life

It was the marriage of his sister Jane Seymour to Henry VIII that brought Seymour to political prominence. During the 1540s he made a name for himself on the battlefield, but as Edward's uncle it was obvious that he would be part of the Regency Council that Henry set up to rule after his death until Edward came of age to rule on his own.

Appointment as Lord Protector

Henry had wanted to have a balanced council, with no dominant individual, to rule on behalf of Edward.

However, Henry's death was kept quiet and the will altered. The council, many of whom received rewards, voted to appoint Seymour as Protector, and gave him virtual royal power.

Somerset's rule

Somerset was not a particularly competent ruler, although he used his position to enrich himself. His social policies, particularly setting up an Enclosure Commission, encouraged unrest, and in the summer of 1549 some 27 counties witnessed uprisings, notably in East Anglia and the West Country. Somerset was blamed by many landowners for the unrest and his failure to deal with it quickly, but many were also fed up with his personal rule and their own exclusion from power. In the autumn he attempted to stage a coup, seizing Edward, but was defeated and dismissed.

Downfall

Somerset was released and restored to the council, but he plotted against his successor, the Duke of Northumberland, and was arrested again and put on trial. He was found guilty and executed.

 KEY FIGURE

Lord John Russell (c.1485–1554/5)

A Catholic member of the Privy Council, he was sent to put down the risings in the West Country.

proved a serious weakness that he had not foreseen. **Lord John Russell**, who had estates in Devon, was the high steward of the Duchy of Cornwall and Lord Privy Seal but spent most of his time in London. The most powerful Cornish landowner was Sir John Arundell, a former privy councillor, but out of favour with the Protestant regime. In any case, he was living at his country house in Dorset. The onus for dealing with the risings in Devon and Cornwall therefore fell to the sheriffs, JPs and local mayors, but they were simply not strong enough to contain the rebellion.

The Duke of Somerset decided to send Sir Peter Carew, a former sheriff of Devon and an experienced soldier, to persuade the rebels to disperse, but this proved to be a disastrous decision. Carew was impetuous, lacked diplomacy and was a devout Protestant. When he tried to reason with the Catholic rebels at Crediton, one of his men set fire to a barn and thereafter the rebels believed that the gentry intended to 'spoil and destroy them'. What had started as a local protest against the new prayer book had quickly become something much more serious.

In the same year, the Lord Lieutenant of Norfolk, the Marquis of Northampton, was ordered to deal with Kett and his rebels. As in Devon and Cornwall, there was no resident privy councillor in Norfolk, the prominent Howard family was in disgrace and none of the leading gentry was willing to take a stand against the rebels. Moreover, the sheriff, Sir Edmund Wyndham, had no troops with which to threaten the host and had retreated to the comparative safety of Norwich Castle.

Elizabethan Privy Council

Elizabeth's council took prompt action when disturbances occurred in north Oxfordshire in November 1596. Earlier that year, the Privy Council had alerted all sheriffs, lords lieutenant and JPs of probable food riots, and told them to be on the lookout for gangs seizing grain and food supplies. The Oxfordshire county gentry had been informed of a possible plot to attack Sir Henry Norris's house and four men were arrested before the revolt gathered momentum. Essex's rebellion of 1601 was similarly dealt with before it got out of hand. The Privy Council knew that Essex was planning something dramatic: either a coup, which would entail seizing the queen and capturing the Tower of London and its arsenal, or a demonstration of noble force in the city. The sheriff and Lord Mayor of London therefore took appropriate defensive action. They ordered the closure of the city gates, heavy artillery from the Tower was prepared and the Earl of Nottingham deputed to draw up sufficient cannon to blast a hole in Essex's house if he resisted arrest. When Essex saw that his attempted revolt had failed to get the backing of Londoners, he submitted without a fight.

Henry VII's personal supervision

Unlike other Tudor rulers, Henry VII dealt with most serious disturbances himself. He appointed Sir Giles Daubeny to lead his forces against Simnel, the Cornish rebels and Warbeck, and on each occasion the king was present in the field or heading towards the rebels' camp when they dispersed. Henry was unsure whom to trust and only relied with certainty on his closest advisers and men who had been with him in exile. Sir Richard Edgecombe, Controller of the Household, and Sir William Tyler, Keeper of the Jewels, were therefore sent to apprehend Lovel in the North Riding of Yorkshire in 1486.

A year later, when **commissions of array** were issued to defend the more troublesome areas of England that might support Simnel, Henry relied on nobles who had fought with him at Bosworth and a handful of ex-Ricardians whom he was prepared to trust: the Earl of Northumberland secured the far north, the Earl of Oxford watched over East Anglia, the Earl of Derby reported on south Lancashire and the Duke of Bedford held the Welsh borders. When Yorkshire broke into revolt in 1489 and the Earl of Northumberland was murdered, Henry assembled a force even larger than the one that had fought at Stoke, and the rebels fled as the royal army approached York.

 **KEY TERM**

Commissions of array
Authority given by the Crown to nobles to raise troops.

The Cornish rebellion of 1497 also required a military solution but was altogether a more threatening affair. When Henry first heard that a large group of rebels was marching towards London, he expected the leading families in the south-west and south of England to deal with it. At the time, his attention was directed towards Scotland and the threat of war presented by James IV in support of the pretender Warbeck. Already a royal army was heading north, although its designated commander, Daubeny, was still in London. News that the Cornish rebels had been able to pass through Devon, Somerset, Wiltshire and Hampshire without any noble resistance alarmed the king. Henry acted decisively. He moved from London to Woodstock and then to Wallingford before gathering troops at Henley, well out of range of the rebels. He also recalled Daubeny and wrote to Edmund de la Pole in Oxfordshire, Rhys ap Thomas in south Wales and the Earl of Oxford in Norfolk to raise as many men as possible. It was these men who defeated the rebels at the Battle of Blackheath.

Ireland

The Tudors treated Ireland like the northern counties. The council in Dublin received its instructions from London and military aid might come from England, but the Crown's representative, the Lord Deputy, had no JPs, only a sheriff and local nobles to call on as his first line of defence, and they were not always willing to help. Moreover, he rarely had sufficient resources to deal with disturbances. Until 1534, there was only a small garrison of around 700 troops in the Pale near Dublin and although this number was periodically increased, reaching 2000 in the 1570s, there were never enough troops to deal with rebellions if they broke out simultaneously in different provinces.

The principal strategy was to defend English interests and areas under English rule and to play for time.

Elizabeth preferred diplomacy to military solutions: it was cheaper and might pave the way for long-term solutions. Her treatment of Shane O'Neill illustrates this point. In 1558, Shane murdered his half-brother when he heard that Mary Tudor had conferred the earldom of Tyrone on him. On Elizabeth's accession, she invited Shane to London but he refused to come until 1561, when she accepted his confession to the murder and to causing rebellion in Ulster. In return, Elizabeth recognised him as Captain of Tyrone and Lord of Tyrconnel. In 1563, she went so far as to acknowledge him as 'the O'Neill', unwisely ignoring the sound advice of Sussex, her Lord Deputy in Ireland, who warned, 'If Shane be overthrown, all is settled; if Shane settle, all is overthrown'. On his return to Ireland, Shane continued to disregard the law: he raided the lands of rival clansmen, kidnapped hostages and dabbled in high treason. In 1566, Elizabeth finally abandoned her attempts to reconcile him and turned to a military solution.

Tactics

Buying time and avoiding confrontation

Tudor governments had limited resources at their disposal: they had no standing army, no police force and, at times, very little money. Their main weapons were their claim to be legitimate rulers (at least ***de facto*** if not *de jure*) and the fact that they had been anointed with holy oil and so derived their authority from God. Anyone who fought against them would therefore be condemned as a sinner as well as a traitor. All governments stressed the need to uphold order and used a range of tactics to persuade rebels to disperse. In essence, governments sought to buy time until they had enough troops to call the rebels' bluff, and then and only then did they consider fighting a battle.

Governments wanted to avoid violent confrontations: the outcome was uncertain and they were always expensive, whether in terms of finance or casualties. It was common for pardons to be offered to rebels if they would first disperse, and this tactic certainly weakened the morale of some rebels and reduced their numbers. Rebels at Stoke, Blackheath, Clyst St Mary and Dussindale were all offered a general pardon on the eve of battle if they surrendered, and a royal herald on two occasions in 1554 gave Wyatt's rebels a chance to go home in peace. Moreover, endemic disorder reflected badly on any administration. Most governments saw no mileage in negotiating with rebels: it was a sign of weakness and would only serve to encourage future rebel leaders. Yet confrontations had to be skilfully handled and, as Wolsey discovered to his cost, circumstances could easily spiral out of control.

Wolsey and the Amicable Grant

Wolsey received reports in the first week of April 1525 that a small number of people were refusing to pay the Amicable Grant. At first, the king's minister took an uncompromising stance towards reluctant taxpayers and sympathetic commissioners. He told the Lord Mayor of London, Sir William Bailey, 'beware and resist not, nor ruffle not in this case, for it may fortune to cost some their heads', and Lord Lisle was threatened with execution if he failed to collect taxes in Berkshire. When the Duke of Suffolk reported that protesters were becoming more vociferous, Wolsey advised stiff retribution and accused the duke of being oversensitive.

By 25 April 1525, it was clear that Wolsey's bullying tactics were not working. Henry may well have seen for himself the growing discontent in London, and informed the Lord Mayor and aldermen that the Amicable Grant would be halved. However, none of the commissioners outside London was informed and soon there were reports of hundreds of protesters gathering in Kent, Warwickshire, Essex, Norfolk and Suffolk. When some 4000 protesters gathered at Lavenham in Suffolk, it fell to the dukes of Suffolk and Norfolk to handle

KEY TERM

De facto By deed, as opposed to *de jure*, 'by law'.

this crisis. And they had a problem. Suffolk's army of retainers was much smaller than the rebels' forces and he was unsure of the reliability of his own men. He informed Wolsey: 'They [his retainers] would defend him from all perils, if he hurt not their neighbours, but against their neighbours they would not fight.' While he waited for Norfolk to join him with more troops, Suffolk tried to contain the rebellion by destroying bridges, 'so that their assembly was somewhat letted [impeded]'. On 11 May, Suffolk and Norfolk heard a deputation of 60 rebels at Bury St Edmunds, warned them of the heinous consequences of rebellion and finally succeeded in persuading them to submit before anyone died.

Henry VIII and the Pilgrimage of Grace

Henry VIII and Cromwell took the same hard line in 1536 when they faced rebellions in Lincolnshire, Yorkshire and other northern counties. The size of the rebel armies and the involvement of nobles, gentry and clergy so alarmed the king that he allowed the **Duke of Norfolk** to negotiate with them on condition that they agreed to go home. More than two weeks passed before Norfolk and Shrewsbury had enough troops to advance north of the Trent. Their 8000 men, however, were dwarfed by over 30,000 rebels waiting at Pontefract Castle. Norfolk decided to arrange a truce with the gentry, promise whatever was needed to disperse their army and, once the leaders were separated from the rank and file, pacify the disaffected areas in revolt. The king favoured a military solution from the outset but bowed to Norfolk's more diplomatic approach. Moreover, the duke had assured Henry that 'whatsoever promise I shall make unto the rebels (if any such be the advice of others make) for surely I shall observe no part thereof for any respect of that other might call mine honour'. When he met the rebels' spokesmen on 27 October, he talked only to the gentry and nobles, and Darcy later reflected how the commons feared they might be betrayed 'because we tarried a while about the entreaty'. Norfolk had succeeded in stemming the advancing rebels, separating the rank and file from the leaders, and escorted four of them to Windsor to meet the king.

Henry's tactic now was to stand firm and browbeat the emissaries into submission. He refused to discuss their petition, which he found 'general, dark and obscure', he rejected pleas to reverse his policies, which he claimed had been misrepresented, and he told them to go away and clarify their grievances before arranging a second meeting with Norfolk. It was not what the rebels wanted to hear. Moreover, their representatives were kept waiting in London for over three weeks and many of the commons and several gentry suspected they might not return. A meeting between 40 pilgrims and Norfolk finally took place on 6 December 1536, when the duke promised that a parliament would resolve the issues behind the rebellion, there would be no more monastic suppressions and the rebels would receive a general pardon. Aske accepted the terms, tore off his badge, and declared, 'We will wear no badge nor sign but the badge of our sovereign Lord'. The rebel captains followed suit and the rebellion was over – or

KEY FIGURE

Duke of Norfolk (1473–1554)

A powerful noble and loyal commander of the army. He was opposed to Protestantism and Thomas Cromwell.

Thomas Cromwell

1475?	Born in Putney, Surrey
1503	Fought at the Battle of Garigliano for the French
1523	Became an MP
1524	Worked for Wolsey
1531	Became a member of the Privy Council
1532	Master of the Court of Wards and Master of the Jewel House
1533	Henry VIII's chief minister and secretary
1540	Arrested and executed

Early life and career

Cromwell's father was a blacksmith and worked as a cloth worker in Putney. Cromwell had no formal education. However, he travelled widely and became a mercenary soldier, fighting for the French. He also worked for Florentine bankers and gained a knowledge of trade and accountancy. Although he had no legal training, he built up a successful legal practice and this brought him to the attention of Cardinal Wolsey.

The fall of Wolsey and its impact

Although Cromwell had been associated with Wolsey, he was able to distance himself from the disgraced former chief minister. Cromwell realised that Wolsey had fallen because he had failed to get Henry his divorce. Cromwell saw that if he could bring about Henry's divorce he would be promoted. It is likely that it was Cromwell who suggested to Henry that he break with Rome and establish himself as Head of the Church, but it is also likely that this fitted with his own religious views.

The Reformation of the 1530s

Cromwell was sympathetic to the new religious views of Martin Luther and, along with Thomas Cranmer, helped to bring about some religious changes in England. He also made Henry the Supreme Head of the Church and through the dissolution of the monasteries made him very wealthy. He also brought about changes in the government of England. However, some of the changes created opposition, particularly among the nobles who disliked an upstart as the king's chief minister.

The fall of Cromwell

It was Cromwell who arranged Henry's fourth marriage, to Anne of Cleves, as England looked for Protestant allies against a possible Catholic invasion. However, Henry disliked the marriage and blamed Cromwell. This gave his enemies their chance and they used the attractive, young Catherine Howard to draw him away from Cromwell, as well as accusing him of heresy. The Privy Council drew up an Act of Attainder against Cromwell, who was arrested and executed.

so they thought. In fact, Henry spent the next month gathering information, interviewing the gentry and nobles involved in the uprising, and deciding what to do about the north.

Somerset and the Western rebellion

The Duke of Somerset's response to the news early in July 1549 that Exeter was under attack was to send a series of letters to the rebel camp urging them to desist, offering them a free pardon if they did and threatening dire punishment if they did not:

- A proclamation dated 11 July threatened to forfeit their land and property with the intention of creating 'a terror and division among the rebels themselves', but it had no effect.
- On 12 July, he pardoned any guilty of 'riotous assembly' if they made a 'humble submission'. None did.
- On 16 July, another proclamation pardoned submissive rioters but future offenders were threatened with martial law. There was still no reaction.

Somerset, perhaps unwisely, had not only promised to listen to the rebels' grievances, but even guaranteed to let the leaders sit on committees to implement reforms. He may have been sincere in his intentions since he did read the rebel grievances and, in the case of the Western rebels, believed they had acted 'rather out of ignorance than of malice', but his fellow councillors begged to differ. William Paget consistently criticised his leniency and both Herbert and Warwick favoured swift repression. Pre-emptive action had worked in Oxfordshire, Leicestershire and Kent, where rioters were summarily executed, and they pressed Somerset to send troops to Devon and Norfolk. He preferred conciliation and for several weeks ignored their advice.

Propaganda

Propaganda was widely used by governments in trying to persuade rebels to give up and return home.

Cromwell employed a team of writers to condemn rebellion in 1536 and one of them, Richard Morrison, attacked the rebels in his pamphlet *A Lamentation in Which is Showed What Ruin and Destruction Cometh of Seditious Rebellion*. 'Obedience is the badge of a Christian man', he declared. Henry himself replied to the Lincoln Articles on 10 October, rejecting their petition and ordering them to disperse. They were, he said, 'one of the most brute and beastly of the whole realm', and he warned that Suffolk was gathering a 100,000-strong army which he would command. This was a wild exaggeration. Later that month, the king, in response to the Pilgrimage of Grace, penned *Answers to the Rebels*, in which he defended his policies and ministers, and ordered Morrison to hit them with some choice words. His *Remedy for Sedition* condemned disobedience in the body politic and he asked rhetorically, 'when every man will rule, who shall obey?' Unfortunately, it had little if any impact on Aske and his supporters.

The Edwardian government in 1549 also undertook a lively propaganda campaign both during and after the summer disturbances.

 **KEY FIGURE**

Thomas Cranmer (1489–1556)

A Cambridge priest who became Archbishop of Canterbury and granted Henry VIII his divorce from Catherine of Aragon. He also wrote the prayer books of 1549 and 1552.

Thomas Cranmer attacked the Western rebels' religious ignorance and brazen effrontery, and compared them to magpies and parrots that 'be taught to speak and yet understood not one word what they say'. Philip Nichols, a Devon Protestant, was commissioned to write a lengthy criticism of the rebel articles, which he condemned on moral and religious grounds. One of the more skilful pieces of propaganda was John Cheke's *The Hurt of Sedition*, in which he compared the conduct of Exeter and Norwich. The citizens of Exeter, he declared, were to be commended because 'being in the midst of rebels unvitteled, unfurnished, unprepared, for so long a siege did hold out the continual and dangerous assault of the rebels'. In contrast, the people of Norwich were censured, and their behaviour 'white livered' because they had 'sought more safeguard than honesty, and private hope more than common quietness'. Significantly, the mayor of Exeter was later knighted, whereas the mayor of Norwich was obliged to explain his cooperation with Kett's rebels.

A print of Thomas Cranmer based on a painting of 1545–6 by Gerlach Flicke.

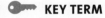

KEY TERM

Polemics A strong, often controversial written attack.

Writing **polemics** against rebellion, of course, had only a limited impact; few could read and rebels were not interested in lessons on morality. Perhaps the circulation of court propaganda did more to buttress the morale of the government than alter the views of rebels. Governments also used speeches and sermons to persuade rebels to disperse, although these too had only a limited impact. When Russell arrived at Honiton in east Devon to confront the Western rebels, he took with him a handful of preachers whom Somerset advised should proclaim the Gospel to the rebels. The decision to send Protestant preachers to assuage Catholic rebels seems at best wildly optimistic and, of course, their words were roughly received.

Somerset also sent preachers to appeal to Kett's rebels at their camp on Mousehold Heath, near Norwich.

Robert Watson, a Protestant, tried to appease the rebels and, although they shared his theological views, they were not prepared to listen to platitudes about duty and obedience. Archbishop Cranmer saw the need to broaden the message and prepared sermons to be read in parish churches that emphasised the sin of rebellion. He declared, 'If they [the people] will be true gospellers, let them be obedient, meek, patient in adversity and long-suffering, and in no wise rebel against the laws and magistrates.' This may have had some effect after the rebellions had ended but cut no ice with the rebels at the time. As Matthew Parker, a young Cambridge scholar, discovered when he visited Kett's camp, the rebels were in no mood to be placated or lectured into submission, and he narrowly escaped being captured.

Pre-emptive measures

Governments from time to time also applied political pressure to undermine rebels and so weaken their cause.

Measures taken by Henry VII

Henry VII in particular took pre-emptive measures against any suspects before they became too dangerous. In 1487, a papal bull that excommunicated all rebels was translated, printed and publicly proclaimed by the clergy. He produced the same papal condemnation on the eve of the Battle of Stoke (Simnel rebellion) and at Blackheath (Cornish rising), and many rebels surrendered rather than risk eternal damnation. At Easter 1487, the real Earl of Warwick was paraded at St Paul's Cathedral in London and introduced to visiting ambassadors to convince them that Simnel was an impostor, a proclamation ordered all rumour-mongers to be pilloried, and the king made two significant arrests. The estates of the queen mother, Elizabeth Woodville, were seized and she was confined to a nunnery, and her son by a former marriage, the Marquis of Dorset, was put in the Tower of London. This was a judicious move. Both had a history of intrigue and Henry was aware that a Yorkist, the Earl of Lincoln, was leading the rebellion. Similarly, to combat the subsequent threat of Warbeck, pressure was put on diplomats to deny him political support wherever he went in the 1490s. Charles VIII of France expelled him and his supporters, Kildare in Ireland was persuaded to renounce him, trade sanctions were imposed on Burgundy until he was ejected, and James IV of Scotland, after playing host between 1496 and 1497, expelled him when Henry threatened to go to war.

The king was equally busy domestically. In the summer of 1493, he went to Warwickshire to inform potential troublemakers that there was no future in supporting Warbeck. Fifteen counties were under suspicion and investigated by commissioners. When Desmond offered his support in Ireland in 1494, Henry deprived him of his office of Constable of Limerick Castle and put his arch-rival in his place. In January 1495, Clifford had discovered the names of several English nobles and gentry willing to back the pretender. Among them were Sir William Stanley, the Lord Chamberlain and the king's step-uncle, and Lord Fitzwater, Steward of the Household. In all, fourteen men were attainted and four executed, including Stanley. When Warbeck did try to land in England in 1495, Henry's men were waiting. Fifty-one were caught and hanged, and a further 150 put on trial. For his part, Henry preferred to be on the move. He visited the Midlands and travelled to Stanley's lands in the north-west, before returning to Nottingham. Ever vigilant, Henry was never outwitted.

Measures taken by Mary I

Mary also demonstrated the virtues of a pre-emptive strike. Her councillors first heard whispers that there was a conspiracy to depose her in December 1553. The council acted speedily. They interrogated **Sir Edward Courtenay** and identified Carew, Suffolk, Croft and Wyatt as the main leaders. Circular letters

 **KEY FIGURE**

Sir Edward Courtenay (c.1527–56)

Great-grandson of Edward IV, he had been seen as a possible husband for Mary Tudor as he was English, but when she married Philip it was rumoured that Wyatt and his plotters planned to marry him to Elizabeth.

were sent to the relevant counties in January 1554 denouncing the plot, and local authorities took preventive measures. The sheriff of Devon garrisoned Exeter, which so alarmed Carew that he fled to France; the Earl of Huntingdon searched for Suffolk in the Midlands, which discouraged others from joining him; and Croft lost his nerve and disappeared into north Wales. By late January, the council seemed to have the situation largely under control. Only Wyatt remained a problem.

Measures taken by Elizabeth I

Elizabeth also acted decisively when required. She first heard rumours at court in the summer of 1569 that several disgruntled nobles were plotting to bring down her chief secretary William Cecil, secure the succession of Mary Stuart, and marry Mary to the Duke of Norfolk. Elizabeth acted quickly. Norfolk was denied permission to marry and nobles such as Arundel, Pembroke, Lumley and Leicester all disassociated themselves from an alleged plot. In November, Norfolk sent a letter to his brother-in-law, the Earl of Westmorland, forbidding him from starting a revolt in his name. When news reached the queen that a rebellion had broken out, she took further steps to safeguard her throne. Norfolk was lodged in the Tower, Mary was moved 30 miles south to a new location near Coventry, and the President of the Council of the North, Sussex, was ordered to suppress the uprising.

Ireland

Tactics in handling rebellions in Ireland were similar to those employed in England. Rebels were offered pardons and promises, rival clan chiefs were encouraged to assist the Crown through offers of reward, and steps were taken to raise a sufficiently large loyalist army, while most commanders tried to avoid a military confrontation. Wet marshy terrain, poor communications, problems in recruiting troops and the increasing hostility of native Irish towards the English all contributed to the government's difficulties. Unlike in England, Irish rebellions had to be treated like wars of attrition that could last for several years and still end without a satisfactory outcome. The Munster rebellion went on for four years and Fitzmaurice eluded capture; the Geraldine rebellion lasted for nearly five years, even though Fitzmaurice was killed within weeks of its start; and the national rising of Tyrone, which lasted for more than eight years, ended only when the earl reached a deal with the lord deputy.

Raising troops

The decision to raise troops was not taken lightly and, in several cases, governments delayed giving the order, for a variety of reasons. Paying troops was an expensive business and if the men were not paid they became as much of a threat as the rebels themselves. Somerset, for instance, faced the prospect of having to suppress revolts and rebellions in over half of all English counties in the summer of 1549 as well as waging war against Scotland. Not only was the Treasury short of money, Somerset was short of soldiers. From the outset, he was more concerned about disturbances in Oxfordshire, Buckinghamshire, Berkshire, Cambridge, Hertfordshire and Lincolnshire, which were much closer to London. As a result, he had to deploy his troops prudently, which explains why the two major rebellions in Devon and Norfolk took so long to suppress and why Somerset was the only ruler to employ foreign mercenaries.

The government relied on the nobility and gentry to provide retainers for their army but this brought hazards. Licences were required to hold more than a reasonable number of retainers and if any noble put his men in armour and prepared to fight without first receiving a royal commission, he knew he was technically committing treason. This dilemma faced Henry VIII's commanders in October 1536. The Earl of Shrewsbury knew that he was likely to be called on to serve the king, and in his keenness to appear as patriotic as possible and raise a large retinue he mustered troops in anticipation, writing to his friends 'to get as many able men as ye can make, well horsed and harnessed'. The Earl of Huntingdon, on the other hand, preferred to wait for official authorisation. In fact, Henry seriously underestimated the size of the rebel host in comparison with the small number of loyalist troops available to his commanders. He bragged that at least 40,000 would soon arrive from the Midlands and Wales, when in practice the Duke of Suffolk had half this number and many of his men were poorly equipped.

Troop shortages

A shortage of troops was a perennial problem. In every rebellion where rebel armies were drawn up, at some stage their numbers exceeded those of the Crown.

Henry VII and Simnel and the Cornish rebellions

Henry VII was fortunate in that he had six weeks in which to prepare for battle against Simnel's forces, and the king showed his skill at military organisation. He set up his command at Kenilworth Castle in Warwickshire. From there, he could deal with an invasion from either the east or west of England, or quickly return to London if necessary, while he was busy raising money to pay for retainers, urging nobles to muster as many men as possible, and sifting intelligence reports from his agents. When he finally prepared for battle at East Stoke in Nottinghamshire, he had the cream of the English aristocracy with him: a duke, five earls, a viscount, four barons and their retainers numbering 15,000, perhaps twice the size of the rebel army. In contrast, ten years later, Daubeny was unable to prevent the Cornish rebels from reaching Blackheath because he had insufficient men, and held back until he was joined by Rhys ap Thomas, the Earl of Oxford and the king himself.

Henry VIII and the Pilgrimage of Grace

Henry VIII was caught by surprise in October 1536. No sooner had he detailed the Duke of Suffolk to scale down his military operations in Lincolnshire than news reached the council that the East Riding of Yorkshire was in revolt. Plans for royal troops to assemble in Bedfordshire to deal with the earlier rising had been cancelled and there was word that further revolts had broken out in Richmond and Lancashire. Worse, Henry heard that many gentry and some lesser nobles had defected to the rebels or gone into hiding. Not until 13 October does Henry seem to have realised just how serious was the situation. At last, letters were issued commissioning nobles to raise armies, and the Duke of Norfolk was told to take as many men as he could, join the Earl of Shrewsbury and hold a line of the River Trent. The king had a number of problems. He did not know whom to trust. He always doubted the honesty of Lord Darcy, which was confirmed when he surrendered Pontefract Castle to the rebels. He also had his doubts about the Earl of Derby, although these proved groundless. More than two weeks were to pass before Norfolk and Shrewsbury had enough troops to advance north of the Trent.

Western rebellion

In 1549, Lord Russell faced worse odds when he arrived at Honiton in east Devon to deal with the Western rebellion. He had with him a retinue of some 300 men but ranged against him were 6000 rebels. In the course of the next few weeks, he raised some 2000 soldiers but since most of the gentry in nearby counties were unwilling to volunteer their services, all he could do was wait for reinforcements and hope that the besieged city of Exeter could hold out. He had to wait for over five weeks. Finally, at the end of July, Wilton appeared with 400 English troops and some 1400 German, Swiss and Italian mercenaries, whom Somerset originally planned on sending to Scotland. Only then was Russell prepared to risk a battle. A similar situation arose in Norfolk. Once Somerset recognised that a military solution was the only option, he decided to send an army under the Marquis of Northampton. He was accompanied by two privy councillors, two peers, a secretary of state, five JPs and leading Norfolk gentry, which Somerset deemed strong enough to deal with the rebels, but Northampton was given only 1500 troops. He had no trouble entering Norwich because the rebels had withdrawn to their camp a few hundred metres away, but his army was outnumbered ten to one. It only took one day of fierce fighting before he decided to leave for the safety of Cambridge and await reinforcements. Not until 24 August did the Earl of Warwick with 7500 troops appear in Norfolk with Northampton in tow, and together they reoccupied the city.

Wyatt's rebellion

Mary's council in 1554 believed they had reduced the threat from Wyatt and his co-conspirators to a manageable size, but his sudden appearance at Rochester, Kent, with 2000 men revealed the frailty of the government's position. The queen compounded her problems by insisting that the Duke of Norfolk should lead her army. Although a veteran of many military campaigns, the duke was now over 80, uninspiring and unable to discipline his 500 'whitecoats', most of whom deserted to Wyatt's army. Worse, neither the sheriff of Kent nor the principal landowner in the county, Lord Abergavenny, was able to raise many men. As rebel forces were reported to be gathering in several towns, Mary also learned that hordes of London-trained bands had changed sides. In this crisis, she revealed her Tudor character. She bought time by twice offering Wyatt a truce to negotiate with the rebels and appointed lords Pembroke and Clinton to raise an army. On 1 February, she played her trump card. She spoke to a crowd at the Guildhall, declared that she would only marry Philip with her council's consent and called on the assembled citizens to support her. Her speech had its desired effect as Londoners rallied behind their legitimate ruler. London Bridge was blocked, other crossing points were damaged and barricades were thrown up around the city. When Wyatt tried to enter London on 7 February, some 40 men died in the fighting. Pembroke repelled the attack and Wyatt surrendered, unwilling to sacrifice any more of his supporters.

Northern Earls' rebellion

Sussex, President of the Council of the North (see page 157), realised that he faced a difficult task when he heard that the northern earls were in revolt in 1569. He could raise 400 cavalry and a small number of county militia of doubtful reliability, but ranged against him were 1600 cavalry and 3400 infantry. Ralph Sadler, Chancellor of the Duchy, underlined the problem when he informed Cecil in London: 'If we should go to the field with this northern force only, they would fight faintly; for if the father be on this side, the son is on the other; and one brother with us and the other with the rebels.'

Elizabeth, perhaps alarmed at the potential unrest indicated by early reports from the north, exaggerated the dangers of a lawless mob that had been enlarged by vagrants and **masterless** men. Parliament duly responded by voting more money to pay for a very large army, but it took time to assemble. By December 1569, Sussex had gathered 12,000 troops in York, **Lord Hunsdon** was preparing to move south from Newcastle with a small army, and lords Warwick and Clinton were collecting 10,000 men to the south. These royal forces under the command of lords lieutenant far outnumbered the rebels and when Sussex started to move towards them, they fled north into Scotland. Only **Lord Dacre** continued to resist until Hunsdon killed or captured 500 rebels at Carlisle in 1570.

Irish rebellions

Raising troops to deal with rebellions in Ireland brought its own problems. In time, troops were based in garrisons in the Pale, Ulster, Munster and Leinster but they were never sufficient to deal with large-scale disturbances, and lord deputies had to rely on recruiting Irish volunteers and the retainers of clan chiefs:

- **Sir William Skeffington** raised 2300 troops in 1534, which was enough to defeat Silken Thomas, but only after fourteen months of attrition.

KEY TERM

Masterless Adolescents who were not apprenticed to a master or an employer and so were more likely to be itinerant and ill-disciplined.

KEY FIGURES

Lord Hunsdon (1526–96)

Cousin of Elizabeth as his mother was Mary Boleyn, he was in charge of the Queen's forces.

Lord Dacre (c.1533–73)

A supposed supporter of Elizabeth; however, he held out against the royal army and when his force was finally defeated he fled into exile.

Sir William Skeffington (1465–1535)

Lord Deputy in Ireland.

- Elizabeth sent 700 troops under Edward Randolph in 1566 to establish a garrison in Ulster, but Lord Deputy Sidney depended mainly on the earls of Kildare and O'Donnell to bring about the defeat of Shane O'Neill.
- **Lord Wilton**'s army of 6500 in 1580 was more than enough to suppress the Geraldine rebellion, and demonstrated that when the government in London put its mind to tackling the Irish problem, well-led professional forces could achieve a decisive result. His troops captured Smerwick from Irish and Spanish rebels and rounded up the ringleaders.

The national uprising of the 1590s, however, proved the biggest test for Elizabeth. England was at war with Spain and there were serious domestic problems such as runaway inflation, food shortages, rising unemployment and recurrent plague. Elizabeth was aware of the strategic importance of Ireland – Spain had landed troops before and Philip intended assisting Irish rebels again – but suppressing rebellions was an expensive business and in the 1590s both money and men were in short supply. As a result, the scale of Tyrone's rebellion was allowed to grow. By 1596, it traversed all four Irish provinces and the size of the rebel armies exceeded 6000, which was far too large for Elizabeth to defeat. Moreover, her frequent change of political leaders in Ireland – seven in eight years – did little to ease the situation. Not until 1599 was a force of 17,000 sent, under the command of Essex. This would have been large enough to combat the revolt if he had deployed the troops effectively but he proceeded to divide his army, putting half in garrisons and sending the rest into the provinces, without ever forcing Tyrone to submit. By 1603, when Tyrone finally surrendered to Lord Mountjoy, Elizabeth's deputy in Ireland, more than 30,000 English troops had been sent to Ireland.

The fate of the rebels

Not all rebellions ended in battles even if both rebel and government forces had troops in the field. The overwhelming desire of all concerned was to avoid military confrontation; life may have been nasty, brutish and short but there was little point in bringing it to a premature end. There are therefore numerous examples of rebel leaders backing away from confrontation:

- Warbeck arrived at Taunton in 1497 with about 6000 men, mainly from Cornwall, but soon realised that he had walked into a trap. The Earl of Devon waited at Exeter, Willoughby de Broke gathered ships at Portsmouth to block any escape by sea, Daubeny started to gather troops and Henry prepared to move west from Woodstock. Rather than risk battle, Warbeck fled at the approach of Daubeny's army.
- A military confrontation also seemed likely in October 1536, when rebel pilgrims in Lancashire called on the Earl of Derby's army to settle their differences at Clitheroe Moor. When he heard about this, Aske wrote hastily to the rebels urging them not to break the truce he had negotiated, and the Earl of Shrewsbury ordered Derby to disband. Derby complied and there was no battle.

KEY FIGURE

Lord Wilton (1536–93)

Lord Deputy in Ireland and was sent to put down the Geraldine rebellion.

- On 14 July 1553, the Duke of Northumberland, in support of Lady Jane Grey, decided to confront Mary and try to defeat her in battle. The 2000 men he took with him to Cambridge, however, were never going to be enough, and his problems increased when some of them deserted. The critical moment came on 18 July when the Earl of Oxford, Lord Lieutenant of Essex, defected. Next day, the Privy Council declared for Mary, and the Lord Mayor and aldermen of London followed suit. Although Northumberland could still count on the earls of Huntingdon and Warwick, the Marquis of Northampton, and lords Clinton and Grey, he decided the game was up.
- Similarly, in 1554, having seen a number of friends killed at Ludgate, Wyatt surrendered to the Earl of Pembroke's troops rather than risk a full-blooded battle in the streets of London.
- The northern earls, in 1569, also lost heart when confronted with the prospect of fighting a pitched battle even though they could muster over 5000 men. Instead, they took a chance at trying to evade the gathering royal armies: Westmorland succeeded but Northumberland was captured in Scotland.
- Finally, 30 years later, the Earl of Essex held back from engaging royal troops in central London after failing to get past Ludgate.

Military casualties

Battles were fought only when rebels refused to surrender. It was not the government's wish to fight its own subjects, although this was necessary from time to time. When battles did occur, casualties were usually high. Some 4000 rebels, mainly Irish and German mercenaries, were killed at East Stoke in 1487. Over 1000 Cornish rebels died at Blackheath in 1497. More than 700 of Sir Francis Bigod's supporters may have fallen when they attempted to storm Carlisle in February 1537 and a further 800 rebels were taken prisoner at the hands of the Duke of Norfolk after the end of the Pilgrimage of Grace. Heavier casualties were reported in 1549. According to an eyewitness, John Hooker, at least 4000 men fell at the battles of Clyst St Mary and Sampford Courtenay in the Western rebellion. In Norfolk, the Earl of Warwick made his intentions clear as soon as he entered Norwich in August 1549: when Kett turned down another offer of pardon, Warwick hanged 49 prisoners, and at nearby Dussindale, the rebels suffered an estimated 3000 casualties at the hands of the royal army strengthened by 1400 Swiss and German mercenaries. The last rebellion in England to witness heavy casualties occurred when 500 of Lord Dacre's 3000-strong rebel army were killed or captured at Naworth near Carlisle in February 1570, at the end of the Northern Earls' rebellion.

Few battles were fought in Ireland. Most rebellions consisted of skirmishes between clans and frequently ended with the murder of one of the leaders. Sometimes military clashes did occur, as in 1567 when Shane O'Neill's rebels were defeated in Ulster. Cork was relieved in 1569 and Spanish troops were beaten at Smerwick in 1580 and again at Kinsale in 1601. The Battle of Yellow Ford in 1598 was exceptional in so far as the English commander, Sir Henry Bagenal, commanded 4000 troops and still suffered a heavy defeat.

Trials and retribution

The extent to which governments sought justice, vengeance or a mixture of both varied from ruler to ruler. Some, like Henry VII and Mary, were notably lenient; others, such as Henry VIII and Elizabeth, could be quite vindictive. Those rebels who indulged in treason knew that the penalty was death but not all rebels were subsequently executed. In Ireland, in contrast, English officers treated rebels with contempt and many of the punishments were excessive and barbaric.

Henry VII

Henry VII assessed each rebellion on its merits and dispensed justice accordingly. Sir John Conyers, for example, who was suspected of being involved in the Lovel revolt and was a major office holder in Yorkshire, lost his stewardship of Middleham and had a £2000 bond imposed; and the Abbot of Abingdon, who had secured **sanctuary** for the Stafford brothers, faced a 3000-mark bond of allegiance. Imposing **bonds and recognisances** was a favoured policy of the king, which was widely employed in the months leading up to the Battle of Stoke. In February 1487, for instance, a large Sussex contingent including the mayor of Winchelsea was bound over for sums up to £1000. In the aftermath of the battle, Henry travelled around the Midlands and north of England before returning to Warwickshire, and finally London. He needed to thank those who had been loyal – some 70 men were knighted – and to punish or threaten any who had not. In general, he was anxious to appease his northern subjects and avoided excessive reprisals. Thirty-three gentry had their lands attainted and fines were paid by several Yorkshire gentry and clergy between 1487 and 1489. Henry's preferred punishment, however, was to bind men under surety of good behaviour, and bonds up to £1000 were quite common. More unusual was the treatment given to lords Scrope of Bolton and Masham, who were bound over for £3000 each, and Sir Edmund Hastings for £2000; in addition, each faced a spell in prison. Although they had not fought against Henry, the king felt they had been sympathetic towards the rebels and he was not yet ready to trust them.

Most of the ringleaders of the Yorkshire and Cornish tax revolts were rounded up, tried and executed, but the rank-and-file rebels were allowed to return home and await the king's judgement. In the case of Yorkshire, some 1500 men were pardoned and only six were executed, including John Chamber, the leader of the revolt. The tax (see page 125), however, was not collected. Henry spent three years investigating the Cornish rebellion, interrogating those involved as well as the gentry who failed to halt the eastward advance, before determining the fate of the rebels. Eventually, heavy fines were imposed on both active and passive suspects, most of whom came from Somerset and Cornwall. Over 4000 people in Somerset, mainly small tradesmen and craftsmen but also several monks and abbots, were fined in 1500. Bridgwater, Taunton, Wells and Bruton paid £1400, and ex-sheriffs Lutrell and Speke, £100 each. In Cornwall, a huge fine of £14,000 was levied on the county as a whole and families such as the Trefusis, Godolphins and Trewynnards were bound over to keep the peace.

 **KEY TERMS**

Sanctuary A place that provided a haven for outlaws. Every parish church, cathedral and monastery had the privilege to offer sanctuary, although in practice certain crimes such as treason were rendered ineligible.

Bonds and recognisances Bonds were written obligations binding one person to another (often the Crown) to perform a specified action or to pay a sum of money; a recognisance acknowledged that someone was bound to fulfil a commitment.

In October 1497, Henry visited Wells and Exeter with an escort of 10,000 troops to reassert his authority in the area. Many of the officials in Wells were later fined or had bonds of loyalty imposed but at Exeter, the city was presented with a sword and ceremonial cap of maintenance for its loyalty during the crisis. Perhaps wisely, the king did not visit Cornwall. The county was reportedly 'still eager to promote a revolution if they were in any way provoked', and significantly none of the bodies of the men slaughtered at Blackheath was sent home for burial. Only in 1504 was Henry willing to draw a line under the rebellion: 24 attainders were passed on the leading rebels and 38 received a royal pardon. The king forgave those who had subsequently shown their loyalty to the regime, but he was still determined to squeeze lands and fines out of the guilty.

Henry VIII

Thomas Wolsey intended showing the ringleaders of the Amicable Grant no generosity: they had given him so much grief and must pay for their crime. Eighteen ringleaders were therefore taken to London to await trial. He wanted revenge as, in his opinion, it would be 'convenient for the king's honour and our estimations' and called for the indictment of a further 525 men on charges of riot and unlawful assembly. The leading rebels duly appeared before Wolsey in the **Star Chamber**, where he reprimanded them for their treasonous activity and then, no doubt to their surprise, freed them. Either he realised how impoverished they were (which is what he declared) or he was forced to release them by the king (which is what Wolsey's critics claimed), and the rebels returned to Suffolk with 90 pieces of silver as compensation paid by the prison keeper on Wolsey's instructions. It was a bizarre end to an episode that brought no credit to either the king or his chief minister.

Henry VIII showed his vindictive side, however, when he determined the fate of the rebels involved in the Lincolnshire, Pilgrimage and Bigod's rebellions. The king left no doubt as to his intentions when he told the Duke of Norfolk in 1537 that the accused in Carlisle and York were to be tried by commissions without a jury and a summary verdict without appeal announced. Although the duke professed he was 'unlearned in the law', he nevertheless justified the use of martial law. 'If I should proceed by indictments', he informed Cromwell, 'many a great offender might fortune be found not guilty.'

Anyone who was involved in the recent troubles or who was suspected of knowing something had to take an oath disclosing the names of the rebel captains, and these were then arrested and sent to London for interrogation. The king had also instructed Norfolk to hang any monks who had repossessed their dissolved monasteries and he identified those rebels he wanted to question personally.

Seventy-four men were executed in Carlisle and surrounding villages. In Lancaster, the Earl of Sussex executed the Abbot of Whalley and four monks,

KEY TERM

Star Chamber The name given to the place or court where members of the council dealing with legal matters met.

four canons from Cartmel and nineteen husbandmen. In Lincoln, Sir William Parr arrested twelve ringleaders and sent them to London, and sentenced 34 others to death, including Sir Thomas Moigne, the Abbot of Kirkstead, fourteen monks and six priests. Further trials took place in May in York and Lincoln in the absence of the accused, where juries were carefully selected and loyal subjects urged to convict.

Lords Darcy and Hussey were tried by a special court of peers in London and executed. Darcy had failed to distance himself from the pilgrims and Hussey had simply not tried hard enough to stop the Lincolnshire rising. Robert Aske, the Percy brothers, George Lumley and gentry, like Sir Robert Constable and Sir John Bulmer, were judged to have been in contact with Bigod and so broke their pardon. Nicholas Tempest and Stephen Hammerton, on the other hand, admitted helping monks to return to their abbeys. All the accused were executed in the summer of 1537. In total, 46 were hanged as a result of the Lincolnshire rising and 132 from the Pilgrimage of Grace and Bigod's rising. However, not everyone brought before the courts was found guilty. Fifty-six rebels were pardoned and a few were acquitted by sympathetic juries. Nevertheless, while the vast majority of the nobility and gentry escaped death, the clergy was less fortunate. All twenty clerics tried at Lincoln in March 1537 were executed, whereas only fourteen out of 67 laymen were given death sentences. Henry expected his clergy to set an example to his lay subjects and if they did not, then he made an example of them.

Edward VI

Once Lord Russell and his colleagues, William Herbert and Lord Grey, had suppressed the Prayer Book rebels at Sampford Courtenay, Edward VI's Privy Council was determined to silence the western counties once and for all. Russell was ordered to execute 'the heads and stirrers of rebellion in so diverse places as you may to the more terror of the unruly'. Over 100 rebels were hanged in Devon and Somerset towns. Sir Anthony Kingston, the provost marshal, imposed martial law in Cornwall. Among his victims were eight priests. The ringleaders were sent to London, housed in the Fleet prison. In January 1550, **Arundell**, Winslade, Bury and Holmes were executed. Six other leaders were pardoned, with the exception of Robert Welsh, vicar of St Thomas's, who was hanged on his own church tower in Exeter dressed in his Catholic vestments and decorated with popish ornaments.

The Edwardian government was equally determined to punish Kett and his rebel captains. The ringleaders who survived the Battle of Dussindale were tried and executed, some under the Oak of Reformation, others on the city gallows. Kett was taken to the Tower of London, held for six weeks, tortured, tried, convicted and returned to Norwich to hang from the city walls in December 1549.

 **KEY FIGURE**

Humphrey Arundell (c.1530–50)

The leader of the Cornish rebels in the Western rebellion, he was executed at Tyburn after the rebellion.

Mary I

Mary's response to Northumberland's revolt was to show leniency towards the rebels. Only a handful were punished: Northumberland and two of his close associates, Sir John Gates (vice chamberlain) and Sir Thomas Palmer (captain of the guards), were executed, and Lady Jane Grey, her father and Northumberland's sons were imprisoned. Mary was similarly generous towards most of Wyatt's rebels in 1554. More than 1000 rebels were indicted, but 600 were pardoned and, of 480 convicted of waging war against the queen, only 71 were executed. Among the victims were Wyatt, Suffolk and his brother, and Jane and her husband. Renard, the imperial ambassador in London, reassured Philip of Spain that the rebellion was really a minor religious disturbance and that Englishmen looked forward to the forthcoming wedding, but behind the scenes investigations into the revolt continued. The Privy Council was divided over the extent of Princess Elizabeth's and Courtenay's involvement. Some Catholics, like Rochester, Waldegrave and Englefield, wanted to put her on trial; others, like Paget, Arundel, Pembroke and Sussex, came to her defence. After several weeks' deliberation, the government decided to place her under house arrest at Woodstock, while Courtenay was confined to Fotheringay Castle. Both detainees were released in 1555: Elizabeth returned to court and Courtenay went into exile in Venice. Throughout the spring of 1554, arrests were made, fines levied and pardons granted. Most of those held in the Tower were not released until January 1555, but the queen and her council were less concerned at exacting revenge and more interested in winning over the hearts and minds of the people.

Elizabeth I

Elizabeth was far less forgiving towards rebels. Once victory was secured over the northern earls, she demanded revenge: Sussex and Hunsdon were encouraged to take raiding parties into Scotland, where they burned 300 villages and sacked 50 castles. The Earl of Northumberland went into hiding but was eventually captured and ransomed to the English for £2000 in 1572, and then executed. Martial law was declared and many innocent parties appear to have been caught up in the aftermath. Dacre and Westmorland evaded capture but 700 rebels were arrested and about 450 hanged. Nevertheless, George Bowes, who was one of the officers required to exact punishments, acted more discriminately and claimed that he had hanged only 81 out of 256 tried in Darlington and Richmond. Most of those who died were commoners. The gentry and lesser nobles, on the other hand, had their lands attainted and castles seized. The severity of punishments meted out to the Oxfordshire rebels in 1596–7, however, merits an explanation. Five ringleaders were taken to London, interrogated by the lord chief justice and other privy councillors, imprisoned for six months, tortured and then sentenced to death for making war against the queen. In June 1597, two rebels – Bradshaw and Burton – were hanged, drawn and quartered; the fate of the others is unknown. On four occasions, the council ordered the Lord Lieutenant of Oxford to make extensive arrests even though he believed no more than twenty men were involved. As a result, many innocent men found themselves in London prisons. Clearly, the council overreacted out of fear that the Oxfordshire rising was part of a larger conspiracy or that a similar incident might occur elsewhere. In a climate of suspicion and uncertainty, it had decided against taking any chances. Over 100 suspects involved in Essex's rebellion in 1601 were arrested and detained in London prisons and private houses belonging to loyal councillors. The council acted quickly to examine the accused and judges were told to hear these cases before setting off on their regular circuits. Thus, within a few weeks, trials took place and verdicts were given. Essex and two associates, Merrick and Cuffe, were executed for waging war against the queen, and 36 others were fined. Some rebels paid dearly: Rutland had to pay £30,000, and Bedford and Neville £10,000 each. The Earl of Southampton was also fined and given an extended spell in the Tower of London. Although several hundred rebels had taken part in the uprising, no one else was punished.

Trial and retribution in Ireland

Martial law was invoked whenever rebellion broke out in Ireland. This allowed English troops to shoot to kill and execute without trial anyone they suspected was involved. Between 1535 and 1537, some 70 English and Irish supporters of Silken Thomas were hanged, the earl and his five uncles were executed in London, and over 200 rebels were fined and their lands attainted. During the Munster rebellion, Lord Deputy Sidney executed 800 rebels between 1569 and 1572, and over twenty castles were captured and lands seized. During the Geraldine rebellion, Lord Wilton, Lord Deputy from 1580 to 1582, massacred the entire garrison of Smerwick and hanged as many rebels as he could find in the course of two years. The head of the Earl of Desmond, who was killed in 1583, was forwarded to Elizabeth and put on display on London Bridge. After each rebellion, lands were seized, fines were imposed and property was destroyed by vengeful troops. The Tudors never showed any sympathy or understanding towards Irish rebels, and as a result treated them quite differently from their counterparts in England.

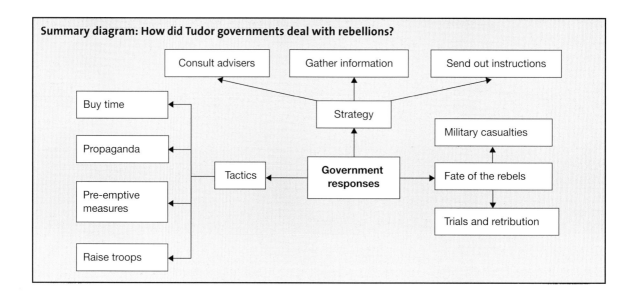

Summary diagram: How did Tudor governments deal with rebellions?

2 The effects of rebellions on government and society

▶ *Why were Crown servants able to survive calls for their dismissal?*

Crown servants

All dynastic rebellions against the Tudors failed and most of the rebellions protesting against government policies and ministers fared little better. The Tudors were resolute in their defence of the Crown; having claimed it under questionable circumstances, they were determined to hold on to it. Crown servants who were the targets of attack – Morton, Bray, Wolsey, Cromwell, Audley, Rich, Cranmer, William and Robert Cecil – all survived. True, Wolsey's relationship with Henry VIII worsened as a consequence of the Amicable Grant protests but he remained in office for a further four years. Nor was Henry inclined to bow to pressure to change the council that had served him so well in the 1530s. Men like Cromwell, Cranmer, Rich and Audley had not caused the Pilgrimage of Grace and he ensured that they were rewarded for their part in defeating it. Cromwell remained Henry's principal secretary and was granted monastic lands and annuities from confiscated estates. When he fell from office in 1540, it was not on account of the rebellion but the consequence of arranging an unpopular marriage for the king to Anne of Cleves. Cranmer continued to serve Henry as his Archbishop of Canterbury, Rich was rewarded with the office of Chancellor of the **Court of Augmentations** and Audley stayed as Lord Chancellor. The Duke of Somerset was the only minister to fall from office as a

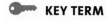 **KEY TERM**

Court of Augmentations
Established in 1536, this administrative and financial court in London handled affairs relating to the dissolved monasteries.

result of rebellion and, ironically, it was not because the rebels demanded it but because he failed to suppress them effectively and was overthrown by his fellow councillors.

Religious developments

The Tudors were also unwilling to reverse or change their religious policies, which had prompted rebellions between 1536 and 1569. If anything, the Pilgrimage of Grace made Henry even more determined to sever links with the Roman Catholic Church. Participation in the revolt by abbots and monks convinced him that their continued existence presented a security risk and led him to support Cromwell's move to dissolve the larger monasteries in 1537–8. Most abbots and abbesses surrendered their convents voluntarily in anticipation of parliamentary legislation. Ironically, the pilgrims, instead of preserving the smaller monasteries, were instrumental in bringing about the closure of the larger ones.

Cromwell's Injunctions of 1538 further confirmed the government's reformed stance in respect of saints, pilgrimages and holy days. The U-turn, which Henry made in 1539 when he endorsed the Act of Six Articles, was a result of popular **iconoclasm** and the conduct of overzealous Protestants (see page 136). If his conservative reaction owed anything at all to the Pilgrimage of Grace, it was his fear of disorder occurring in many parts of the realm that reminded him of the German peasants' revolt of 1525, the more recent **Anabaptist** disturbances in Münster and the **placards incidents in France**.

Edward VI, like his father, did not recall the English prayer book, which had angered the Catholics in Devon and Cornwall, leading to the Western rebellion; in fact, Cranmer proceeded to publish an even more Protestant book three years later.

Mary went ahead with her marriage to the Catholic prince, Philip of Spain, in spite of Wyatt's rebellion, and stepped up her campaign against heretics.

Elizabeth was not intimidated by the reaction and rebellion of northern Catholics to her religious settlement of 1558–9; in 1571, the council introduced penal laws specifically against Catholic recusants. Not a single religious revolt achieved its prime objective.

Policy changes

In a few cases, governments did respond to rebellions by making policy changes. As a result of the Yorkshire rebellion in 1489, Henry VII agreed not to collect the tax nor did he impose any fine on the rebels. The Cornish were also relieved of having to pay their war tax in 1497. Although the county was heavily fined, the king did not attempt to introduce tax novelties again. The most successful of all protests was against Wolsey's Amicable Grant. No one paid any tax, no

 **KEY TERMS**

Iconoclasm The smashing and destruction of religious images and icons.

Anabaptists Radical religious reformers, many of whom also wanted to overturn the established social order and were therefore seen as a threat.

Placards incidents in France On 18 October 1534, posters supporting the reformed religion and attacking mass were put up in Paris, five provincial towns and even in the royal place.

Benevolence A gift that was occasionally requested to help the government overcome a financial crisis.

benevolence was received and a parliamentary subsidy that still had two of its four instalments to be collected was reassessed at more modest rates for fear of reigniting a taxpayers' strike. Of course, failure to impose a non-parliamentary tax did not prevent future governments from trying again, but Wolsey and Henry had learned their lesson. When Henry collected benevolences in the 1540s, he targeted the wealthier groups rather than the poor.

Henry VIII's responses to the Pilgrimage of Grace

The Pilgrimage of Grace produced two positive changes that would have pleased some of the rebels:

- Unlawful enclosures and excessive entry fines had been the cause of rioting in Westmorland and Cumberland in 1535 and accounted for angry outbursts in 1536–7. To try to obviate this, the earls of Sussex and Derby were instructed by the king to examine the landlord–tenant relations in Kendal, the Vale of Eden and Craven, and if they discovered any irregularities, 'to bring such enclosers and extreme takers of fines to such moderation that they and the poor men may live in harmony'. The commissioners appear to have been successful. No further disturbances occurred in this region in the 1540s, when much of the country was experiencing severe social and economic difficulties.
- The gentry and lesser nobility had complained about the Statute of Uses of 1536 (see page 40) and called for its repeal. In 1540, this happened when a new Statute of Wills allowed testators the right to distribute two-thirds of their property without incurring the payment of feudal taxes to the Crown.

Edwardian concessions

The rebellions in 1549 produced several responses from the government:

- The most dramatic event was the arrest and imprisonment of the Duke of Somerset by privy councillors. They held him responsible for the political crisis, partly because of his unwise policies, which were seen as undermining the authority and power of landowners, and partly on account of his failure to deal with the crisis effectively.
- Confidence was soon restored in the City of London and among the gentry, and this was further reflected by legislation passed in November 1549 when the new regime tried to prevent further disturbances. An 'Act for the Punishment of Unlawful Assemblies and Rising of the King's subjects' declared it high treason if twelve or more people gathered to alter existing laws or tried to kill or imprison a privy councillor or refused to disperse within one hour.
- As a result of the unrest, it was also declared a felony if twelve or more people attempted to destroy enclosures, parks, barns or grain stores and refused to disperse, and it became treason if 40 or more people gathered for more than two hours.

- To improve the quality of civil defence in the counties that had proved ineffective in recent times, lords lieutenant were given control of the shire levies. Privy councillors even suggested that 'idle persons' and rebel leaders should be forced to join the county militia to save on expensive mercenaries, but this proposal does not appear to have been implemented.

Although further disturbances occurred between 1550 and 1552, there was no repetition of the 'year of commotion'. JPs were more vigilant, privy councillors and lords lieutenant acted decisively, and a run of good harvests lowered food prices and so reduced social tension.

Social and economic reforms

Tudor governments also took note of social and economic problems, which had been a cause of unrest in 1549 and 1596, and sought to remedy them:

- The Edwardian government in 1549–50 introduced several measures to help the poor. The Subsidy and Vagrancy Acts were repealed and an Enclosure Act was passed that restricted landlords' manorial rights over the commons and wasteland of less than three acres. This was designed to protect rural peasants from future enclosers of woods and marginal land. Further Acts fixed grain prices, prohibited exports and maintained arable land.
- The Elizabethan council also took steps to stop future anti-social disturbances after the Oxfordshire rising of 1596. All bishops were ordered to give sermons that advertised the good work the government was doing in helping the poor; and wealthier subjects were to be reminded that they had a Christian duty to organise special charity collections. Congregations were expected to 'endure this scarcity [food shortage due to bad harvests] with patience' and to reject attempts by 'discontented and idle brains to move them to repine or swerve from the humble duties of good subjects'. Moreover, in 1597, the council prosecuted seven leading Oxfordshire landowners who had enclosed local common and wasteland. Two Acts were also passed to alleviate social distress:
  - an 'Act against the decaying of towns and houses of husbandry'
  - an 'Act for the maintenance of husbandry and tillage'.

MPs were also ordered by the Lord Keeper to return to their counties at the end of parliament to ensure that the recent statutes were implemented. The government's 'carrot and stick' strategy appears to have worked, and there were no further popular risings in Elizabeth's reign.

Measures taken to strengthen royal authority

Henry VII

A major consequence of rebellion was measures taken by the Crown to strengthen its position and weaken that of potential rebels in troublesome areas. Henry VII achieved this in a number of ways.

In 1487, following Simnel's rebellion, the Star Chamber Act established additional legal powers to deal with nobles who disturbed the king's peace, and an Act of Livery and Maintenance attempted to restrict the number of servants retained by lords and used as private armies.

In the aftermath of the Yorkshire revolt in 1489, Surrey was rewarded by being appointed Lieutenant of the Council of the North, a royal council begun by Edward IV but which had lapsed in 1485, and lands that had belonged to the Earl of Northumberland were transferred to the Crown. Over 30 families now held their land by **knight service** to the king, and at a stroke Henry had considerably strengthened his grip on the north of England. Unlike his successors, Henry preferred to travel throughout his realm and stayed for long periods of time in some of the more disaffected areas, such as Somerset, Worcester and York. Gradually, Henry built up close ties with county families, which played a key part in the restoration of order.

After the Cornish rising and Warbeck's rebellion of 1497, there were no more armed uprisings, although Henry still needed to be vigilant. Edmund, Earl of Suffolk, appears to have been conspiring against the king between 1501 and 1506, until Henry imprisoned him in the Tower, and 51 attainders were issued to suppress Suffolk's supporters and strengthen the Crown politically and financially.

Henry VIII and the northern counties

Henry VIII similarly took the opportunity afforded by the Pilgrimage of Grace to build up royal support in the northern counties. Too many gentry and sons of nobles had involved themselves in the disturbances, either willingly or out of compulsion. Although the older heads of noble families had not participated, Henry and Cromwell decided to reform the Council of the North and the administration of the **marches**. The death of the Earl of Northumberland in June 1537 was particularly fortunate: he had held the east and middle marches. The wardenship of the west march was taken from the Earl of Cumberland but because he had not supported the rebellion, he was made a **Knight of the Garter**. Another major reform was the appointment of local lesser gentry as deputy wardens while the king assumed overall responsibility for the marches. Changes also occurred in the commissions of the peace between 1536 and 1539. Henry purged the bench of magistrates who had shown sympathy towards the rebels or in whom he no longer had total confidence. No disciplinary action, however, was taken against nobles like Lord Scrope of Bolton, John Lord Lumley and John Lord Latimer, who had cooperated with the rebels. It was not Henry's intention to destabilise the north any further and he needed noble families to enforce his rule. Loyalty, however, was vital and he reminded these men, 'We will not be bound of a necessity to be served with Lords'.

Henry VIII had promised that a parliament would meet in the north, but it never did. Instead, reforms to the Council of the North strengthened his political hold.

Its judicial and administrative functions were expanded and all JPs and sheriffs north of the Trent (except in Lancashire) were to take orders directly from it. This enhanced its power to act quickly and suppress future disturbances. The council's membership was also reformed. Tunstall, Bishop of Durham, was made president, senior nobles such as Westmorland, Cumberland, Dacre and Shrewsbury were encouraged to attend, but most significant was the inclusion of Ellerker, Bowes and Tempest. Each had taken leading roles in the rebellion but Henry was prepared to give them a prominent part in the political life of the north, and none acted disloyally again.

Elizabethan reforms to the Council of the North

An important legacy of the Northern Earls' rebellion was the reforms to the county militia, commissions of the peace and Council of the North (see Chapter 4, page 157). From 1569, all parishes were ordered to keep a list of men aged between sixteen and 60 who were eligible for military service, and parishes were instructed to improve the quality and size of the county muster. The rebellion had revealed the inadequacies of the militia, and better training was introduced in 1573. Reforms to the Council of the North occurred in 1572. The Earl of Huntingdon, Elizabeth's cousin and a puritan with no local connections, became the new president. He was authorised to ensure that JPs enforced the penal laws against Catholics, removed illegal enclosures, punished unlawful retaining and assisted the poor. From 1570, most northern counties had their magistrates purged. JPs who had shown leniency towards the uprising were replaced by more reliable men. Although this purge could not be applied in every case, as there were insufficient alternatives, a constant turnover of JPs in the 1570s gradually built up a more dependable bench. It was hoped that these measures would minimise the likelihood of future disturbances and remove the influence of Catholic families from the political social scene in the northern counties. In this way, the Crown turned one of the prime objectives behind the earls' rebellion to its own advantage, and the absence of any further religious or political revolts in the north suggests that it succeeded.

Ireland

Silken Thomas's rebellion of 1534 was a watershed in Anglo-Irish relations. Henry VIII decided to end the dominance of the Geraldines and, thereafter, English officials replaced Irish office holders in Dublin. A small permanent garrison was established and border fortresses were restrengthened. Although periodically cuts were made, a military presence came to symbolise English rule in Ireland for the next 400 years. The seizure of Kildare's lands and those of his supporters opened the way for granting lands to English loyalists, and the refusal of the Irish parliament to meet the cost of the rebellion led to Henry seizing Irish monastic and bishops' lands instead. There was no immediate reaction to the reprisals, which were fairly lenient, and most Anglo-Irish endorsed Henry's religious changes, but opposition by Gaelic lords and

Palesmen to religious reforms did lead to a revolt in 1539 against the Archbishop of Dublin. Although it failed to gather much support and within a year had fizzled out, it was an early indication of nationalist and papist opposition that would characterise Elizabethan Irish rebellions.

From time to time, rebellions in Ireland could be a security risk but they never presented a serious challenge to English rule, and domestic troubles and foreign wars were always given priority. Nevertheless, in comparison with the costs involved in suppressing disturbances in England, Irish rebellions were far more expensive. Henry VIII spent £40,000 dealing with Silken Thomas's rebellion whereas fifteen years later, in the 'year of commotions', the Edwardian government spent £27,000 suppressing a multitude of English revolts. The costs spiralled out of control in Elizabeth's reign: the Geraldine rebellion cost the government £254,000 and Tyrone's national uprising an estimated £2 million. Moreover, the Tudors increasingly struggled to suppress disturbances in Ireland; after fighting the Earl of Tyrone for more than eight years, victory was limited. Although the earl renounced his title of 'the O'Neill' and agreed to support English sheriffs and garrisons in Ulster, he was granted a pardon and recovered all that he had held at the start of the rebellion.

Foreign affairs

Rebellions also had an impact on Tudor foreign affairs:

- The Yorkshire uprising distracted Henry VII at a time when he was preparing to go to war with France over Brittany. Raising money was proving hard and, although Yorkshire's contribution to his war preparations would have been relatively small, Henry felt obliged to visit York to try to prevent future disturbances when his time would have been better spent in London. Support for Warbeck from foreign powers in the 1490s also affected Henry's relations with Burgundy, France, the Holy Roman Empire and Scotland. Henry signed the treaties of Étaples and Ayton to secure his throne from the claims of the pretender, and put a three-year trade embargo on Burgundy. His preparations to attack Scotland in 1497 were also badly affected by the Cornish rebellion. Troops had to be recalled and Daubeny, who was to have marched north to lead the campaign, found himself defending the south of England instead. Eventually a truce was declared between James IV and England but the revolt had proved particularly embarrassing for the government, and encouraged Warbeck to choose Cornwall as the starting point for his own campaign.
- Failure to secure the Amicable Grant also had an impact on Henry VIII's plans to invade France in 1525. Without the additional money, which the grant was intended to produce, he could not hope to raise enough troops and equip them for a summer campaign. Within a year, relations with Charles V had deteriorated and those with France improved, and Henry's hopes of leading an army on the continent were dashed. It would be another seventeen years before Henry and Charles were again comrades in arms.

- The rebellions in 1549 also had a serious impact on Somerset's foreign designs and in particular the war against Scotland. The government already had serious financial difficulties and was struggling to meet the costs of what was turning out to be a lengthy and expensive war. Foreign mercenaries were hastily redeployed to deal with the domestic troubles, and the orderly withdrawal of English troops from the Scottish lowlands was thrown into disarray. In addition, news of these rebellions encouraged France to declare war on England, which compounded Somerset's problems.
- Relations with Spain were also affected by rebellion. Wyatt may have failed in his attempt to stop Mary from marrying Philip but his revolt brought to the fore xenophobic feelings among many Englishmen and did little to appease the Spanish prince's own concerns about living in England. The legacy of this ill-feeling, which was enhanced by the Marian persecution of Protestants, continued into Elizabeth's reign.
- Spain also recognised the strategic opportunities that Ireland presented whenever rebellions broke out, and in 1580 and 1601 sent money, troops and priests to assist Irish rebels against the English. Although neither expedition proved successful, they further damaged Anglo-Spanish relations.

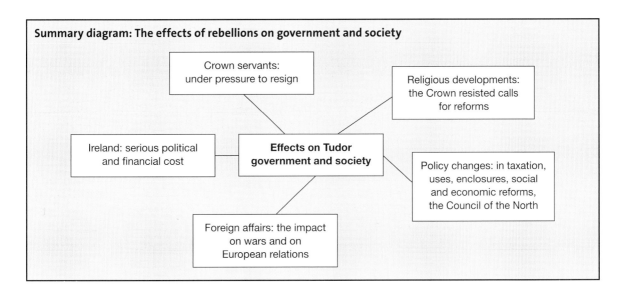

Summary diagram: The effects of rebellions on government and society

- Crown servants: under pressure to resign
- Religious developments: the Crown resisted calls for reforms
- Ireland: serious political and financial cost
- **Effects on Tudor government and society**
- Policy changes: in taxation, uses, enclosures, social and economic reforms, the Council of the North
- Foreign affairs: the impact on wars and on European relations

Conclusion: were Tudor governments ever seriously threatened by rebellion and unrest?

▶ *Were Tudor governments ever seriously threatened by rebellion?*

We have seen in Chapter 2 that the strength of a rebellion depended on several factors and if these worked in unison, they were capable of challenging, even threatening, the stability of Tudor governments. The size and support a rebellion received could prove to be too large for a government to confront directly and, if it had the backing of English nobles or foreign princes, then the threat was very serious. The Cornish, Amicable Grant, Pilgrimage of Grace, Western, Kett and Northern Earls all raised a force greater than the royal army, and could not be easily dispersed. Simnel and Warbeck, although they gathered fewer troops, acquired the support of foreign rulers and, in the case of Simnel, several English and Irish nobles. This rebellion was probably the most threatening in so far as the king had to fight a battle in person to defend his newly acquired throne.

A rebellion's objective largely determined its potential threat. Politically motivated disturbances, such as Simnel, Warbeck, Wyatt, Northern Earls and Essex, were dangerous precisely because they planned to overthrow the monarch. Should a rebellion approach London – as occurred in the Cornish, Wyatt and Essex revolts – then the safety of the government was similarly imperilled. Fortunately for the Tudors, London proved consistently loyal and, as long as the government held its nerve, the citizens were likely to support it. Thus, neither Wyatt nor Essex was able to rally the people against two potentially vulnerable female rulers, and Mary Tudor secured the throne because Londoners backed her legitimate claim against Northumberland's protégée, Lady Jane Grey.

In practice, most rebellions were localised affairs and intent on registering a protest against government policies and ministers rather than seeking to overthrow the monarch. The length of a rebellion could be an irritant, however, which might raise doubts about the government's competence to maintain order and thus weaken its credibility. The reputation of both Wolsey and Cromwell suffered as a result of the Amicable Grant and Pilgrimage of Grace, and the Duke of Somerset fell from office as a direct consequence of the 1549 disturbances. Most disturbances lasted for less than a month, and the Pilgrimage, Western and Kett's rebellions that lasted for more than two months were exceptional. Yet even these rebellions, which wished to reverse government policies and remove unpopular royal councillors, failed to present a serious threat to the government in London.

Governments, then, were never seriously challenged provided they stayed calm under pressure. Strategies of deploying a mixture of propaganda, persuasion and threats usually kept the nobility and clergy on side, and rebels either lost interest in their protest or went home confident that changes for the better would follow. All governments played for time until they were in a position of strength. Once they felt strong enough to exact reprisals, they isolated rebel groups and picked off the leaders at will. If they made a bargain or offered concessions, it was because they felt temporarily vulnerable and had little intention of keeping to promises made under duress.

Only in Ireland did the Tudors have some difficulty suppressing disturbances. The absence of large permanent garrisons, the harsh terrain which made fighting very tough and the growing unpopularity of government policies contributed to an increase in ill-feeling between the native Irish and the English administration and settlers. Yet although the Tudors struggled to keep Ireland at peace, rarely did Irish rebellions present a threat to the government or the monarch. Certainly, Irish nobles and clergy could destabilise political affairs in Ireland. They invaded England in Henry VII's reign in the name of the pretender Simnel, and some Irish received support from Catholic Spain in Elizabeth's reign. Only in the 1590s did the Tudors view the Irish as a serious threat, partly on account of the size and widespread support in Ireland for O'Neill's rebellion but mainly because its potential to receive assistance from Spain endangered national security. For most of the Tudor period, the Irish Channel protected England and Wales from disturbances across the water and ensured that what was 'out of sight' stayed largely 'out of mind'.

Summary diagram: Conclusion: were Tudor governments ever seriously threatened by rebellion and unrest?

Factors that increased a rebellion's seriousness	**Factors that weakened a rebellion's seriousness**
• Size, support, and backing of English nobles and foreign powers • A rebellion's objective, e.g. to overthrow the monarch • Its proximity to London	• Governments held their nerve or made deals they had no intention of honouring • Most rebellions were localised protests • Most of the English nobility and clergy supported the Crown

Chapter summary

All Tudor governments used much the same strategy and tactics to deal with rebellions and unrest. Some monarchs, such as Elizabeth I, were harsher in their treatment of rebels than monarchs such as Mary Tudor. All the governments attempted to avoid resorting to force to deal with unrest, in part because of the cost but also because they had the difficulty of then raising a force to put it down. Although most rebellions did not achieve their primary aim, some rebellions did lead to the government introducing legislation to tackle the underlying problems, particularly social and economic, that had sparked the unrest. However, the government could not, and did not, make concessions when dealing with dynastic rebellions, as these rebellions were a much greater threat because they planned to overthrow the government. Irish rebellions, although usually of greater duration, were usually not a threat to the government or monarch, even if they struggled to put them down.

 Refresher questions

Use these questions to remind yourself of the key material covered in this chapter.

1 Why did Tudor monarchs gather information about unrest?

2 What government strategies were successful in dealing with unrest?

3 Why did governments use pre-emptive measures in dealing with unrest?

4 Why did the government attempt to buy time when rebellions broke out?

5 What were the messages of government propaganda issued during rebellions?

6 Why did the government try and avoid the use of troops to suppress rebellions?

7 Why were rebel casualties during rebellions often so high?

8 Why were some monarchs more lenient than others in their treatment of rebels?

9 What concessions did governments make to rebels?

10 How did the government strengthen royal authority after rebellions?

11 How were foreign affairs affected by unrest?

12 How was the government affected by unrest in Ireland?

In-depth studies and debates

The examination requires you to study three topics in depth and for this unit they are:

- The Pilgrimage of Grace
- The Western rebellion
- Tyrone's rebellion.

This section will go into more detail about the impact of these three rebellions and introduce you to some of the key debates about the impact of each rebellion, so that you will have enough depth of knowledge to be able to evaluate passages that are set on any of these three rebellions.

Key debate 1: did the Pilgrimage of Grace slow down the pace of religious change?

The period after the Pilgrimage of Grace saw a number of changes in the religious position in England, with the passing of numerous reforms. The impact of the Pilgrimage on those changes appears to have been quite significant, with some suggesting that Henry, fearful of further protest and aware of the strength of feeling towards traditional religion, slowed down moves away from traditional Catholic practices, while others have argued that he increased the pace of change because the rebellion had shown that he could not trust the monks or clergy, who were blamed for much of the unrest.

In arguing that the Pilgrimage slowed down the pace of change, it could be said that:

- The government agreed to allow the smaller monasteries, which the Pilgrims had restored, to stand until a new parliament in the north met. However, this promise was not kept.
- In 1537, the Bishops' Book was introduced. This restored many conservative religious practices. It recognised the four lost sacraments that had been absent from the Ten Articles of 1536.
- There was an attack on some reformist practices such as radical preaching and clerical marriage.
- The orchestrator and supporter of radical religious changes, Thomas Cromwell, was removed from power in 1540. The Pilgrimage may have played a role in his fall and certainly his radical beliefs were mentioned in the Act of Attainder against him.
- The religious policies of the 1540s were largely conservative, and more radical religious change would have to wait until the reign of Edward VI.
- The Act of Six Articles, passed in 1539, confirmed a number of Catholic practices including transubstantiation, private Masses and the hearing of confession by priests.
- It may have made Henry more cautious theologically.

However, although it is possible to contend that the Reformation was slowed, most would support the view that this was a period when the pace of religious change increased and that traditional practices came under further attack:

- The most obvious example of the increased pace of change was the closure by 1540 of all the monastic houses. In 1536, when the Pilgrimage had occurred, the legislation had closed just the small houses, and some historians have argued that Henry did not intend to go further, praising the great houses. However, the rising showed Henry that the loyalty of monks could not be assured and therefore a second Act, dissolving the remainder of the houses, was passed. Many had already offered voluntary surrender so the Act simply completed the process and brought to an end the monastic tradition in England when Waltham Abbey was dissolved. It might also be noted that some of the abbots were actually hanged from the walls of their monasteries if they had resisted.
- Cromwell did not fall until 1540. It is therefore unlikely that the Pilgrimage played a significant role; it is more likely that it was due to the failed marriage of Henry to Anne of Cleves.
- Even if the religious changes of the 1540s were conservative, the rebellion did not stop religious reform and the pace increased under Edward.
- As the rebellion was defeated it may have encouraged reformers to press on with their demands.
- The Matthew Bible was published in 1537; this was distinctly reformist and had the king's permission. The Great Bible was published in 1539; this may have had the greatest impact on the Reformation as its frontispiece reinforced the royal supremacy and began a process that, over time, would be difficult to reverse. The Bible was to be placed in all parishes within two years.
- The Injunctions of 1538 discouraged people from pilgrimages, and relics were to be removed from churches, a sign of the rejection of the Catholic belief in purgatory.
- It can also be argued that the Bishops' Book had some reformist elements; the Mass was glossed over, the status of priests was reduced and purgatory was only implied.

Although it is impossible to argue that all of these changes were the direct result of the Pilgrimage, it is also difficult to argue that such a large rising would not have had an impact on the government's religious policy. It should also be remembered that the rising had an impact on financial and agrarian policy and that in these areas the rebels did achieve some gains (see page 126).

Key debate 2: was the Western rebellion a serious threat to the government?

It could be argued that the Western rebellion presented the greatest threat of all Tudor rebellions to the government. The rebellion appeared to be a direct challenge to the government's religious policies and it occurred when the government was particularly weak and under other pressures. The rebels were able to force the government into battle, although they were defeated. However, if the rebellion was more about social and economic grievances and an attack on greedy landowners it might be seen as less of a threat.

There is certainly some evidence to suggest that the Western rebellion was a serious threat:

- The rebellion occurred at a time of a royal minority when many thought that the Protector did not have the right to change religion and that any changes should wait until Edward came of age.
- The rebellion was just one of many incidents of unrest the government faced in the summer of 1549 and, therefore, in that context, it was a greater threat, particularly if the rebels joined forces with other religiously motivated rebels in Oxfordshire and Hampshire.
- The government was ill-informed about developments in the West Country and this meant they were slow to realise the seriousness of the situation and send sufficient forces, allowing the rebellion time to gain momentum and recruits.
- The government was unable to send troops immediately to the West Country, even when it was aware of the situation, as the troops it had gathered had to deal with other unrest *en route*.
- The government considered it serious as it was forced to abandon its Scottish policy and withdraw troops. It also faced the prospect of invasion from France, which made unrest at home even more dangerous.
- The rebels, although apparently not always well armed, were able to force the government into five battles or skirmishes before their final defeat at Sampford Courtenay, showing that the government struggled to suppress the unrest.
- The reaction of the city authorities in Exeter to the rebels and the siege suggests that they considered it a threat and were fearful that the rebels would enter the city, as had happened at Norwich.
- The rebels threatened the main legislation of the government's religious policy and added further evidence to William Paget's comment that the new religion had not won the hearts and minds of the people.
- The rebels' behaviour was often violent, and the wording of their demands showed a lack of respect – 'we will have' – for their superiors.
- The numbers put to death after the rebellion suggest that the government was concerned and wanted to make an example.

Despite these developments, it can also be argued that the rebellion was not a serious threat to the government:

- The rebel force was only 5000 and there was no collaboration with other rebel forces, which would have increased numbers and made it a greater threat.

- The aim of the rebels was not to overthrow the government; it might not even have been a threat to the religious policies if its concerns, as the first list of grievances suggests, were more social and economic.
- It was only government action that made matters worse: the actions of Carew and the burning of the barns at Crediton.
- The number of rebels killed in the battles was some 3000, which weakened resistance.
- Exeter was able to resist the rebels for some six weeks and remained loyal to the government.
- The rebellion remained in the West Country and did not move towards London and threaten the seat of government.
- The government was able to raise sufficient forces, including mercenaries, and they were able to push the rebels back and defeat them at Sampford Courtenay.

It might also be argued that the governments saw the rebellions of 1549 in a wider context and that the decision to remove Somerset as Protector was due to his poor handling of the rebellions, suggesting that they were fearful that such unrest could be repeated. It is also worth considering whether any of the social and economic legislation brought in by Northumberland (see pages 126–7) was in direct response to the rising. Much will depend on whether you see the rising as having social and economic causes.

Key debate 3: how serious a threat to Elizabeth was Tyrone's rebellion?

Tyrone's rebellion was the longest lasting of all sixteenth-century rebellions and it was also the most costly in terms of finance and the number of men required to deal with it. It might be argued that Irish rebellions were less of a threat because they were so far away; on the other hand, it might be seen as serious because it could provide a springboard for an invasion of England. However, very few historians would suggest that the rebellion was not a threat and the debate centres around the extent of that threat. Rebellions in Ireland were always difficult to suppress because of the terrain and the nature of warfare.

In arguing that Tyrone's rebellion was a serious threat to Elizabeth, it might be noted that:

- It was the first rebellion in Ireland that was able to rouse nearly the whole population in support. The element of nationalism was a new feature and a direct challenge to the Tudor state. This meant that the rebellion had widespread and large-scale support.
- Tyrone was able to take much of Ireland and was close to forcing English forces back to the area around the Pale and other southern counties.

- Tyrone controlled the resource-rich county of Ulster. He also had well-trained troops, some of whom had served in Elizabeth's armies. He was further reinforced by Scottish forces.
- The arrival of Spanish troops made the rebellion a greater threat, which could endanger English national security.
- Tyrone was able to defeat the English forces at Yellow Ford.
- Elizabeth made the major mistake of sending Essex as commander. He wasted time and resources and was also unwilling to risk confrontation.
- The context in which the rebellion took place made it a greater threat as, despite defeating the Armada in 1588, the Spanish were still looking for the opportunity to attack England and sent further Armadas. War with Spain also meant that Elizabeth was unable to fund forces in Ireland to the level needed.
- Irish leaders had lost trust in the English deputies and saw the whole system under threat. They therefore might turn to Tyrone.
- The English government had been divided over the strategy to adopt towards Ireland, with Elizabeth having other priorities and wanting peace, almost at any cost.
- The rebellion was only finally defeated after Elizabeth's death.

It can, however, be argued that Tyrone's rebellion was less of a threat to Elizabeth:

- The rebellion was far away from London and was therefore not a direct threat.
- Once Elizabeth sent Mountjoy, the rebellion was put down with relative ease. His expedition was well planned.
- Mountjoy was also skilful and better at conciliating the Irish and therefore won back support.
- Many in Ireland had become fed up with the power of Tyrone.

Study skills: thematic essay question

How to answer turning-point questions

The mark scheme used by examiners is exactly the same for turning-point questions as it is for other thematic essays. This suggests that the approach should be exactly the same as it is for other theme essays and that the structure should be thematic and not chronological. It is much easier to compare the significance or importance of different turning points if a thematic approach, rather than a chronological one, is adopted.

Look at the following question:

'The rebellions of 1549 were the most important turning point in introducing legislation in response to unrest.' How far do you agree with this view?

A range of events might be considered to be the most important turning point in introducing legislation, including:

- the Western and Kett's rebellions of 1549
- the Pilgrimage of Grace 1536
- the rebellion of the Northern Earls
- the Cornish rising 1497
- the Oxfordshire rising 1596.

In theory, an essay could analyse, evaluate and compare each of these events (in order to show synthesis), but it would make for a very cumbersome structure and would be difficult to undertake in 45 minutes.

It would be far easier to adopt a thematic approach which would allow you to compare the events. The following themes could be considered:

- political legislation
- economic legislation
- social legislation
- religious legislation.

You would then select examples from the period and compare their relative importance and significance in terms of being a turning point for each theme, and reach a judgement as to which event was politically, economically, socially and religiously the most important, before going on to reach an overall judgement as to which event was the most important turning point.

This means that the skills you have considered in the previous chapters are just as applicable to turning-point questions as to other essays.

Consider the following responses to the question above.

Response A

The rebellions of 1549 were an important turning point as a large amount of legislation was introduced in the following years under the Lord President of the Council, John Dudley, Duke of Northumberland. The government was aware of the social problems that were behind the unrest, and in 1549 and 1550 several measures were introduced; the Subsidy and Vagrancy Acts were both repealed as they had been unpopular: the peasants had complained about the levels of taxation, while the Vagrancy Act was known as the Slavery Act. It was an important period not just for social, but also for economic legislation. A major cause of the unrest had been enclosure, as seen by the number of enclosures that were attacked. The government response was to introduce an Enclosure Act, which was aimed at protecting peasants from the future enclosure of the commons, as had been demanded by Kett. The rebellions were also followed by a large amount of religious legislation, most of which was contrary to that demanded by the Western rebels as it saw a dramatic move towards Protestantism. However, it could be argued that this was in response to the more reformist demands of the East Anglian rebels. The large amount of legislation that followed in the years 1549–53 shows how important a turning point the rebellions were. The government appeared more willing to tackle the social and economic issues and appeared to be taking on greater responsibility for the social ills of the country, making it an important turning point.

Analysis of Response A

Strengths:

- The paragraph shows good knowledge of the legislation that followed the unrest in 1549.
- The knowledge is used to support an argument about the significance of the rebellions in prompting legislation.
- The paragraph offers a clear view about the significance of the unrest.

Weakness:

- There is no synthesis or comparison of 1549 with other rebellions to establish whether it was the most significant turning point. It simply lists possible turning points and is more like a Period Study essay.

Response B

In terms of economic and social legislation, the most important turning point was the 1549 rebellions[1]. **This was more important than the legislation that followed the Pilgrimage of Grace, which also saw some reform. The legislation that followed the unrest in 1549 was more far-reaching and dealt with a wider range of issues than the legislation passed in 1536. The legislation passed in 1536 did abandon the 1534 subsidy, in the same way that the Subsidy Act of 1549 was abandoned. However, in 1536 little else was done to tackle the social and economic ills, other than on entry fines, whereas there was a large amount of legislation during Northumberland's rule and Mary's reign. The issue of enclosure of common land, which had also been an issue in some regions in 1536, was tackled after the 1549 unrest. Moreover, there was legislation to tackle the conversion of land from arable farming, while the government also modified its treatment of vagrants, an issue that was largely ignored after 1536 and may even have been made worse by the closure of the monasteries[2]. The 1549 risings were also more significant than the Oxfordshire rising of 1596, as although two Acts against the decaying of towns and the maintenance of tillage were passed, the legislation did not tackle other issues such as taxation, which was a concern given the heavy demands of the wars against Spain, whereas after both 1549 and 1536 taxation was dealt with[3].** There was some indication at the start of the period that legislation was introduced to deal with rebel grievances; after the 1497 rebellion the Cornish did not have to pay their war tax, but **this success was limited** as the Cornish were fined heavily, **whereas after both 1536 and 1549 the Subsidy was abandoned, further supporting the view that the impact of 1549 was a far greater turning point[4].**

Analysis of Response B

Strengths:

- The whole period from 1485 to 1603 is covered.
- A clear view is offered: the 1549 risings were more important than the Pilgrimage of Grace [1].
- There is comparison between the 1549 risings and the Pilgrimage of Grace, which is seen in the emboldened text.
- The view is explained and justified [2].
- There is comparison with the Oxfordshire rising, which also witnessed significant legislation [3].
- The significance of the changes brought about by the 1549 rebellions is then compared with the changes at the start of the period [4].
- There is considerable comparison between periods and the significance of a range of events is evaluated.

Activity

Sample paragraph B compared 1549 as a turning point for social and economic legislation. Now write thematic paragraphs which compare the importance of the 1549 rebellions with other events in terms of social and economic, political and religious legislation.

Essay questions

1 To what extent was Elizabeth's reign a turning point in how Tudor governments dealt with rebellions?
2 'The most important turning point in Government strategy in dealing with rebellions occurred in the reign of Edward VI.' How far do you agree?
3 'Tudor monarchs maintained the obedience of their subjects in the same way.' How far do you agree?

Study skills: depth study interpretations question

How to evaluate

This chapter continues to look at how to evaluate, or apply own knowledge, to one of the interpretations to judge its strengths and weaknesses. In the first paragraph in answer to this type of question, you will have explained the two interpretations and placed them in the context of the wider historical debate about the issue (see page 56), and in the second paragraph you will have evaluated the strengths and weakness of the first interpretation (see page 97).

In the third paragraph you will evaluate the second passage and consider both its strengths and weaknesses by using your own knowledge. Read Passage A below, about the threat of the Tyrone rebellion.

PASSAGE A

The rebellion in Ireland led by the O'Neill chieftain, the Earl of Tyrone, was a serious matter. In 1598 Tyrone captured a key fort on the River Blackwater, guarding one of the main entries to Ulster. He defeated and killed the English commander at Yellow Ford in 1598 and only half the English troops returned safely to their base in Armagh. He was now able to seize Munster and drive out the English settlers and take control of most of Ireland. This was a real threat and prevented any further action against Spain from being contemplated. Tyrone had the rich resources of Ulster to supply his troops. His native soldiers were well trained and often led by captains who had served in Elizabeth's armies. He had reinforcements in the shape of mercenaries from Scotland. He was a competent leader skilled in the old Irish art of warfare by ambush. Elizabeth saw the peril. But she dealt with it by sending Essex. But Essex did not prove equal to the task and wasted his time and his troops in needless manoeuvres. She replaced Essex with Charles Blount, Lord Mountjoy. Mountjoy moved rapidly and effectively. This was easily the greatest threat to the Tudors in Ireland and was only overcome by heavy expenditure and the talents of Mountjoy.

(Adapted from Nicholas Fellows and Mary Dicken, England 1485–1603, *Hodder Education, 2015.)*

Response A

The passage puts forward the view that Tyrone's rebellion was a serious threat. It argues that Tyrone's capture of a key fort, which guarded the entry to Ulster, and his victory over the English forces at Yellow Ford meant that he had control over much of the northern part of Ireland with its resources. This view is valid as the defeat meant that the English could have been forced back into the Pale and the southern counties and this was only prevented by the actions of Mountjoy, who replaced Essex. The passage also argues that the rebellion was a threat as it prevented England from taking further action against the Spanish. This is also true as England was concerned about the Spanish as more Armadas were sent in the 1590s and there were fears, which were later justified, that the Spanish would land in Ireland and aid the rebels, as happened at Kinsale. The sending of Essex to Ireland was a mistake, as the passage suggests. This is made clear by Essex failing to engage Tyrone with his full force of 17,000 men. He preferred to divide his forces and put half in garrisons and send the rest into the provinces, thus allowing the rebellion to continue and link with the Spaniards, making it a greater threat, although the passage largely ignores the importance of the Spanish threat in Ireland.

Activities

1 What are the strengths of Response A?
2 Identify places where the passage is evaluated.
3 What other information could you use to either support or challenge the view offered?

Now read Passage B, on the seriousness of Tyrone's rebellion, and consider the following question:

> Evaluate the interpretation in Passage B and explain how convincing you think it is as an explanation of the seriousness of Tyrone's rebellion.

Remember in the examination you will have to evaluate two passages and reach a judgement as to which you think is more convincing, but this exercise will help you to develop the required skills.

PASSAGE B

By 1595, Tyrone was in open rebellion and looking for help from Spain. Philip II was not one to throw away money on lost causes, but Tyrone's effective and modernized army interested him – especially when it became clear that Elizabeth's forces were finding it a formidable opponent. In 1597, an Armada was dispatched for Ireland, only for it to be scattered by the winds. Undaunted, Tyrone inflicted a remarkable defeat on a 4000-strong English army at Yellow Ford in 1598. Indeed, it could be argued that the successes of Tyrone revealed the folly of Elizabeth's past meanness. All the penny-pinching, free-enterprise scheme, all the inadequate but still substantial monies provided for the campaigns of the Lord Deputies, all the attempts to 'civilize' the Gaelic Irish, all in jeopardy and all potentially wasted. Indeed, if Tyrone were to succeed in linking up with a Spanish invasion force then the English might well be forced back into the Pale and the surrounding southern counties. The perilous position for the English in Ireland was redeemed only by the appointment of Lord Mountjoy as military commander. He managed to motivate the dispirited English forces and succeed in pushing Tyrone back towards Ulster, only to be faced with a formidable Spanish invasion of 3400 crack troops at Kinsale. Turning to besiege Kinsale, Mountjoy ran the risk of finding himself surrounded by Tyrone. It was, indeed, a close-run thing. Tyrone made an error in risking full-scale battle and was heavily defeated. By January 1602, the Kinsale garrison had surrendered.

(Adapted from John Warren, Elizabeth I: Religion and Foreign Affairs, *Hodder Education, 2002.)*

Activities

Apply what you have learned in the study sections so far to respond to Passage B. Before you start you should reread pages 96–8 and 144.

It might be helpful to consider the following questions before you write an evaluative paragraph:

1 What is the view of Passage B about the seriousness of the Tyrone rebellion?
2 What evidence is there in the passage that supports this view?
3 What own knowledge do you have that agrees with the view?
4 What own knowledge do you have that challenges this view?
5 How convinced are you by the view offered in the passage? Explain your answer.

Having answered these questions you are now in a position to evaluate the passage.

CHAPTER 4

The maintenance of political stability

This chapter is concerned with the maintenance of stability and seeks to explain how the Tudors ruled their kingdom. It will consider how the monarchs and governments attempted to maintain stability within the kingdom in the absence of either a police force or standing army. It will assess the actions of both central and local government in achieving stability and examine the range and role of institutions available to them. It will discuss the relative importance and successes of these institutions. The chapter will also consider the extent to which governments changed their policies in order to maintain law and order in the kingdom.

The chapter will analyse these issues under the following headings:

★ Institutional developments

★ Tudor policies: continuity and change

★ Conclusion: the maintenance of political stability

It also considers the debates surrounding the three in-depth topics:

★ Why were the Tudor authorities so concerned about the Pilgrimage of Grace?

★ Was the Western rebellion a response to recent political instability in the area?

★ Why was Ireland such a threat to stability?

Key dates

1487	Act of Maintenance	1558	Reform of the militia
1495	De Facto Act	1563	Statute of Artificers
1529	Reformation parliament started to meet	1572	Council of the North reformed and Poor Law Act
1534	Office holders swore oaths of allegiance and supremacy	1593	Repeal of anti-enclosure legislation
1549	Appointment of lords lieutenant	1598	Poor Law Acts: Act for the Relief of the Poor and Act for the Punishment of Rogues and Sturdy Beggars
1553	Northumberland issued a proclamation denying Mary's right to the throne		

Revolts and rebellions were exceptions to the general rule of order. In general, rulers were able to develop institutions and address the key problem areas that commonly gave rise to rebellion. Continuity was more evident than change in respect of Tudor institutions. When changes did occur, they were often short lived and met specific needs rather than forming part of a coherent programme of reform. The 1530s, however, did see major constitutional, religious and administrative changes, which historian G.R. Elton once described as 'revolutionary', but this was an exceptional decade. Generally, Tudor institutions underwent more subtle, evolutionary changes. The main objective of governments was to maintain political stability and this could best be achieved through continuity.

Institutional developments

▶ *How did the monarchy affect popular perceptions of authority?*

The monarchy

The institution of the monarchy was the most important element in the maintenance of stability:

- The monarch was the source of unity and authority in the kingdom.
- The monarch was directly responsible for the protection of his or her subjects.
- The monarch was responsible for ensuring that the laws of the land were upheld.
- The monarch held power from God and, as Henry VIII proclaimed, owed allegiance to no one else.

It was commonly believed, and the Tudors never tired of reminding their subjects, that an act against the monarch was not just treason, it was a sin against God. Thus, William Baldwin could write in the *Mirror for Magistrates* in 1559:

> *Full little know we wretches what we do*
> *When we presume our princes to resist.*
> *We war with God against His glory too,*
> *That placeth in His office whom he list.*

Respect for the monarchy

The power of the monarchy, both real and imaginary, did not depend simply on the awe and mystique that surrounded it. Governments stressed the relationship between subject and master, the need to keep one's place in society and respect the authority of one's superior. Those in authority constantly underlined this idea through the concept of the **Great Chain of Being**. Each link in the chain, they claimed, connected humans upwards towards God and downwards to the

 **KEY TERM**

Great Chain of Being
A theoretical defence of the existing social order, under which all classes were interdependent.

animal kingdom, plants and minerals. Everyone and everything had a place in society and any attempt to usurp one's position was likely to result in chaos. In 1509, **Edmund Dudley** had stated in *The Tree of Commonwealth*:

> Let not them [the commons] presume above their own degree nor any of them pretend or counterfeit the state of his better.

Not all subjects understood or accepted this philosophy, as uprisings and revolts clearly demonstrated, but respect for authority was increasingly publicised by the Tudors, particularly in the second half of the sixteenth century. As **Richard Hooker** explained in his *Laws of Ecclesiastical Polity*, written in 1593:

> Every degree of people, in their vocation, calling and office, has appointed to them their duty and order. Some are in high degree, some in low, some kings and princes, some inferiors and subjects, priests and laymen, masters and servants, fathers and children, husbands and wives, rich and poor, and every one has need of [the] other.

All Tudor monarchs recognised that if they were to be effective rulers then they had to work at enhancing the respect and aura surrounding the monarchy:

- From 1534, both spiritual and lay office holders swore oaths of allegiance and supremacy, and under Edward, oaths of uniformity were added, which were reversed under Mary and reinstituted by Elizabeth. Like medieval oaths of fealty that bound subjects to the Crown, the **oaths of succession and supremacy** were taken throughout the country by individuals and by corporate institutions such as universities and cathedral chapters.
- The Tudors also made increasing use of **proclamations**; nearly 900 were issued during this period. These could be turned into parliamentary statutes but most were issued in the absence of parliament when speed was of the essence and the Crown wished to impart information immediately. Thus, Henry VII issued a proclamation in 1509 to end speculation surrounding the claims of a pretender and in 1553 the Duke of Northumberland authorised one to deny Mary's right to the throne. Copies were sent to every county, where the message was read out in parish churches and marketplaces. In this way, the Crown kept informed as many of its subjects as was practicable.

Propaganda

Propaganda was an important weapon in the Tudor armoury and helped to consolidate the monarch's aura of power and authority:

- Henry VII claimed descent from King Arthur, developed the Tudor rose as a symbol of political unity, and decked his servants in his coat of arms and royal badges. His Burgundian-style court with its lavish displays and entertainment impressed foreign visitors and English nobles alike and added to the majesty of the king.
- Henry VIII preferred more visual imagery to highlight his physicality, wealth and imperial bearing. Coins that portrayed a 'closed' crown were minted to show Henry's '**imperatur**' status, and larger coins contained finer

details of his facial features. Illustrations accompanied official documents, portraits by Holbein suggested his grandeur, and stately buildings, such as Hampton Court, Nonsuch and Greenwich palaces, were monuments to his magnificence.

- Neither Edward nor Mary glamorised the monarchy to the same degree: a sickly boy and an introverted woman were not suitable subjects. Nevertheless, Edward was portrayed in paintings in the image of his father and Mary's image on her Great Seals reflected a regal bearing.

- Elizabeth, on the other hand, realised the potential of elevating the image of the monarchy while still maintaining close links with her subjects. Unlike her father, brother and sister, most summers she visited royal castles and manor houses, stayed with county gentry, hunted with her nobility and travelled to provincial towns. Wherever she went, she developed bonds of affection with her people who lined the route of her advertised progresses. Although she never visited Ireland, Wales, or the north and south-west of England, she built up a strong rapport with southern, central and eastern England, which was where most people lived. The queen encouraged pageantry that idealised her as a symbol of eternal stability. Painters focused on her wisdom, beauty, justice and good governance, poets represented her as **Belphoebe and Astraea**, and her court developed an endless round of rituals and ceremonies designed to celebrate her majesty.

🗝 **KEY TERM**

Belphoebe and Astraea
Mythical women celebrated for their beauty and sense of justice, respectively.

Through its use of patronage, the Crown had at its disposal the means to win over and keep the political nation subservient. Its capacity to award honours such as peerages and knighthoods, to grant monopolies, land, annuities and pensions, and to make appointments to the Church, court, judiciary, administration and armed forces, gave the Crown an enormous potential to

'Armada portrait' of Elizabeth I painted about 1588. Why do you think the queen would have wanted to be portrayed as a young woman?

149

reward loyal and competent subjects. They, in turn, were expected to reward the monarch with unbending service and obedience. The main beneficiaries were the nobles, courtiers and gentry, who may have numbered some 2500 in Elizabethan England. In theory, offices were not sold but money certainly changed hands in the form of fees, gifts and unrecorded payments as royal servants benefited from their privileged position and built up a network of clients in central and local government. In this way, the interplay between dispensers and receivers of royal patronage bound the counties to the central administration and was a key reason for long periods of stability under the Tudors. Men and women were drawn to the power, wealth and influence of the court, and, as long as the channels of patronage remained fluid and were not monopolised by one individual (which occurred under Wolsey in the 1520s and **Robert Cecil** in the 1590s), the politically active classes stayed loyal to the Crown.

The Church

Throughout the Tudor period the Church consistently supported the Crown and was an important institution in the maintenance of stability.

The reign of Henry VII

At Henry VII's accession he was anointed with holy oil, crowned by the Archbishop of Canterbury and imbued with divine authority. For his part, the king looked to his bishops for advice and assistance in administering the realm and appointed the archbishop as his Lord Chancellor. Henry was a devoted son of the Church and expected the pope to support him against rebels and impostors. Pope Innocent VIII duly obliged. Anyone who fought against Henry at Stoke and Blackheath was threatened with excommunication. The use of sanctuary, which Henry believed Lovel and the Staffords had abused, was denied to traitors and rebels by Henry's judges, and the pope made no objection to this ruling.

The reign of Henry VIII

Until 1529, Henry VIII continued to use clerics as his administrators, advisers and diplomats. Bishops Warham, Fox and Tunstall were key royal servants but they paled into insignificance alongside Wolsey. When he was Lord Chancellor between 1515 and 1529, the Church enjoyed a high profile in central administration. Wolsey made active use of the courts of Chancery, Star Chamber and Requests (see pages 158–9) and his clients, many of whom were in holy orders, sat on royal commissions and helped to maintain order in the country. Henry VIII's divorce and subsequent break from Rome, despite actions by some Roman Catholics, did not weaken Church–Crown relations. If anything, the relationship was strengthened as bishops continued to be appointed by the Crown and after 1533 they owed their office and loyalty solely to the Crown. Henry, in turn, continued to use them as administrators and advisers – Tunstall,

 **KEY FIGURE**

Robert Cecil (1563–1612)

Son of William Cecil, he became a member of the Privy Council in 1591 and did most of the work of secretary before being officially appointed in 1596.

Bishop of Durham, for instance, became the new President of the Council of the North and Lee, Bishop of Coventry and Lichfield, presided over the Council of Wales – but laymen trained in civil law displaced bishops as his Secretary of State, Lord Chancellor and Lord Privy Seal.

The reigns of Edward VI, Mary I and Elizabeth I

Apart from a brief period under Mary when Cardinal Pole was Lord Chancellor, all political offices in Edward's and Elizabeth's reigns were held by non-clergymen. The clergy's role as law enforcers, which had been of vital importance before the fall of Wolsey, was over – at least until the 1630s.

The Church and the doctrine of obedience

The alliance between Church and the Crown, however, remained strong. The Church's support for the monarchy is well illustrated by its public avowal of the doctrine of obedience and non-resistance, which was first fully developed in the sixteenth century. In the 1530s, priests received detailed injunctions as to the content of their sermons and were instructed to preach at least four times a year on the subject of obedience. **Stephen Gardiner**, an orthodox Roman Catholic, had serious misgivings about the royal divorce and the efficacy of the English Church separating from Rome, but he acknowledged that the king-in-parliament had no superior as far as the law was concerned. He argued in *De Vera Obedientia Oratio*:

> *God, according to his exceeding great and unspeakable goodness toward mankind ... substituted men, who, being put in authority as his **vicegerents**, should require obedience which we must do unto them with no less fruit for God's sake than we should do it (what honour soever it were) immediately unto God himself.*

The accession of a minor to the throne in 1547 raised doubts about the Privy Council's legitimacy to rule on his behalf and prompted Cranmer, the Archbishop of Canterbury, to write a series of **homilies** by which the clergy would educate their congregations. The *Homily on Obedience* reminded people that in obeying the king, they were actually obeying God. It declared:

> *Let us all therefore fear the most detestable vice of rebellion ever knowing and remembering that he that resists common authority resists God and his ordinance.*

Bishop Latimer in his *Sermons* summed up the Church's doctrine of obedience in 1548:

> *When laws are made against God and his word, then I ought more to obey God than man. Then I may refuse to obey with a good conscience: yet for all that, I may not rise up against the magistrates, nor make any uproar; for if I do so, I sin damnably.*

Although timely in their publication, neither Cranmer's *Homilies* nor Latimer's *Sermons* could prevent the outbreak of widespread revolts. Cranmer's reaction was to circulate copies of his sermons to be read out in parish churches throughout the kingdom. Their purpose, he explained, was 'to preserve the

 **KEY FIGURES**

Stephen Gardiner (1487–1555)

Bishop of Winchester and Lord Chancellor in 1529, he supported the royal supremacy, but not Protestantism. He was imprisoned by Edward VI but restored under Mary I.

Bishop Latimer (1485–1555)

A priest and scholar, he was Bishop of Worcester but was burned along with Cranmer for his Protestant beliefs by Mary I.

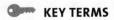 **KEY TERMS**

Vicegerent Someone exercising authority on behalf of a ruler.

Homilies Lessons that could be read directly or improvised into a sermon.

people in their obedience and to set out the evil and mischief of the present disturbances'. In citing the Old and New Testaments, he reminded people that they had a duty to be 'patient in adversity' and to be 'long-suffering'. Bishops relayed a similar message in the 1590s, at the height of an economic and social crisis. Their sermons spoke of the efforts that the government was making to combat the problems, they reminded wealthy subjects of their Christian duty to help the poor, and they instructed everyone to endure the famine 'with patience'. The Church therefore played an important role in reiterating the need to obey the law.

Sermons helped to shape public opinion and ensure the townspeople and peasantry were kept informed of government policies.

The oppressive rule of Mary led to a minority of English writers developing theories of disobedience towards the monarch on the grounds that rulers had an obligation to be just and true to the Christian Church. If they acted like a tyrant or sinned against God, then it was argued rebellion could be justified, but only if led by a magistrate, such as a noble, justice of the peace (JP) or mayor. These ideas, however, became irrelevant to most Englishmen once Elizabeth came to the throne. Although some Calvinist and Catholic writers on the continent went on to develop more advanced theories of resistance, the Church of England held firm to the doctrine of non-resistance. Archbishop **Parker**, who was probably responsible for the *Homily against Disobedience and Wilful Rebellion* published in the aftermath of the Northern Earls' revolt, spoke for the majority when he declared:

> *The first author of rebellion (the root of all vices and mother of all mischiefs) was Lucifer … Thus rebellion, as you see, both the first and greatest and the very root of all other sins, and the principal cause both of all worldly and bodily miseries … and, which is infinitely worse than all these … the very cause of death and damnation also.*

Role of the local clergy

At a parish level, the Church played a vital role in local politics. Increasingly, the parish came to be the focal point for administering poor relief and tackling social problems (see pages 176–7). Clerics were encouraged to inform their bishops of any signs of trouble and relevant matters were forwarded to the Privy Council, and the parish clergy were expected to instruct the people on their moral and legal obligations. Not everyone attended church, but those who listened to feast day and Sunday sermons will have received enough reminders from their parish priest of their duty to be obedient and a good neighbour. Moreover, children in learning the catechism were instructed 'to honour and obey the king, and all that are put in authority under him'. Although respect for the Church was undermined by a decline in its political status in the course of the period, the clergy no longer had a majority in the House of Lords after 1540, and Elizabeth expected her bishops to reside in their dioceses and not engage in high politics,

 **KEY FIGURE**

Matthew Parker (1504–75)

A Cambridge-educated priest and moderate Protestant, chaplain to Anne Boleyn, he was Archbishop of Canterbury under Elizabeth.

she nevertheless gave them her support and they supported her in keeping the country stable and peaceful.

Parliament

Parliament was not an integral part of Tudor administration. It met infrequently and only when the monarch commanded: for instance, just seven sessions were held during Henry VII's 24-year reign and thirteen occurred in Elizabeth's reign of 45 years. Its main purpose was to vote the Crown financial grants and discuss bills that royal councillors and members of parliament (MPs) had proposed, yet each of the Tudors recognised that parliament could be a useful tool in preventing disorder and in dealing with rebels and conspirators who threatened the stability of the country.

Parliament, or more precisely, the House of Lords, acted as a court of law. Nobles had the right to be tried by their peers, and Hussey and Darcy (1537), Suffolk (1554), Dacre (1570), Northumberland (1572) and Essex (1601) were all tried and convicted for making war against the Crown. Parliament was also used to bring bills of attainder against rebels. Henry VII's parliaments passed 138 Acts and his successors each authorised statutes in the wake of rebellions. Once lands had been attainted, only an Act of Parliament could restore them. Henry VIII and Mary were quite generous, unlike Henry VII and Elizabeth, but it did not serve the Crown to be overly oppressive. For example, much of the resentment felt by nobles and gentry towards Henry VII may have been due to the way he treated them in his later years. Contrary to traditional practice, he only reversed one-third of attainders.

The reign of Henry VII

From time to time, Acts of parliament were passed to maintain order and deter would-be malcontents. Early in his reign, Henry VII made clear his intention to clamp down on illegal retaining, which was the root cause of so much violence and disorder. The Star Chamber Act, Act of Livery and Maintenance and subsequent Statute of Liveries confirm the king's support from parliament in pursuit of this objective. His De Facto Act of 1495, on the other hand, was intended to draw a line under past indiscretions and acts of disobedience committed by Yorkists against the Crown, and may have helped to restore stability in the wake of Stanley's treason.

The reign of Henry VIII

In the 1530s, Henry VIII and Cromwell implemented religious and political reforms through parliament, which ensured minimal resistance and considerable support. It is hard to gauge how far the Commons and Lords agreed with the doctrinal changes. Most Catholic clergy naturally felt uneasy about the break from Rome and some but not all abbots objected to the closure of their monasteries. Parliament as a whole approved of the dissolution, and the subsequent disposal of monastic land went a long way towards retaining the support of MPs and peers, many of whom were beneficiaries. In fact, the Reformation parliament of 1529–36 probably marked a watershed in the history of English parliaments. Thereafter, changes to existing religious laws had first to be approved by parliament.

Since religion could be such an emotive subject, as was evident in the 1536 and 1549 rebellions, Edward, Mary and Elizabeth understood the political value of having MPs endorse proposed changes, as can be seen below. These were the men who in the past might have led protests against undesirable reforms; after 1536, MPs and the gentry they represented stood squarely behind the government and suppressed any extra-parliamentary disturbances. Potential poachers had become keen gamekeepers.

The reigns of Edward VI and Mary I

In the 1550s, the House of Commons provided a forum where the grievances and concerns of the gentry and nobility could be expressed. Whether or not MPs and peers were able to affect policy-making, their voices were heard at the highest level.

The reign of Elizabeth I

The growing support from MPs for the Crown was evident in Elizabeth's reign. Every parliament called on to vote subsidies did so, even when they were multiples of two, three and four times the normal request. From 1571, MPs legislated to protect the queen and country from Catholic plots, and in 1581 from Jesuits who, it was alleged, had entered England 'to stir sedition'. The Act to retain the Queen's Majesty's subjects in their due obedience (1581) and the Act for the Queen's Safety (1584) reflected the increasing patriotic fervour among many MPs. A sea change had occurred in the Commons. At the start of the Tudor period few men aspired to be an MP: there was no salary, it entailed travelling to and finding accommodation in London, and much of the parliamentary business held little interest. By Elizabeth's reign, many gentry wanted to become an MP and wished their sons to follow them. Pressure to create more parliamentary seats steadily grew, and the Crown responded by establishing 80 new seats between 1509 and 1558 and a further 62 between 1558 and 1603. Few MPs were interested in high politics and the affairs of state, but they were concerned about economic and social issues that affected their boroughs and they saw parliament as a way of tackling these problems and preventing rebellion. The 1563 Statute of Artificers is a good case in point. Privy Councillors proposed the bill to establish seven-year apprenticeships but it was MPs who extended the bill to include the urban economy as well as agriculture. Similarly, the Elizabethan poor laws owed much to the initiative of MPs. Parliament did not always agree with royal policies or support Crown-sponsored bills but in the realm of law and order, it proved a valuable ally and sounding board for the political nation.

Royal councils

The Tudors governed their kingdom through councils, initially the king's council (*curia regis*), which became the Privy Council in the 1530s, and, in the course of the period, through the addition of regional councils in the north of England, Welsh borders and Ireland (see pages 156–7). For a brief spell between 1539 and 1540, there was a Council in the West headed by Sir John Russell that administered the south-west counties of England. The prime function of all these councils was to transmit the monarch's wishes into actions and ensure that the country was effectively governed.

The Privy Council

The royal council changed in its size, character and work in the course of the sixteenth century.

The Privy Council under Henry VII

Some 227 men attended Henry VII's council during his reign, although fewer than twenty councillors were in regular attendance. His principal advisers were bishops, nobles and courtiers, of whom the most important were the Archbishop of Canterbury, who was also Lord Chancellor, the Lord Privy Seal, who acted as the Chancellor's secretary, the Lord Chamberlain, who oversaw the court, and trusted household servants who held key administrative and financial offices.

The Privy Council under Henry VIII

Henry VIII added more nobles to the council, although clerics continued to hold important posts, especially during Wolsey's ascendancy in the 1520s. By 1540, a small, select group of councillors had emerged into a Privy Council. Its genesis was due to the rebellions that beset Henry in 1536 and its membership came to reflect noble factions according to the king's changing matrimonial circumstances. Thus, senior members of the Boleyn, Howard, Seymour and Parr families assumed prominent roles. The size of the council increased from 30 to 40 members under Edward and Mary and continued to contain a mixture of nobles, bishops, law officers and household servants of principally Protestant and Catholic persuasions according to the monarch's faith.

The Privy Council under Elizabeth I

Under Elizabeth, numbers in regular attendance fell back from around twenty to fewer than twelve, with five or six men doing most of the work. Gradually, the frequency of meetings and composition also changed. At first, the council met three times a week, contained six nobles and no bishop; by 1603, it was meeting every day, was heavily influenced by the secretary and treasurer, and was dominated by members of the household and sons of government officials who had risen through state service and professional training. Cromwell, in the 1530s, had given the office of Secretary of State a key role in the central administration and, although its relative importance had declined after his

William Cecil

1520	Born in Lincolnshire
1547	Entered service of Duke of Somerset
1548	Secretary of State under Somerset
1550	Appointed to the Privy Council
1553	Signed the Devise; retired when Mary succeeded to throne
1558	Appointed Secretary of State by Elizabeth
1571	Created Lord Burghley
1572	Made Lord Treasurer
1598	Died

Early life and career

Born into a gentry family, Cecil was educated at local grammar schools before going to Cambridge University. He trained to be a lawyer at Gray's Inn in London. He married his first wife, Mary Cheke, in 1541, but she died two years later. He then married again in 1545.

His role under Edward VI

Cecil's rise to power came through entering the service of the Duke of Somerset, who then appointed him Secretary of State. He survived Somerset's fall and was promoted by Northumberland to the Privy Council. He signed the Devise to bring Lady Jane Grey to the throne and therefore retired when Mary Tudor triumphed.

Promotion under Elizabeth

When Elizabeth came to the throne in 1558 she made him Secretary of State again. He was the most important of her councillors, drafting correspondence, creating an intelligence service and a propaganda system. He also managed parliamentary business and ensured that there was an effective administrative system. In 1571, he was created Lord Burghley and moved from being an MP to the House of Lords, from where he continued to run government business. He was made Lord Chancellor in 1572 but continued to play a dominant role in decision-making, including the execution of Mary Queen of Scots.

Importance to Elizabeth

Elizabeth valued Cecil's advice and her admiration for him was seen when she fed him on his deathbed. He was completely loyal and honest. She knew that he always gave his opinion, but then enforced her decisions even if he did not agree with them.

fall, Elizabeth's dependence on Cecil and Walsingham, who held the post from 1558 to 1572 and 1573 to 1590, respectively, ensured that it survived as a vital administrative office. Walsingham, in particular, assumed responsibility for maintaining stability in the kingdom.

The Council of Wales

The Council in the Marches of Wales and the Council of the North took their orders from the Privy Council in London but also developed in the sixteenth century into administrative and judicial councils in their own right, with a president, secretary, chief justice and clerks. Until 1536, there were no changes in the administrative organisation of the Welsh marches and lordships. The Crown held most of the land in Wales and there were few independent lordships, although some lords such as the Duke of Buckingham (until 1521) and Henry Somerset were powerful figures. Henry VII restored a council at Ludlow in 1487, placed his uncle Jasper in charge, and invited the leading Welsh and English nobles to attend. After Jasper's death in 1495, its presidents were often bishops, men like William Smith, John Veysey and Rowland Lee, but effective power rested with local landowners until the 1530s, when Lee restored royal authority by rebuilding castles and enforcing justice more effectively. He was assisted by the statutes of 1536 and 1543, which created twelve new counties in Wales and extended the council's authority to cover five English border counties. Wales now had an English administrative and judicial system and elected 24 MPs to Westminster.

The Welsh lords accepted the political and religious reforms under Henry VIII and caused no problems for his successors. No doubt their Welsh descent helped the Tudors, but bribes of church land and offices were probably more crucial. The gentry were keen to become JPs and serve the Crown as well as enhance their own position locally. Although order and justice appear to have been of variable standards, there were no revolts or rebellions against the Crown in Tudor Wales. In the 1590s, George Owen proudly wrote in his *The Dialogue of the Government of Wales*:

> No country [sic] in England so flourished in one hundred years as Wales has done, since the government of Henry VII to this time … so altered is the country and countrymen, the people changed in heart within and the land altered in health without, from evil to good, and from bad to better.

The Council of the North

Henry VII revived the Council of the North after a four-year lapse. The Yorkists had created it in 1473 and at Henry's accession it was dominated by the Clifford, Neville, Percy and Dacre families. The appointment of the Earl of Surrey as his lieutenant in 1489 heralded the king's intention to develop greater control over the northern counties but the council's influence remained limited until the 1530s.

Twice the Council of the North was remodelled – in 1525 and 1530 – and received judicial functions in 1537, acting as a regional Star Chamber under the presidency of Cuthbert Tunstall, Bishop of Durham. Henry VIII invited leading nobles to attend and kept a watchful eye on proceedings by assuming himself the wardenship of the marches, which bordered Scotland, and appointing gentlemen rather than nobles as his deputies of the east, middle and west marches. Nevertheless, the Duke of Norfolk was probably correct when he declared that the 'wild people' of the marches could only be controlled by men of 'good estimation', which may explain the ennoblement of two deputy wardens in 1544.

Although Edward and Mary restored the Dacres and Percys as wardens, Elizabeth from 1563 started to appoint more southern nobles and northern gentry to the wardenship, which greatly assisted the council in attempting to maintain stability in the north.

The council, however, underwent further reforms in the light of its failure to deal effectively with the revolt of 1569. The Earl of Huntingdon was appointed president (from 1572 to 1595) and the council's authority was increased to cover all northern counties except Lancashire. Even though there was local sympathy for Mary Queen of Scots and Catholicism continued to be a potential source of conflict, the council played a major part in upholding order and dispensing justice in the north of England. After 1570, there were no more revolts or disturbances in Elizabeth's reign.

The judiciary and the law

One of the most important requirements of any government is to ensure that the law is respected and upheld. Without this there can be no stability. From the outset, the Tudors understood that the success of their dynasty largely depended on the restoration of the law. The Yorkist kings had gone some way towards achieving this in the years following the Wars of the Roses, and Henry VII largely built on their foundations. He had at his disposal a range of common law and prerogative courts.

Common law courts

- The common law courts comprised the Court of King's Bench, which heard serious criminal cases, civil cases that involved personal injury, suits in which the Crown had an interest and cases of appeal from other courts.
- The Court of Common Pleas heard civil cases concerning debt, fraud and property.
- The Court of Exchequer handled disputes concerning the Crown's revenue and in the course of the sixteenth century also dealt with private suits.
- Parliament occasionally met to hear cases of treason.

These courts were well established but in the fifteenth century, when the Crown commanded less respect, juries had been threatened and judges bribed by powerful litigants.

An Act of Maintenance in 1487 was designed to end the pressure nobles could bring on the judicial system, but the Crown put more store in supplementing the common law courts by using **prerogative** courts.

Prerogative courts

Courts such as Star Chamber, Requests and Chancery had no jury, gave rulings according to the evidence presented to the king's councillors and flourished during the Tudor period. Wolsey as Lord Chancellor established regular sittings and a recognised procedure in Star Chamber and Requests, which led to an increase in litigation in both courts as the period progressed. For instance, the number of cases brought before Star Chamber in the first half of the sixteenth century rose from an annual average of twelve to nearly 150. The number of Chancery petitions also increased as the court, unlike the common law courts, could hear cases of appeal from inferior jurisdictions, notably the borough courts.

The Tudors also established law courts to meet particular needs. Some courts had a long history; others were short lived. The Councils of the North, Welsh Marches and Dublin each acquired its own judicial status and heard both criminal and civil cases; the Court of High Commission was established in the 1580s to deal with ecclesiastical issues.

 **KEY TERM**

Prerogative Powers held by the Crown. Prerogative courts were presided over by royal councillors who dispensed justice in the interests of the Crown.

Some courts only functioned for a few years:

- Henry VII created the General Surveyors court to oversee his royal estate and the Council Learned in the Law, which investigated cases of suspected malpractice among his tenants-in-chief, many of whom were nobles. Both courts ceased in 1509, although the General Surveyors was revived later in Henry VIII's reign.
- Financial courts that Cromwell established in the 1530s, such as Augmentations and First Fruits and Tenths, were amalgamated into the Exchequer in 1554, but the Court of Wards retained its separate status and organisation to become one of the Tudors' most important judicial and financial courts.

Each of these prerogative courts in time came to be resented by the common lawyers, who viewed them as a threat to their livelihood, but the Tudors saw the advantage of encouraging both systems. If they wanted to be certain of winning a case, they brought it before a prerogative court and, although such courts lacked the authority to give a death sentence, once a verdict had been reached it was possible to transfer the case to a common law court for sentencing.

In practice, however, the Tudors were not despots. They understood the value of presiding over a judiciary and legal system that was respected and, as far as possible, independent and free from corruption. When, for instance, Henry VII attempted to get his King's Bench judges to give a ruling on sanctuary in advance of the trial of Humphrey Stafford, he was rebuked for interfering in the judicial process. This did not, however, prevent the king from intervening in cases of retaining where, in advance of the indictment, he intimated the fines and recognisances awaiting the accused. Thus, the Tudors took full advantage of the law to strengthen their authority and maintain order in the country.

Martial law, sedition and treason

- Henry VII and Henry VIII used parliament to pass bills of attainder against rebels and traitors, whereby trials were held and sentences given on absentee offenders.
- Martial law was also introduced at particular times of crisis, for instance during the rebellions in 1536–7, 1549 and 1569.
- Mary also used it in 1558 to arrest and prosecute anyone carrying **seditious** or heretical books.
- In 1589, Elizabeth granted her **provost marshals** the power to stop and detain any vagrants.

Unlike Acts of attainder and treason laws, martial law did not allow the property of the accused to be seized, so it was used sparingly against the landed classes. However, it did have several advantages: it dispensed with the niceties of witnesses and evidence, which could be hard to obtain in times of rebellion; it dispensed with trial by juries, which could be very unreliable; and it delivered justice quickly and in the Crown's interest.

 **KEY TERMS**

Seditious Liable to cause an affray or act of disorder.

Provost marshal A senior administrative officer, probably a senior magistrate.

The law of sedition and the treason law in particular were extended by the Tudors to increase compliance and reduce the likelihood of disorder.

The spreading of rumours

The spreading of rumours was a common occurrence in revolts and rebellions and the authorities treated severely those found guilty of causing sedition:

- Whipping, imprisonment and public declamation awaited anyone who spread rumours of Henry VII's death or claimed to know of the existence of impostors.
- Cromwell, in the 1530s, insisted that rumours, prophesies or false stories should be thoroughly investigated and the perpetrators punished. For instance, in 1538, the vicar of Muston in Yorkshire was executed for predicting that the pope would soon 'come jingling with his keys' to England, the king would 'flee into the sea', and the Percys would 'shine kindly again and take the light of the sun'.
- In 1542, rumour-mongering became a **felony**. Seven years later, in the wake of widespread rebellions, the Privy Council declared that rumour-mongers would be chained to the galleys, which was virtually a sentence of death.
- Mary introduced the decapitation of the right hand and Elizabeth went further in 1581 by making sedition a capital offence.

Treason

The treason law was also broadened and became more intrusive. Since 1352, treason had constituted compassing or imagining the king's death and levying war against the king in his country:

- In the 1530s, two Acts extended treason to denying the Act of Succession, refusing to take the oath of supremacy and criticising Henry's marriage to Anne Boleyn. Most significant was the 1534 Act which stated that treason could be 'by words' as well as 'by deeds'. Treason by words was not an innovation but its application was extended to cover recent developments. By 1540, nearly 400 people had been charged with treasonous words and at least 52 had been executed.
- Although this law was repealed in 1547, Northumberland restored it to apply to anyone who declared 'by writing, printing, painting, carving or graving' that the king was a 'heretic, schismatic, tyrant, infidel or usurper of the Crown'.
- In 1554, Mary widened the Act to cover any allegations made against her marriage to Philip or the welfare of the two sovereigns.

Elizabeth extended the Treason Act even further:

- In 1571, anyone who possessed papal objects, obtained, published or received papal documents, or claimed the queen was a heretic in writing or by words could be indicted for treason.

 **KEY TERM**

Felony An offence that carried the death penalty.

- In 1585, a group of people – the Jesuits – were declared to be traitors even before treason was committed in word or deed. And such severe measures were not confined to Roman Catholics.
- In 1597, parliament declared that any group assembled to destroy enclosures was guilty of treason. In the same year, judges ruled that conspiring with arms was high treason on the grounds that 'rebellion is all the war which a subject can make against the king'.

The vast majority of people never came before assize judges, who twice a year attended county sessions. Indeed, few will have appeared at **Quarter Sessions** where JPs presided. In most cases, disputes were dealt with in local courts such as the sheriff's court, manorial, borough and hundred courts or, in the case of matrimonial disputes, sexual impropriety and disputed wills, in the diocesan courts. Whenever possible, arguments were settled out of court, subjects were 'bound over' to keep the peace and the community acted to see that social harmony was maintained. At the beginning of the Tudor period, some people believed it was acceptable to act disorderly in order to achieve justice; by the end of the period, fear of popular disorder was very real. The overall feeling was that the proper way to proceed was to use the judicial system and act lawfully. It was quite a transformation.

Royal Commissions

One of the most important methods of administration used by the Tudors and one frequently underrated by historians was the instigation of commissions to perform particular tasks within the counties. Under the early Tudors, members of the royal household and departmental officials often headed the commissions but in the second half of the period lords lieutenant regularly supervised their work. The range of their activities illustrates the importance that the Tudors attached to them as organs of royal administration:

- Henry VII used commissions of *oyer et terminer* when he wanted to investigate and take action against suspected rebels in 1497, and commissions of array were used to authorise nobles to draw up troops to deal with Simnel's rebellion.
- Henry VIII appointed commissions to assess subsidy payments, survey monasteries and chantries, and sell Crown lands.
- Enclosure commissioners were sent around the country by Wolsey, Somerset and Cecil.
- After 1570, most counties had commissions to investigate the extent of **recusancy**.

Elizabeth made extensive use of special commissions as an effective way of being kept informed of developments at county level. Teams of officials conducted their enquiries quickly, made recommendations directly to the Privy Council and thus made a significant contribution to the maintenance of stability in the country.

KEY TERMS

Quarter Sessions General courts held in a county every three months.

Oyer et terminer A commission directed to justices that empowered them to 'hear and determine' indictments for specific crimes committed in a particular area.

Recusant A Catholic who denied the royal supremacy or refused to attend the services of the Anglican Church.

Justices of the peace

The commissions of the peace (or justices of the peace) were by far the most important commissions to develop under the Tudors. JPs had existed since the fourteenth century, but the nature of their work and the number operating in each county increased dramatically under the Tudors, such that it is hard to see how law and order would have been upheld without them. In 1485, most counties had fewer than ten JPs and commissioners often served two adjacent counties, such as Devon and Cornwall. By the end of the sixteenth century, most counties had over 50 – Norfolk had 61, Yorkshire 57 and Wiltshire 52 – and JPs were no longer itinerant. The increase in numbers in part reflected an increase in their workload but it was also due to the pressure from the gentry. Many became JPs and enjoyed the authority and prestige that went with the office and the financial and political opportunities it afforded them. Although unpaid and subject to annual appraisal, most JPs held office for life, but periodically commissions were remodelled:

- Wolsey, for example, deliberately appointed non-northerners to several northern counties between 1513 and 1525 to effect greater stability in the region.
- Between 1536 and 1539, nearly one-third of all JPs in areas affected by the Pilgrimage of Grace were replaced.
- Edward, Mary and Elizabeth changed JPs in particular counties for religious reasons.
- There were wholesale changes in 1569 and 1601 in areas where JPs had supported rebellions.

Functions of justices of the peace

JPs performed two main functions: judicial and administrative. Their judicial role was extensive. For instance, they could:

- order sheriffs and bailiffs to search for robbers
- examine felons
- commit those who disturbed the peace to jail
- review the empanelling of juries; collect recognisances for upholding the peace
- fine recusants and arrest papists
- detain and punish vagrants and rioters
- hear cases concerning burglary, petty larceny and assault
- resolve disputes between masters, apprentices and servants.

Much of their time was spent in travelling the county 'out of session', dealing with cases presented by constables and hundred courts, but four times a year they presided over the Quarter Sessions in the county courts. At these formal gatherings, a cross-section of the county society attended to witness Tudor law in operation. In a typical session these would comprise: the sheriff or his deputy, the county gaoler, constables, bailiffs, coroners, jurors, witnesses and accused. While cases involving the Crown and serious charges of rape, murder and treason were forwarded to the Assizes, JPs fulfilled a vital role in dispensing justice at a local level. Not all JPs were honest and hard working, but most worked for the good of their community and were loyal subjects of the Crown.

Their administrative role was arguably more important than their work as law enforcers. According to the 1602 edition of William Lambarde's *Eirenarcha*, a handbook for JPs, they were expected to administer over 300 statutes, although clearly some were more important than others. These ranged from:

- ensuring that roads, highways, bridges and sea defences were properly maintained to clearing blocked sewers and drainage ditches
- monitoring weights and measures on market days to fixing the price of grain in times of famine
- assessing subsidy tax returns to overseeing the welfare of the poor
- licensing alehouses to assisting officials at the county muster.

In fact, there was very little that a JP was not expected to do.

Sheriffs and lords lieutenant

The decline of the sheriffs

Since the fifteenth century, sheriffs, who were originally responsible for maintaining order in the counties, had been in decline. In 1485 they still played a key role in supervising parliamentary elections, serving royal writs, mustering of troops, organising Quarter Sessions and assizes, transporting prisoners, empanelling juries, presiding over monthly meetings of the county court and enforcing sentences passed down by JPs and assize judges, and these duties continued throughout the sixteenth century.

However, the Tudors never fully trusted their sheriffs to exercise political and military power. Henry VII had viewed with alarm their capacity to undermine royal authority in the shires and sought to weaken their influence. In 1495, he gave JPs the power to monitor their activities and encouraged them to report any malpractices to the royal council. Gradually, the sheriff's authority became more honorific and the maintenance of stability in the counties fell to the increasingly overworked JPs. The outbreak of rebellions in the 1530s and 1540s, moreover, demonstrated that the sheriffs' ability to muster soldiers and suppress serious disturbances left much to be desired – some had even joined the rebels – and reform was required.

The rise of the lords lieutenant

In 1549, in the wake of serious disturbances in central and southern England, lords lieutenant were appointed to oversee counties where there had been rebellions or where subjects might become troublesome. Intended as a temporary measure, the Duke of Northumberland in 1551 saw the political advantage of their existence to buttress his position as President of the Privy Council. Lieutenants like Russell in the south-western counties and Northampton in East Anglia performed military as well as police duties, and the absence of any rebellions between 1550 and 1553 suggests that the twelve men appointed by Northumberland fulfilled their role competently, although their unwillingness to support his coup against Mary is a telling comment on the illegitimacy of his claim to rule the country.

The office of the lords lieutenant lapsed at Mary's accession but was revived with the advent of war in 1557, when she divided the country into ten lieutenancies. Elizabeth similarly saw no need to appoint lieutenants on a permanent basis and only appointed them in times of crisis, notably in 1569 during the Northern Earls' revolt and in 1585 at the outbreak of war with Spain. However, the continuance of war and the threat of invasion in 1588 resulted in most counties having a resident lord lieutenant, and since most officers were privy councillors, as many as two to six deputies per county were appointed to carry out their duties in their absence.

By the end of the period, lords lieutenant had become a regular feature of county administration. Sometimes they were used to supervise recusants, distribute grain in times of shortage and collect loans on behalf of the Crown, but their main function was to muster and train the county militia.

The county militia

In the course of the sixteenth century and largely as a result of the rebellions between 1536 and 1570, the Tudors came to realise the inadequacy of the county militia. The law required every free man aged from sixteen to 60 years to carry a weapon to defend himself and his country in the event of an invasion. Although this was clearly inadequate, and in most cases never implemented, the Crown, without a standing army and police force, necessarily relied on the nobility and gentry to supply retainers and, where possible, weaponry and armour. The number of retainers had greatly diminished since the advent of the Tudors and many were reluctant to fight for commanders other than their own lord or to act against their neighbours (see pages 166–7). Moreover, the logistics of the Crown raising, equipping and organising troops proved very haphazard when put to the test. In theory, every summer the sheriff mustered all able-bodied men in the county, recorded and checked their weapons, and gave them basic training in warfare. In practice, the Crown had little idea how many men could be put on a war footing ready to suppress rebellions or repel invaders. Wolsey conducted a survey in 1522, which revealed that the most common weapon was the **billhook**, and a survey in the 1540s suggested that few men possessed complete sets of armour and harnesses.

Reform of the county militia

Mary tried to improve the condition of the militia by passing two Acts in 1558. These first required everyone to contribute according to their means towards the

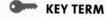

KEY TERM

Billhook A curved blade attached to a wooden handle that could be used to slash and cut an adversary.

provision of men, equipment and horses, and secondly, attempts were made to achieve a more regular attendance at the muster. If any improvements occurred, they were clearly inadequate to deal with the 1569 revolt and so it fell to the lords lieutenant to overhaul the whole system of raising and training troops.

In 1572, a Militia Act was passed to address the problem. Men aged from sixteen to 60 years were required to be trained in the use of arms: they were paid 8*d.* (3p) a day for about ten days' training a year and their equipment was to be provided by the county. However, as this would cost the Crown at least £400 a year per county, only ten per cent of men were selected for training. The lords lieutenant and their deputies appointed muster masters and provost marshals for raising, equipping and training the troops, and by the late 1580s England had some 26,000 trained bands ready for active service. Their prime task was to fight any Spanish invasion but they could be used to suppress riots and disturbances, although Elizabeth was reluctant to send them overseas or even to use them against Tyrone's rebellion in Ireland. Nevertheless, by 1603 the Crown had at its disposal a civil defence force that was independent of the servants and retainers that the aristocracy had supplied for centuries. It is difficult to assess the competency of the trained bands as a whole but when they were first put to the test in the Midland counties in 1607, the gentry found 'great backwardness' and relied far more on their own retainers.

Lords lieutenant and their deputies worked closely with the JPs and gentry and were a pivotal link in the chain of command between the Crown and county administration responsible for ensuring that the country remained stable and peaceful. The absence of any major rebellion after 1570 in Elizabethan England does not prove that they were an effective deterrent against popular disorder, but a permanent Crown appointee in each county enabled the government to be better informed of local issues and undoubtedly better placed to resolve difficulties before they became too serious.

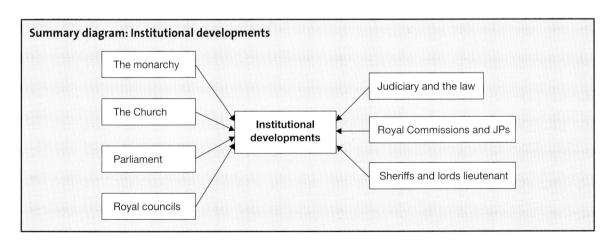

Summary diagram: Institutional developments

- The monarchy
- The Church
- Parliament
- Royal councils

→ **Institutional developments** ←

- Judiciary and the law
- Royal Commissions and JPs
- Sheriffs and lords lieutenant

Tudor policies: continuity and change

> ▶ *How and why did the role of the English nobility change during the Tudor period?*

We have seen how the stability and order of the kingdom depended to a great extent on Tudor institutions and administrators, but it was also the case that the policies undertaken by Tudor governments played a vital part in keeping the people under control. Political, religious, economic and social issues needed to be addressed if recurrent disturbances and rebellions were to be avoided.

The nobility

The political role of the nobility underwent a dramatic change during the Tudor period. In the second half of the fifteenth century, families such as the Howards, Percys, Staffords and Nevilles owned vast tracts of land, often consolidated in one area of the kingdom, where they ruled their tenants like petty kings. The Percys in the north, for instance, controlled the lives of some 10,000 tenants. Many lords had private armies, waged war against their neighbours from fortified castles and had little respect for the king's laws. While the Wars of the Roses had certainly depleted the resources of many nobles and in a few cases wiped out families altogether, there still remained a small number of nobles who were unwilling to accept Henry Tudor as the rightful king. Moreover, many had become accustomed to governing the country with or without the king and, as leaders of the political community, Henry knew they were indispensable if he was to survive. As long as they were competent and loyal, the king would leave them alone; but if they acted independently or against his best interests, he would rein them in.

Henry VII and Henry VIII sought to reduce the incidence of disorder perpetrated by the nobility by dismantling castles in non-strategic sites, confiscating supplies of gunpowder and decommissioning cannons. Most nobles complied, although they were encouraged to keep their suits of armour and harnesses in good condition ready for royal service.

Henry VII spent most of his reign trying to eliminate the threat of pretenders and rival claimants and in so doing trammelled the English and Irish nobility into a state of subservience. Statutes of 1487 and 1504 attempted to confine retainers to licensed holders and harsh fines were imposed on nobles who ignored the law. Lord Burgavenny, for example, was fined £71,000 and Sir James Stanley £245,000 in 1506. It was not Henry's intention to eliminate retaining – he needed troops to suppress disturbances and fight foreign wars – but to punish the worst cases of abuse.

Other Tudor rulers took the same view:

- Henry VIII relied on 700 of Norfolk's retainers and Lord Ferrers provided 1000 men to counter the pilgrims in 1536.
- Mary issued over 2000 licences for retaining.
- Elizabeth needed nobles' retainers to deal with the 1569 uprising. Private feuding still existed, especially in the Welsh marches, Scottish borders and outside the Irish Pale, although there is evidence that the number of cases involving **livery and maintenance** declined significantly in the course of the sixteenth century.

By the end of the period, the Crown, in the words of the historian Lawrence Stone (1964), may have gained 'a royal monopoly of violence' from the aristocracy, but some nobles were still capable of raising and equipping troops independently if they so wished.

The Crown, nobility and land

The Crown preferred to seize nobles' lands if an act of treason had been committed. Henry VII passed 138 Acts of attainder and, contrary to customary practice, only reversed a minority of them. Henry VIII, Edward and Mary were more generous in restoring lands but few nobles after 1536 were involved in treasonous activities. Bonds and recognisances were also imposed on the nobility by all of the Tudors. These required Crown servants on taking office, many of whom were nobles, and any subjects who had infringed the law, to stand surety for hundreds and sometimes thousands of pounds. It has been estimated that two-thirds of the English nobility and gentry were at the king's mercy by 1509 and, although Henry VIII cancelled all bonds in a gesture of unprecedented generosity, bonds were the preferred method of controlling unreliable nobles and were again introduced after the rebellions of 1537, 1549, 1554, 1570 and 1601.

All of the Tudors tried to prevent major families from building up large tracts of land and exercising political dominance in their counties:

- Henry VII discouraged English heiresses from marrying powerful and potentially threatening nobles, made the Welsh lords sign indentures of good behaviour and kept a close watch on Burgavenny, the most powerful baron. When the fourth Earl of Northumberland was murdered in 1489, the king took possession of the young heir as a royal ward to gain control of the Percy estates in Yorkshire and Northumberland.
- Henry VIII similarly tried to strengthen royal control of sensitive areas. In the 1530s, he endowed Russell and Suffolk with lands in the south-west and East Anglia, respectively, and transferred the wardenship of the northern marches from traditional noble families to lesser gentry. The appointment of local gentry who owed their office to the Crown made steady inroads towards reducing the lawlessness in the north. The perceived view was that

KEY TERM

Livery and maintenance
Wearing a lord's tunic bearing his coat of arms, and the practice in which some lords attended a law court in order to influence the judge and jury.

the northern magnates promoted disorder by either ignoring disturbances or actually encouraging them.

● However, the demise of the great northern families – the Nevilles, Percys and Dacres – came as a result of the Northern Earls' revolt in 1569, when many of their lands were seized and regranted to gentry from the south of England.

The Crown, nobility and rewards

Henry VII did not favour ennobling his subjects. He raised only four men to the peerage, two of whom were relatives, and in the course of his reign the overall number of peers fell from twenty to ten. In contrast, Henry VIII, Edward and Mary behaved more generously. Henry rewarded his nobility with lands and titles and was responsible for creating over half the peerage by 1547, but he skilfully balanced new creations with the promotion of existing nobles, and confined his generosity to a small group of courtiers. During Edward's reign, his regents rewarded themselves and many of their associates with peerages. In 1547 alone, Thomas Wriothesley became the Earl of Southampton, John Dudley the Earl of Warwick, William Parr the Marquis of Northampton, and Thomas Seymour, Richard Rich, William Willoughby and Edmund Sheffield all became barons. Elizabeth, like her grandfather, was ungenerous in her creation of peers. Only ten new peerages were created and as a result the total number fell from 57 in 1558 to 55 in 1603.

In the course of the Tudor period, the nobility also appears to have undergone a metamorphosis that had a significant bearing on their relationship with its tenants, the Crown and society in general. Instead of military honour, war and violence, which had influenced their social customs in the fifteenth century, many by 1603 espoused good lordship, peace and civility. Part of this transition can be explained by the steady decline in feudal relations with their tenants; land tenure came to be based on **copyhold and customary rights** rather than on the 'honour' and 'will' of the lord, and lords retained far fewer servants. The demise of large households in the second half of the sixteenth century for economic reasons further weakened the bonds of personal ties. The change can also be attributed to an increasing interest in **humanism**, learning and European culture, and a desire to study at one of the universities and Inns of Court. Thus, most nobles ceased to be politically ambitious or aggressive towards their neighbours and instead focused their efforts on managing their estates and working with the Crown to attain political and social stability in the counties.

The nobility and government

The Tudors relied heavily on the nobility as councillors, administrators and military leaders. Henry VII convened five Great Councils of the nobles, and Henry VIII and Elizabeth held assemblies of nobles in the 1530s and 1580s to discuss matters of state. Parliament, of course, was an occasion when the peers were invited to advise the monarch and all Tudor councils contained nobles. In 1526, for instance, seven out of twenty royal councillors were peers, in 1540

KEY TERMS

Copyhold and customary rights Copyholders were tenants who held a copy of their tenancy but in practice had only limited rights. Customary rights were more secure and reflected traditional local practices and customs.

Humanism The study of architecture, art, language, rhetoric and literature that enabled the individual to become more civilised and better prepared to play an active role in the political life of the state.

eight were in attendance, and fourteen in Edward's enlarged council in 1553. Only in Elizabeth's reign did the number of peers decline, from six in her first council to one in 1601. But if Elizabeth was less dependent on her peers in the Privy Council, they served her in other ways.

Every peer and leading gentleman was expected periodically to attend the royal court to pay their respects to the queen. Some nobles resided permanently as servants of the household and chamber; others served as ambassadors and fulfilled diplomatic duties. Some became JPs, some served on special commissions and many more became lords lieutenant. Stanley in Lancashire, Hatton in Northamptonshire and Talbot in Derbyshire, for instance, were the queen's principal sources of authority in these counties. Nobles also presided over the regional councils in Wales, the North and Dublin, and used their influence to impose order in the region. Above all, the Tudors relied on nobles to put down rebellions. Surrey, Oxford and Pembroke assisted Henry VII; Norfolk, Suffolk and Shrewsbury suppressed rebellions in Henry VIII's reign; Russell, Warwick and Grey led armies against the Western, Kett and Oxford rebels; and Pembroke, Clinton and Norfolk were sent to deal with Wyatt and his rebels. Elizabeth similarly depended on Sussex, Clinton and Hunsdon to combat the northern earls, she sent lords Grey, Essex and Mountjoy to suppress the Irish rebellions, and the Earl of Nottingham was called on to arrest Essex himself in 1601.

Religious changes

Reforms under Henry VIII

Ecclesiastical and doctrinal reforms could be a potent source of conflict, as both Henry VIII and Edward VI discovered. All governments feared rapid change and much effort was made to explain and justify religious reforms and minimise popular instability. Although uniformity of belief was the preferred goal, a more realistic objective was to implement changes with as little disruption as possible and only to target extremists who could not be accommodated in the English Church. As a result, Henry persecuted a minority of Roman Catholics who would not be reconciled to the new headship and Protestant reforms, and those sects that threatened the unity of the Church of England such as Anabaptists and **sacramentarians**. After the Pilgrimage of Grace he faced no more religious uprisings, partly owing to his decision in 1539 to halt further Protestant reforms in the face of growing iconoclasm and partly because few English and Irish were prepared to rally to the papal cause. The government nonetheless remained on its guard against popular insurrections. In 1543, for example, an Act for the Advancement of True Religion declared that 'no woman (except noble women in private) nor artificers, prentices, journeymen, serving men of the degrees of yeoman and under, husbandmen or labourers' was to read the Bible because these 'lower sort' might acquire 'naughty and erroneous opinions, and by occasion thereof fall into great division and dissention among themselves'.

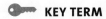 **KEY TERM**

Sacramentarians
Protestants who denied the real presence of Christ in the Eucharist.

Edwardian reforms

Apart from the Western rebellion and disturbances in counties such as Hampshire and Oxfordshire in 1549, there was little negative reaction to the Edwardian religious reforms. Although the government played down the radical nature of religious change, the dukes of Somerset and Northumberland introduced reforms slowly and cautiously. They were, for instance, concerned that itinerant preachers and unlicensed printing might be provocative, and from September 1548 banned all preaching. A year later censorship was introduced to prevent the printing of radical tracts, sermons and ballads. In fact, reforms were greeted more by apathy and indifference than by active opposition. Of course, it may be that by 1552, when the country experienced the most radical doctrinal reforms to date, people who might have opposed the changes were biding their time in anticipation of a Catholic restoration under Mary. It is equally possible that the introduction of legislation, which made the gathering of twelve or more people a felony, deterred potential protesters.

Catholic restoration

Mary Tudor, in spite of her harsh treatment of Protestants, faced no religious revolts. Wisely, she and her council encouraged recalcitrant Protestants to emigrate rather than spread opposition internally. Of course, the government's decision to burn nearly 300 heretics must have deterred some would-be rebels,

A portrait of Mary I at the age of 28 painted in 1544 by Master John.

although it was concerned that public burnings might generate popular protests, and a proclamation in 1556 attempted to bar servants, apprentices and young people from attending these ceremonies. Also, the knowledge that Mary was childless and would be succeeded by her Protestant sister perhaps convinced many people that it was better to suffer in silence. In reality, outside London and certain dioceses such as Canterbury, York and Winchester, where Catholic bishops were keen to enforce a Counter-Reformation, the religious reforms in the 1550s had little impact on the spiritual condition of the people. Both Catholic and Protestant gentry are known to have acquired monastic and chantry property, there was no real appetite by clerics or laymen to see a restoration of the papacy, and as many as 2000 priests resigned or retired from their benefices after 1554 rather than give up their recently acquired marital status.

The Elizabethan Church settlement

Elizabeth famously announced that she would 'open windows into no man's soul'. Her principal desire to achieve outward conformity and to establish a religious settlement that was acceptable to the vast majority of the nation largely explains the absence of popular resistance and revolts in her reign. Only a small number of Catholic priests were unwilling to subscribe to the oaths of supremacy and uniformity. A minority of English counties, notably Lancashire, Sussex, Hampshire and Cornwall, and most of Ireland had a Catholic core but none was prepared to revolt against the Elizabethan Church. Significantly, none of these areas joined the northern earls in their pseudo-religious revolt of 1569.

The arrival in England of Mary Queen of Scots in 1568 and the excommunication of 1570 increased the potential for Catholic conspiracies and disturbances, which the government effectively countered:

- Counties known to favour Catholic beliefs had their JPs systematically remodelled.
- Assize judges were ordered to readminister the oath of supremacy to all JPs in 1579.
- Walsingham's agents alerted the Privy Council to plots linked to Mary.

In practice, few Catholics sympathised with Mary's plight or showed much interest in the activities of Jesuits and missionaries who were roaming the country in the 1580s.

Anti-Catholic penal laws from 1571 made it clear that Catholics had to choose between obeying the queen and obeying the pope, and the majority of the noble and gentry families stayed loyal to the queen. In return, she periodically protected them from attempts by zealous Protestants in parliament to increase the severity of the penal laws. In 1571, for instance, the Commons and the Lords passed a bill to force Catholics to take Anglican Communion once a year or pay a £66 fine. The queen vetoed the proposal. Similarly, no concerted attempt was made to force the Church settlement on Ireland. As a result, religion was never a serious issue with Irish clans in spite of its potential to cause instability.

Protestant challenges

Wherever religious grievances underpinned rebellions against Tudor governments the protagonists were Catholics. English Protestants, in contrast, were consistently loyal to the monarchy: a minority in 1549 wanted further reforms, none rebelled against Mary and even puritans acknowledged Elizabeth's entitlement to be the Supreme Governor of the Church of England. In fact, Elizabethan Protestantism was not that popular: it was too academic and unattractive to most rural people who disliked long sermons and had little time for Bible reading. Attendance at church was generally low and some parishes had difficulty keeping order during services. In practice, playing football, hunting and going to the pub were preferred Sunday activities in many parishes. Although by law everyone should have attended Sunday service, the authorities were reluctant to proceed against absentees. The emergence of Protestant nonconformists in the 1580s, however, led to the government taking action to stamp out possible dissension. Sects like the Brownists and Barrowists were forced into exile, leading members who returned from the continent were arrested and the Court of High Commission was used to censor literature and issue licences to preachers. At a time of growing national crisis, the government again took no chances. An Act of 1593 restricted all recusants to a five-mile radius from their homes and imprisoned indefinitely known troublemakers, both puritan and Catholic. Although none of the radicals posed a threat to civil or religious stability this Act may have been a factor in ensuring that dissidents were kept under control.

Economic developments

The Tudors did not have a coherent economic policy; they simply reacted to events as they unfolded. Governments were, however, influenced by the need to raise revenue to administer the country and by a desire to prevent disorder and look after their subjects' welfare. Grievances over taxation, enclosures, high food prices and unemployment were the root cause of several rebellions and generated riotous behaviour in most English counties at some stage under the Tudors. No government set out to provoke disquiet, and in most cases Tudor governments only intervened in economic affairs to rectify a problem. Even then, the main objective was a short-term fix, not complete reform. As a result, over 300 statutes were passed, mainly to improve trade and industry, and to control labour relations and social welfare, which JPs were expected to enforce. In practice, few cases seem to have been presented to JPs at a local level and even fewer prosecutions were brought by the Crown, which suggests that once legislation had been introduced the Crown was more interested in its own fiscal welfare. It is also likely that JPs were reluctant to prosecute for fear of exacerbating unemployment and fomenting trouble.

Government finance

Raising taxes was always unpopular: then, as now, people resented handing over their money. The government's response was to try to justify the need and to avoid making excessive or innovative demands. The Amicable Grant amply demonstrated the danger of trying to collect a non-parliamentary tax and farmers expressed similar concern in 1536 and 1549 when rumours circulated that the government was planning to increase indirect taxation. Medieval rulers had been expected to 'live of their own', to utilise their own lands, profits of justice and customs duties to meet the costs of running the country and maintaining the royal household – but by the end of the Tudor period this was no longer the case. To meet the rising costs of administration, which more than doubled in the sixteenth century, governments employed a variety of expedients:

- Henry VII and his successors used parliamentary grants to pay for wars, and the practice of receiving peacetime subsidies began in the 1530s.
- Henry VIII and Edward debased the coinage, sold off Crown lands and negotiated loans from continental bankers.
- Mary and Elizabeth cut back on expenditure, made their administrations more efficient and avoided wars for as long as possible.

Above all, Elizabeth made no attempt to reform the system of self-assessment whereby land, property and goods were rated for tax and confirmed by JPs at levels well below their acknowledged value. Since 1547, MPs and peers had begun to revise their parliamentary assessments downwards. By 1558, the assessed landed income of nobles had on average fallen by 25 per cent, and continued to fall such that, in the 1570s, those rated at £100 or more were taxed at around ten per cent. William Cecil, for example, had estates and goods rated at £133 a year that were valued at over £4000, and he was the Lord Treasurer! This collusion between landowners, merchants, nobles and gentry ensured that, while the wealthy classes did pay taxes from time to time, as long as the government kept its demands within reasonable limits, there was never going to be any serious resistance or opposition. Even during the last decade of her reign, when Elizabeth requested very large subsidies, MPs approved. War needs and national security outweighed any thoughts of complaining. Indeed, by judicious financial management and by avoiding excessive demands, neither Mary nor Elizabeth experienced tax revolts.

Enclosures

The enclosing of land was not a major issue, except when it occurred illegally or in times of economic hardship, and then only in areas where fertile land was in short supply. Every Tudor government legislated against unlawful enclosures. Thus, Acts were passed in 1489, 1533, 1549–50, 1555, 1563 and 1597 to prevent the conversion of arable land to pasture, the engrossment of farms and the destruction of common rights. Commissions of enquiry were periodically held in 1488, 1517, 1548, 1549 and 1565–6 to ensure that illegal enclosures had not occurred, and there is evidence to suggest that plaintiffs increasingly turned to litigation rather than violence to right a wrong:

- Wolsey charged 264 landlords and corporations with unlawful enclosure.
- The Privy Council took action against illegal enclosures in the wake of the Pilgrimage of Grace.
- Northumberland, in contrast, sided with the landlords in 1550 and took action to deter protesters, although the collapse of the wool trade and a series of good harvests may explain the absence of complaints in the 1550s.

Generally, enclosures became less of an issue in Elizabeth's reign, such that by 1593 the government was confident enough to repeal all existing anti-enclosure legislation. Unfortunately, the repeal coincided with the start of five poor harvests, grain shortages, rising inflation and urban unemployment. Yet even allowing for this downturn in the economy and the disturbances in Oxfordshire in 1596, there was no strong call to reverse the law. In fact, an Act was passed that made protests against enclosures treasonous, which no doubt contributed to a spate of enclosure activity in the last years of Elizabeth's reign.

Food supplies

Economic historians have estimated that one in every four harvests failed in Tudor England and that at least one-third of the population lived at or below starvation level. If this is so, it is perhaps surprising that the period did not see more grain riots and rebellions due to rising prices and the scarcity of food. Part of the explanation lies in the lack of interest shown by nobles and gentry in leading rebellions or participating in local riots; but principally the answer is to be found in government legislation, the enforcement of statutes and proclamations by JPs, and the initiatives taken by municipal authorities in tackling the problems locally:

- Acts were passed in 1534, 1555, 1559, 1563, 1571 and 1593 to limit the export of grain and encourage imports.
- Measures were taken in 1527, 1544, 1545, 1550, 1556 and 1562 to prevent the hoarding of grain.
- In many cases, towns such as Norwich, London and Ipswich bought up cheap corn, stockpiled it and sold it to the poor at below market rates in times of dearth.
- JPs were also ordered to search houses for grain, and farmers were forced to sell corn at a fair price.
- Books of Orders were issued by the royal council in 1527, 1550, 1556 and 1586, that gave detailed advice on how to deal with food shortages, and Orders in the 1590s required towns to transport surplus corn to the most affected areas.

Perhaps on account of the sensitive nature of food prices and the fluctuating availability of grain, the government was more willing to intervene when there were food shortages than in other fields of economic activity. Its success rate, however, is hard to judge. It remains true that in spite of continuing poor harvests and food shortages in the last twenty years of Elizabeth's reign, there was little sign of disorder. JPs did their best to enforce regulations but towns often looked no further than helping their own citizens and some merchants were primarily interested in profiteering.

Unemployment

The steady rise in population and fluctuating trade markets meant that levels of unemployment rose during periods of depression, which increased the likelihood of unrest. The 1520s, 1550s and 1590s saw short-lived but significant slumps in the woollen cloth trade and resulted in corresponding bursts of government interventionism. Admittedly, the Crown had a personal interest in maintaining high levels of cloth production since its customs revenue was directly affected by exports of wool and cloth. The problem of large numbers of unemployed fullers, carders, weavers and dyers only became serious in the 1550s. Northumberland's council issued rules in 1552 to control the quality of manufacturing different types of cloth in an attempt to raise export sales, and Mary's government passed laws in 1555 designed to force weavers to join guilds and maintain a good standard of work.

By far the most important legislation came in 1563. The Statute of Artificers introduced a range of measures intended to restrict the movement of labour as the unemployed travelled from town to town in search of work, and to ensure that relations between employers and workers were put on a fair basis. Thus, the Act declared that:

- no one could practise a craft without first completing a seven-year apprenticeship
- workers and servants could not be hired for less than a year
- masters were not allowed to dismiss a servant nor servants leave their employment without good reason
- JPs must set maximum wage rates for every occupation
- all unemployed people aged between twelve and 60 were to be found work in their parish; men in agriculture and women in domestic service.

The statute represented a real attempt to control the economy, to find work for the unemployed and to preserve order across the country. It is, however, difficult to say how effective it was in practice. There were no revolts or rebellions involving unemployed workers and farmers in the second half of the sixteenth century but JPs appear to have been reluctant to impose regulations strictly, and only in years of severe economic depression, notably in the 1590s, were laws enforced. In reality, JPs usually sided with the masters, employers and craft guilds, and only fully applied the laws when it was in their interest to do so.

Social reforms

How best to deal with the rising number of beggars, vagrants and poor people was a concern for all Tudor administrations. Although the poor were unlikely to cause a rebellion, they could swell the ranks of protesters and exacerbate social and economic problems for the authorities, particularly in towns and cities. The measures that were taken by central and local governments reflected the need to tackle a problem before it got out of hand. Not all remedies were successful and in retrospect some seem quite inadequate, yet Tudor society for the first time in 300 years introduced reforms that remained on the statute books until 1834. Moreover, in spite of the population doubling in the course of the period, severe trade depressions that increased the numbers of unemployed and the closure of the monasteries that had been a source of relief for many destitute beggars, urban and rural authorities succeeded in keeping the poor under control.

Reforms under Cromwell

The first Tudor administration to address the growing number of beggars was that of Cromwell in the 1530s. Until then, itinerant beggars were put in the stocks for three days and then returned to their place of birth or previous known residence. Impotent beggars were allowed to stay but none was permitted to roam the countryside. The depression of the 1520s led to large numbers of unemployed taking to the roads, which galvanised the government and some towns into action:

- In 1531, an Act made a distinction between the impotent and idle poor; the former were licensed by JPs to beg, the latter were to be whipped.
- London took a more benevolent approach and introduced voluntary alms' collections in 1533, a measure that was extended nationally by an Act of 1536, which also required parish authorities to find work for the able-bodied but lazy poor. In practice, however, few collections were made, village constables were given neither money nor raw materials to set the poor to work and, like so much Tudor social legislation, the reforms proved ineffectual.

Edwardian reforms

The Edwardian government also made little headway in helping the poor:

- Vagabonds continued to be punished, most notably between 1547 and 1549 when a proclamation sentenced them to two years' slavery for a first offence of begging and life imprisonment thereafter.
- The genuine poor, on the other hand, were to receive dole money from church donations, but as these remained discretionary and the threat of being admonished by the parish priest or bishop awaited non-contributors, this attempt in 1552 at stopping begging was a failure.

Already cities such as Norwich and York had instituted a compulsory poor rate levied by the parish and it is clear that measures adopted by town authorities were much more effective than government legislation. By 1553, several hospitals in London had been founded and endowed with ex-monastic and chantry property, and important distinctions were made between different types of poor:

- Bridewell housed vagabonds.
- Christ's looked after 400 orphans.
- St Thomas's and St Bartholomew's took in the sick, aged and impotent.

Elizabethan reforms

Later in Elizabeth's reign, cities like Norwich, Ipswich and Exeter came to accept their responsibility for funding and managing the welfare of their citizens.

The most important legislation occurred in Elizabeth's reign:

- The 1572 Act recognised that the 'deserving poor' – the aged, sick and impotent – were to be helped, and vagabonds severely punished (they were whipped and had their ears bored), but it required JPs to assess how much was needed to keep them and for the first time overseers were appointed to collect compulsory parish taxes. Since the onus fell on the parish to provide for the poor, parishioners developed a collective responsibility for maintaining order and were naturally keen to discourage begging and vagrancy. A fundamental flaw in the Act – it made no provision for men and women who wanted to work but were unable to find any – was rectified four years later.
- The 1576 Act required parishes to provide wool, flax, iron and hemp so that all able-bodied people had to work. A run of five bad harvests between 1594 and 1598, large numbers of young people who were 'out of service' (that is, neither apprenticed to a master nor employed in a household) and many disbanded soldiers and sailors, combined to alarm the government to pass a comprehensive poor law in 1598.
- The 1598 laws modified and codified previous legislation, and introduced two new reforms. First, the 'Act for the Relief of the Poor' replaced overworked JPs with churchwardens to oversee the welfare of the genuine poor and unemployed. Second, the 'Act for the Punishment of Rogues and Sturdy Beggars' separated vagabonds into two groups: dangerous vagabonds were to be rounded up by provost marshals and sent to the galleys or banished; other beggars were to be returned to their parishes of birth (if known) or placed in houses of correction and made to work.

Much had been achieved in the course of the Tudor period to reduce the likelihood of the poor disturbing the peace and, coincidentally, to alleviate their distress. By 1603, the deserving poor had been distinguished from the wilful vagrants, and the wandering poor from the settled poor. Local overseers administered relief that was compulsorily levied on parishioners and went towards food, clothing, providing work and treating the sick, elderly and infirm.

Vagabonds were discouraged from begging or becoming nomadic, and punished if they refused to work. Once again, it fell to the JPs to ensure that this system of social welfare actually worked. The genuine poor were therefore assisted by a combination of state, municipal and private charitable relief and, although the range of statutes and proclamations may not have been consistently enforced, enough was done to ensure that the poor did not pose a threat to the stability of the country.

Ireland

The maintenance of permanent order in Ireland was all but impossible. The only effective areas of law enforcement were the lowlands of Munster and Leinster centred around Dublin and the Pale where the Anglo-Irish mainly lived. Feuding between rival clans such as the Geraldines and Butlers, or O'Neills and O'Donnells, was endemic, whether in or out of office. Tudor monarchs were not recognised as sovereign rulers by Gaelic lords, who controlled most of the island, and instead English kings depended on the most prominent Anglo-Irish family – the Geraldines – to govern on their behalf. Relying on the Geraldines was a high-risk, low-cost strategy. The eighth Earl of Kildare, Gerald, acknowledged Simnel and Warbeck as kings of England and his brother, Thomas, died fighting Henry VII at Stoke. Moreover, the family used its political status to extend its power at the expense of rival clans and, although revolts were commonplace, a semblance of order was maintained. Disturbances in Ireland were, after all, not in the Kildares' best interest because they could not govern without a royal commission, and this could be revoked as in 1492, 1522 and 1528. However, attempts to rule through the Kildares' rivals, the Butlers, proved equally unsatisfactory as they were unable to command much respect from the other lordships. In practice, English laws were only occasionally enforced and Gaelic customs and language were encouraged by the Irish administration. In return, the Crown's landed interests were protected and the cost of governing Ireland was met by the feudal dues paid to Kildare.

Both Henry VII and his son sent troops to Ireland when trouble flared up: Edgecombe went there in 1487, Poynings in 1494 and Surrey in 1520, but the conquest of Ireland was never seriously considered by the early Tudors. Poynings took only 400 men and Surrey had 500 troops and the king's Yeomen of the Guard.

Nevertheless, in 1519 Henry VIII took a more proactive interest in Irish affairs, establishing a council in Dublin and sending Surrey to see 'how Ireland may be reduced and restored to good order and obedience'. The earl made a shrewd assessment of the situation when he reported that the Irish 'will not be brought to no good order, unless it be by compulsion, which will not be done without a great puissance of men, and great cost of money, and long continuance of time'. As Henry had neither men nor money to spare, he returned to a policy of relying on the Irish magnates.

Changes in Anglo-Irish relations

The year 1534 marked a turning point in Anglo-Irish relations. Until then, the main colonial grievance had been royal neglect: no Tudor ever visited Ireland, the administration was expected to be self-funded, and rulers seriously underestimated the difficulties that faced the lord deputies and deputy lieutenants in maintaining peace. After 1534, the main colonial grievance was royal interference. English-born officials held all the principal offices, which naturally caused resentment among Old English families, who had hitherto monopolised royal patronage, as well as among Gaelic lords, who resented the increasing interference in their way of life. Moreover, Henry VIII's Reformation brought religion into the political arena. The new Lord Deputy, Leonard Grey, made clear his intentions in 1536: he called a parliament, attainted Kildare, imposed Henry's Reformation Acts, ordered the collection of First Fruits and Tenths and sold off half of all monastic lands. Although the garrison in Dublin was reduced from 700 to 340 troops, the cost was borne by the locals and army captains were granted lands on the borders of the Pale.

The appointment of Anthony St Leger as deputy in 1537 heralded further changes. He increased the garrison to 2000 men (although it was again reduced to 500 in 1543) and tried to get the Gaelic chiefs to recognise Henry as the King of Ireland rather than 'Lord'. In 1541, his diplomacy eventually worked. The chiefs agreed to surrender their lands to the king and he regranted them according to English laws and customs. They swore an oath of allegiance and rejected the authority of the pope. For his part, Henry gave up claims to land under Gaelic occupation and surrendered many feudal rights, which gave the Irish greater security of tenure as their lands were now hereditary. Progress was also made in getting the Gaelic chiefs to attend Irish parliaments, adopt English customs and refrain from tribal conflict. The idea of a united and non-partitioned kingdom of Ireland was slowly taking shape.

Under Edward VI the garrison was again enlarged to 2600 troops and more fortresses were built in the marcher borderlands. Both Somerset and Northumberland took an aggressive stance towards Ireland, which won them more enemies than friends. When disturbances broke out between the O'Connors and O'Mores, for example, the lands confiscated from the warring families were granted to new English settlers at low rents and subject to English law. Resentment further grew as more Englishmen in Dublin saw the opportunity to gain lands and wealth at the expense of the Irish.

In Mary's reign more garrisons were built in Leix and Offaly, plantations (proto-colonies) were set up in the vicinity, and **purveyance** and military service imposed on local tenants and Irish natives. The Anglicisation of Gaelic lordships and the establishment of colonies outside the Pale, accompanied by a growing military presence, increased the likelihood of instability and worsened Anglo-Irish relations.

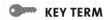 **KEY TERM**

Purveyance The right of the Crown to purchase supplies or to obtain transport for the royal household at prices fixed below prevailing market rates.

Policy under Elizabeth

Elizabeth's policy towards Ireland was characterised by inconsistency. Reluctant to spend money on maintaining her garrisons and regularly changing her deputies, justiciars and lieutenants (between 1580 and 1603 there were six deputies, six justiciars and one lieutenant), the queen condoned numerous experiments to keep effective control of Ireland that were underfunded, poorly organised and guaranteed to antagonise both the Old and New English inhabitants. The Old English favoured a peaceful and gradual expansion westwards; the New English wanted an instant occupation of borderlands which could be best achieved by force. Under Lord Deputy Sussex's administration (1559–65), the Old English complained that 'their kingdom was kept from them by force and by such as be strangers in blood to them'. Their complaints were reminiscent of those later voiced by the English northern earls. Following the suppression of Shane O'Neill's rebellion in 1567, junior branches of the clan were made to surrender their land in Ulster and have them regranted according to English law, the Scots in Antrim were expelled, three garrisons were set up and two English colonies established in Ards by Thomas Smith and Walter Devereux. Both colonies failed largely because of the attitude adopted by the founders. Smith, for example, planned to expel the 'wicked, barbarous and uncivil people, some Scottish and some wild Irish', force remaining natives to work for the colony at low wages and deny them the chance of owning land themselves.

Some lessons, however, were learned and subsequent colonies that were established in Connaught in 1585 and Munster in 1586 were more successful. Each colony was overseen by a provincial council and president, who were keen to extend English law and customs, and was modelled on the councils in the northern and Welsh marches. All landowners, both new and Gaelic, registered their entitlement to land, abolished customary practices and paid a yearly rent towards the administration and defence of the province. Elsewhere, this composition scheme was less well received and Elizabeth's policy of land resumption, which entailed claiming rebels' land as well as concealed properties, led to ill-feeling. Moreover, attempts to enforce recusancy laws in the 1580s were rejected by the Old English, most of whom were Roman Catholic. By the early 1590s, much of Ireland outside Ulster was subject to English rule within acceptable terms of administration. Revolts and disturbances occasionally occurred in Munster, Connaught and Leinster, but they were suppressed by local garrisons and Gaelic chiefs intent on preserving the *status quo*. Colonies were slowly spreading eastwards and provincial councils gave passing credence of a centralised administration. Many of these developments were even infringing into Ulster itself, although the northern province remained an implacably hostile region.

Hugh O'Neill, Earl of Tyrone

1550	Born in Tyrone
1580	Fought with the English against the Fitzgerald rebellion
1587	Visited England and given the lands of his grandfather
1595	Seized English fort at Blackwater
1596	Pardoned by Elizabeth
1597	Defeated the English at the Battle of Yellow Ford
1602	Defeated by Lord Mountjoy
1603	Negotiated a surrender
1616	Died in Rome

Situation in Ireland and Tyrone's support for the Tudors

Hugh, Earl of Tyrone, was the major power in Ulster. This was the area where Gaelic influence was the strongest and English power the weakest. He was unsure initially whether working with the Tudors or breaking from them was the best way to advance his own position. At first, he worked with the Tudors and helped to suppress the Geraldine rebellion of 1579–83.

Tyrone's change of sides

Despite being rewarded, his views changed and he decided to work with Spain and the papacy to remove the Tudors from Ireland. This was made possible because of English neglect of Ireland, but was also encouraged because the English government appeared to be attacking the clan system.

Rebellion

At first, Tyrone harried English forces, but in 1595 he seized the English fort at Blackwater, captured Enniskillen Castle and defeated the English at Clontribet. Elizabeth pardoned him, but he simply used this opportunity to build up his forces and then start a nation-wide rebellion. He inflicted the greatest defeat on English forces at the Battle of Yellow Ford in 1597, which led to the Earl of Essex being sent to Ireland with 17,000 men. Instead of confronting Tyrone, Essex made a truce and returned to London. In 1600, Lord Mountjoy was sent with a large army. Tyrone was joined by Spanish forces, but Mountjoy launched a major offensive and defeated Tyrone, who later negotiated a surrender.

After the rebellion

Tyrone came to England, where the new king, James I, confirmed him in both his title and estates, but on his return to Ireland he fell into dispute with the administration. Invited back to London to resolve the dispute, he was warned that he was to be arrested. He fled to Spain and this was declared treasonous by James. The Irish parliament passed a Bill of Attainder against him in 1613, by which time he had made his way to Rome, where he died in 1616.

By 1603, Ireland was in a poor condition as a result of the lengthy and exhausting Tyrone rebellion. Much of Ulster was devastated, cattle and crops had been destroyed, the colonies in Connaught and Munster had been swept away, and social divisions between the New and Old English and Gaelic natives had resurfaced. Elizabeth had failed to maintain order and stability mainly because she had not been willing to devote enough resources to administer the provinces nor allowed colonial initiatives enough time to succeed. If lessons were learned, they were not always consistently applied. English governors needed to work with Gaelic chiefs, as had occurred in the effective strategy of surrender and regrant. In contrast, the development of colonies and small, underfunded garrisons only caused resentment. And when military solutions were considered, the queen despatched too small an army that failed to protect the Old English or control the borders and Gaelic lordships from rebellious clans.

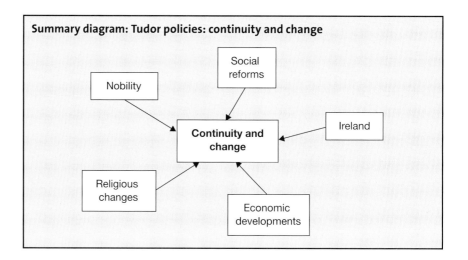

Summary diagram: Tudor policies: continuity and change

Nobility → Continuity and change

Social reforms → Continuity and change

Ireland → Continuity and change

Religious changes → Continuity and change

Economic developments → Continuity and change

 # Conclusion: the maintenance of political stability

▶ *Why did the Tudor period see an increase in political stability?*

The development of central and local administration under the Tudors was instrumental in producing a political and social structure that made government more effective and reduced the likelihood of provincial disturbances. Institutions such as the monarchy, Church, parliament and judiciary strengthened central government and, together with the ubiquitous JPs and newly created lords lieutenant, ensured that there were more direct links between the central and county authorities.

The Tudor period saw many political, religious, economic and social changes. Most people sought stability and never considered challenging the authorities. Those in authority stressed the need for people to know their place and to keep to it, and Elizabethan society in particular was obsessed with maintaining order and degree. In practice, social relations were upheld and stability was maintained not because people were brainwashed by concepts of the Great Chain of Being or frightened by sermons recounting tales of 'hell, fire and damnation', but by being good neighbours, by resolving personal problems privately and by behaving responsibly. A 'reformation of manners' appears to have occurred in which people tried to control their behaviour for the good of the community. They sought compromise, not confrontation. At a local level, those who ensured that order was upheld were yeomen and husbandmen. They bound over potential troublemakers and inculcated a moral obligation to obey the law. If all else failed, individuals might consider litigation, and if this proved unsatisfactory, then possibly civil disobedience as a last resort. The imposition of order was achieved by magistrates and manorial courts, but the maintenance of stability also owed much to the ordinary, 'middling' sort of people, who became parish officers, constables and bailiffs.

By the end of the period, the gulf between rich and poor, and between governors and governed, had widened. Prosperous farmers, merchants and gentry had little in common with day labourers, husbandmen and men 'out of service'. They often had their own property, they had an interest in upholding the social mores and, if they had any grievances, they felt confident enough to use the law courts. Under no circumstances would they lead or join popular demonstrations and disturbances. The increase in town charters, particularly in Mary's reign, and the explosion in local government offices led to towns acquiring greater responsibility for their own welfare. Local people sought to remedy their problems and selected their own citizens to manage the administration, and increasingly these people were yeomen and craftsmen, men whose ancestors might have participated in rebellion. By the end of Elizabeth's reign, they were serving as constables, churchwardens, watchmen and overseers of the poor, and as keepers of the gaols, houses of correction and customs houses, and, like other local officers, assumed a collective responsibility for maintaining order.

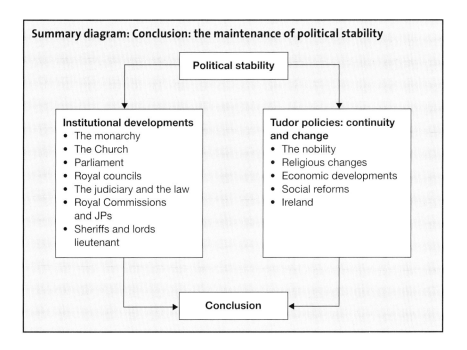

Summary diagram: Conclusion: the maintenance of political stability

Political stability

Institutional developments
- The monarchy
- The Church
- Parliament
- Royal councils
- The judiciary and the law
- Royal Commissions and JPs
- Sheriffs and lords lieutenant

Tudor policies: continuity and change
- The nobility
- Religious changes
- Economic developments
- Social reforms
- Ireland

Conclusion

Chapter summary

In a period of dramatic religious and social and economic change, the maintenance of stability was a major concern of the Tudor authorities. There were several institutions available to the government to help them to maintain stability and order, and during the period a number of bodies were either strengthened or developed to help in the process.

As the period progressed, an ever-increasing amount of legislation was passed to help alleviate the worst elements of the social and economic changes. However, the government was also aided by a number of other developments, such as a 'reformation in manners', which encouraged the peaceful settlement of disputes and a growing gulf between the rich and poor, which discouraged the well-to-do from engaging in unrest.

 Refresher questions

Use these questions to remind yourself of the key material covered in this chapter.

1 How did the monarchy aid stability?

2 In what ways was propaganda used to help bring about stability?

3 How was the Church used to help bring about stability?

4 How did parliament help to bring about stability?

5 In what ways did royal councils bring stability to the more remote areas?

6 In what ways did JPs help to bring about stability?

7 Why were lords lieutenants important in the counties?

8 Why was the local militia reformed?

9 How did the nobility help to maintain stability?

10 In what ways did religious change create instability?

11 Why did Tudor governments introduce so many social and economic reforms in the second half of the period?

12 Why did the social and economic reforms reduce unrest?

13 Why was it difficult to achieve stability in Ireland?

In-depth studies and debates

The examination requires you to study three topics in depth and for this unit they are:

- The Pilgrimage of Grace
- The Western rebellion
- Tyrone's rebellion.

This section will go into more detail about the threat to stability of these three rebellions and introduce you to some of the key debates about the threat to stability of each rebellion, so that you will have enough depth of knowledge to be able to evaluate passages that are set on any of these three rebellions.

Key debate 1: why were the Tudor authorities so concerned about the Pilgrimage of Grace?

The Pilgrimage of Grace was the largest of all the Tudor rebellions and therefore it is hardly surprising that the authorities were so concerned about it. However, it was not just the size and scale of the rising that made it a threat, but also the direct challenge to government policy.

In arguing that the size and scale of the rising was the main reason the government was so concerned, the following issues could be considered:

- The Pilgrimage involved some 40,000 people, whereas the government could raise a force of only 8000 men and therefore had to avoid a military confrontation with the rebels.
- The rebellion involved much of the north of the country and the rebels were able to take the northern 'capital', York.
- The north of England was an area where royal authority was less strong, despite attempts to bolster it through the Council of the North and the reforms that had taken place to the institution in both 1525 and 1530.
- The loyalty of many northern nobles was dubious. Therefore, the government could not rely on the rebellion being suppressed locally and this gave the rebellion the opportunity to grow.
- The rebellion appealed to all groups of northern society and as a cross-class rebellion could present a threat similar to that posed earlier in Henry VIII's reign by the Amicable Grant.
- The rebellion appeared to be co-ordinated and this increased the threat to the government.

However, it might be argued that it was less the scale of the rising that was a threat than its aims:

- The rebellion was a direct challenge to the government's religious legislation.
- The reforms that followed the rising suggest that the government considered the rising a challenge to stability, as all the monasteries were subsequently closed since they were claimed to be behind the rising.

- The Council of the North was reformed and given a judicial function.
- Henry took on the role of warden of the marches, which gave him control over the lands that bordered Scotland. He appointed members of the gentry, rather than nobility, as his deputies as he was wary of the loyalty of the northern nobility.
- The government withdrew the subsidy and also passed legislation to regulate entry fines, suggesting that they had responded to some of the economic demands of the rebels.
- The rebels wanted to restore Mary Tudor to the succession, which was a direct dynastic challenge to Henry.

Key debate 2: was the Western rebellion a response to recent political instability in the area?

As with the Pilgrimage of Grace, a rebellion that occurs on the periphery of the country can be seen as much harder to deal with. The Western rebellion was due, at least in part, to the instability in the region. The political structure of the West Country in 1549 certainly appears to give this view much credence.

In arguing that the rebellion threatened stability:

- The absence of a powerful local family allowed the rebellion to develop and grow. The fall of the Courtenay family meant that there was a power vacuum in the region, with the absence of nobility from Cornwall and Devon.
- The other rebellion that developed in 1549 was Kett's in East Anglia, another region where the local influential noble family, the Howards, had fallen from power, suggesting that the government was dependent on local nobles for the maintenance of stability.
- Sir Peter Carew, the leading member of the gentry in Devon, antagonised the rebels further by his actions at Crediton. He lacked the social status to command respect.
- Lord John Russell, who had replaced the Courtenays, had not had time to build up a following in the counties and was absent in London.
- The government had recognised its lack of influence in the south-west by establishing a Council in the West in 1539–40.
- There had been struggles to control unrest in the region in the previous years, with the murder of the government official William Body in 1548.
- Leaders of the community, such as the mayor of Bodmin, became involved in the unrest in 1549 rather than suppressing it.
- The social divisions within the West Country gave the rebellion an element of class warfare. This has been further developed by John Guy (1988), who believed that 'the 1549 revolts were the closest thing Tudor England saw to class war'.
- The leaders of the rising who have been identified were from the lesser gentry and civic elite. Therefore, the government lacked the support of local office holders, making the rising an even greater threat.

- The change in regime with the death of Henry VIII allowed ambitious men within the county to gain promotion; this meant that those who lost out were alienated and remained passive when unrest broke out in 1549. This view is consistent with studies of other regions, such as East Anglia.

However, it can also be argued that the rebellion was not caused by recent instability, but was due to the nature of the West Country or to government actions:

- There was a tradition of unrest in the West Country, seen in the Cornish rising of 1497.
- Joyce Youings has argued (1979) that the region 'must have seemed very like the edge of the known world'. This suggests that the region, particularly Cornwall, was separate from the rest of the country.
- The area was strongly provincial and therefore resented interference from central government, which was on the increase.
- The area regularly showed defiance towards central government, as reflected in the murder of William Body only a year prior to the rebellion.
- The area was consistently turbulent. There had been a planned uprising in defence of traditional religion at St Keverne in 1537, and in 1538 there had been the Exeter conspiracy. Elton (1977) has also suggested that the Carpyssacke conspiracy of 1537 was an attempt to revive the Pilgrimage of Grace in the West Country. However, all this unrest suggests that the main cause was religious rather than political instability and might therefore be seen as less of a threat.
- Many of the rebels were loyal to the regime, with some singing 'God save our King', while some historians have argued that popular culture used a traditional theatre of protest to object to unpopular edicts, such as religious change, while remaining loyal to the Crown.
- It was government actions that turned a peaceful protest violent – the arrival of Carew and the burning of the barns at Crediton. Without this action it would have remained a peaceful protest like the Pilgrimage of Grace.

Key debate 3: why was Ireland such a threat to stability?

In considering the threat that Ireland posed to stability, the question remains the extent to which it was due to the nature of Ireland and Irish society or whether it was due to Elizabeth's government and her policies. In order to understand this threat, it is necessary to be aware of the changes that had taken place in England's relationship with Ireland and the policies that had been pursued since 1534.

In arguing that it was a threat due to the situation in Ireland:

- Feuding was an everyday feature of the lives of ordinary Irishmen.
- The country was only partly under English rule and there was a mixture of Gaelic and Anglo-Norman cultures.

- The religious divide only added to the problems. Roman Catholicism grew in strength in Ireland as a result of missionary work and an increasing dislike for English Protestantism.
- The papacy and Spain intervened at times on behalf of the Irish, adding to the threat and danger for England.
- Government control in Ireland virtually broke down, which according to Ellis (1998) was due to 'Geographical, cultural and social differences within Ireland and between Ireland and England created conditions which were so extraordinary by English standards as to constitute an intractable problem of government.'
- The Gaelic and Old English families remained loyal to Catholicism and therefore Protestantism was not firmly established.

In arguing that it was due to government policy:

- There was growing Irish resentment over English control, made worse by the decision, imposed on Ireland, to replace the authority of the pope over the Church with that of the monarch.
- These had been increasing English intervention, and attempts at centralisation, since the reign of Henry VIII.
- The English were attempting to impose their culture and traditions on the Irish. The English did not understand the traditions and culture of the Irish.
- The government wanted to reduce the amount of money spent on Ireland but, at the same time, retain control.
- The plantation policy and other policies were not given a chance to succeed because the government wanted to run Ireland on the 'cheap', so not enough money was invested to ensure success. As Ellis (1998) has argued, 'Policies failed in Ireland because they were not given the chance to succeed.'
- Until Elizabeth appointed Mountjoy, she failed to support the reforms of able deputies, such as Sidney.
- Elizabeth appointed some unsuitable men to run Ireland, including Essex and Grey.

Study skills: thematic essay question

How to write a conclusion to a thematic essay

You may have already considered the importance of a conclusion when studying units 1 and 2 of the OCR course. As with those units, a conclusion needs to reach a judgement based on what you have already written and should be briefly supported so that it is not an assertion. It should *not* introduce new ideas – if they were important they should have been in the main body of the essay. It is also important *not* to offer a contrary argument to the one you have pursued throughout the rest of your essay. This possibility will be avoided if you have planned and thought through your essay before you started writing (see page 56 for guidance on planning).

It might be that you are largely restating the view that you offered in the opening paragraph; or, in stronger answers, there might be a slight variation to that judgement so that you confirm your original view, but suggest, with a brief example, that there were occasions when this view was not always correct.

As with unit 1 and 2 answers, if the question has a named factor, then you should give a supported judgement about that factor's relative importance, explaining why it is or is not the most important and the role it played in the events you have discussed. If the question asks you to assess a range of issues, the conclusion should explain which you think was the most important and why, and give some brief support for your claim. Remember, a claim is simply an assertion unless there is some evidence to support it, and a simple assertion will not score highly.

Consider the question below and the sample conclusions in Responses A and B which follow. Response A is an example of a weak conclusion and Response B an example of a strong conclusion.

> 'The Crown was the most important factor in maintaining political stability in Tudor England.' How far do you agree?

The focus of your answer should have been on the role of the Crown in maintaining political stability across the period to show change and continuity. However, you will have needed to compare the role of the Crown with other factors such as the clergy, gentry and nobility. In the main body of the essay, you should look to compare these other groups with the Crown so that you demonstrate any links between the developments and also so that your evaluation of the various factors is comparative.

You may have considered the following issues in your essay:

- The character and personalities of the monarchs: strong personalities of Henry VIII and Elizabeth, compared with the weak 'mid-Tudor' period.
- The divine nature of monarchy and the unity and authority of the monarch.
- The use by the Crown of patronage, propaganda and policies.
- The role of central government, particularly parliament in the later period, to voice discontent.
- The role of local government: JPs, sheriffs, lords lieutenant.
- The role of the gentry.
- The role of the nobility, both locally and centrally.
- The role of the clergy as administrators and preachers.

Response A

The Crown was the most important factor in maintaining political stability in the period. This was evident at the start of the period and in the mid-Tudor period when weak royal authority under Henry VII and under the boy-king Edward VI and the female rule of Mary resulted in unrest and instability, as seen in the large number of rebellions from 1485 to 1509 and again from 1547 to 1558. There were other factors that also helped to maintain stability, such as the nobility who helped with central government and, along with the gentry, imposed laws in the countryside. The Church was also important as bishops helped with administration, whilst the clergy often preached obedience. There were therefore many groups that helped to achieve stability.

Analysis of Response A

- A clear judgement is reached. It explains why the Crown was important, but does not explain why it was more important than other factors.
- There is some awareness of continuity and change or comparison over the period, which is a strong point.
- The relative importance of the factors is not discussed – there is simply a list with no relative judgement.

Response B

The Crown was the most important factor in maintaining political stability in the period. This was evident at the start of the period and in the mid-Tudor period when weak royal authority under Henry VII and under the boy-king Edward VI and the female rule of Mary resulted in unrest and instability, as seen in the large number of rebellions from 1485 to 1509 and again from 1547 to 1558[1]. Although the nobility, gentry and clergy played an important role in both central and local government, their willingness to support the Crown depended on the monarch's personality and capability. They were more willing to uphold the Crown during periods of strong authority, as was seen with Norfolk during the Pilgrimage of Grace, than they were under Edward and Mary, when they caused instability through trying to alter the succession or preach against the Crown's religious policies during Edward's reign[2]. However, the relationship was interdependent and stability did depend on the willingness of the nobility, gentry and Church to ensure that Crown policies and laws were implemented in the localities[3]. It was simply not possible for the monarch to be everywhere, but the willingness of the nobility, gentry and church to uphold the Crown was also linked to the patronage and rewards that the monarch could offer[4].

Analysis of Response B

- A clear judgement is reached that the Crown was the most important factor and why it was more important than [1] or linked to other factors.
- The importance of the personality and character of the monarch is explained [2].
- There are links made between the factors and some support for the claim is made, which supports the judgement [3].
- The student is aware of the link between factors and this is explained [4].

Activity

You should now try and write a conclusion to some of the questions below. Ensure that you reach a clear, supported judgement and that when you have to discuss more than one factor your evaluation of the importance of the factors is comparative.

Essay questions

1 Assess the role of the nobility in maintaining political stability in Tudor England.
2 'Local authorities were more important than central government in maintaining the political stability of Tudor England.' How far do you agree with this judgement?
3 Assess the importance of the clergy in maintaining political stability in Tudor England.

Study skills: depth study interpretations question

How to reach a judgement

This chapter looks at how to reach a judgement about the two passages. In the first paragraph you will have explained the two interpretations and placed them in the context of the wider historical debate about the issue, and in the second and third paragraphs you will have evaluated the strengths and weakness of the two interpretations. However, in order to reach the higher mark bands you must reach a supported judgement as to which passage's view about the issue in the question you think is more convincing.

A good conclusion will:

- reach a clear judgement as to which passage's view about the issue in the question is more convincing
- explain why a particular passage is more convincing and why the other is less convincing
- suggest that there are some parts in both passages which are more or less convincing
- briefly support the judgement so that it is not simply an assertion.

Read the question and Passages A and B below about the threat of the 1549 Western rebellion and then the example conclusions (Responses A and B) that follow:

Evaluate the interpretations in both of the passages and explain which you think is more convincing as an explanation of the threat posed by the Western rebellion.

PASSAGE A

The gentry and local officials could not manage affairs in the West, intervention by the government was imperative. Somerset might have been more successful if the Western Rebellion had been an isolated event, but beginning in the spring of 1549, he faced a series of worsening crises which weakened his authority. Although Somerset was warned to proceed more cautiously, the rush of events overwhelmed the government and forced it to react defensively.

Preachers were sent to the West to proclaim the reformed Gospel, while Somerset waited for the gentry to restore order. Later Somerset dispatched the Carews to help the gentry resist the rebel force. Offenders were to be pardoned. Those who refused pardon were to be apprehended. The Carews could not implement Somerset's policy; and when Sir Peter returned to London he was greeted with indignation.

The Councillors assumed that the rebels could be duped easily and induced to abandon their leaders. These hopelessly erroneous assumptions were made at a time when the rebel army, vastly larger than the government force, was laying siege to Exeter. The government's inept directive may have resulted from Somerset's leniency toward the rebels but was more likely the result of misinformation and poor communication.

(Adapted from Barrett L. Beer, Rebellion and Riot, *Kent State University Press, 1982, pp. 73–5.)*

PASSAGE B

Somerset faced more determined and widespread opposition than any other Tudor government. The harmony of Tudor society collapsed and class hostility flared up. The rebellion had the potential to cause serious problems for the government and if there had been co-ordination between the regions government resources may have been overwhelmed. However, the aims of the rebels were not to overthrow the government, but to bring about changes to government policy. The rebels did not advance on the capital, unlike either the Peasants' Revolt of 1381 or Jack Cade in 1450. Although the number of rebels was quite large, they were no match for government forces, particularly the mercenaries. Some 3000 rebels were killed in battle and further retribution followed, with executions without trials and the confiscation of property. When the government was forced into military action and had sufficient forces it dealt with the rebels quickly and efficiently, without heavy losses of capital or men.

(Adapted from Nicholas Fellows and Mary Dicken, England 1485–1603, *Hodder Education, 2015, pp. 153–5.)*

Response A

In conclusion, Passage B offers a more convincing view of the threat posed by the Western rebellion. The passage offers a balanced answer considering both the threat the rebellion posed and the government's handling of the situation. It correctly suggests that the government, when forced to act, was able to crush the rising relatively easily through battles at places such as Fenny Bridges and Sampford Courtenay. It is also more convincing because the rebels did not threaten the government as they never left Devon and spent most of their time laying siege to Exeter, and Interpretation A ignores this.

Response B

Both passages correctly acknowledge that the rebellion had at least the potential to be a serious threat to the government. However, ultimately they differ in the seriousness of that threat, with Passage A viewing the rebellion as a greater threat than Passage B[1]. Although Passage A is correct to see the threat it caused because of the context of the rebellion, such as war with France and Scotland and the government's handling of it, unlike Passage B it does not consider the ease with which the rebels were defeated at Fenny Bridges and Sampford Courtenay once the government had assembled a large enough force[2]. Passage B, while acknowledging the potential threat to the government, balances that against the rebels' aims, their movements and the ultimate outcome to show that the government's position was not threatened, as the rebels did not aim to overthrow the government. It is therefore more convincing as an interpretation.

Analysis of Responses A and B

Both conclusions offer a judgement and both support their claims. However, Response B is the stronger conclusion:

- Response A focuses almost exclusively on Passage B, with mention of Passage A only in the final line.
- Response B compares the two interpretations in reaching its judgement and is more balanced [1].
- Response B, although it argues that Passage B is stronger, does not dismiss the valid points made in Passage A [2].

Activity

Revisit the questions on the passages in Chapters 1–3 (pages 54, 97 and 144–5) and write a conclusion for those questions.

Timeline

1485–1509	**Reign of Henry VII**
1485	Defeat of Richard III at Battle of Bosworth
1486	Lovel rebellion
	Stafford rebellion
1486–7	Simnel rebellion
1487	Battle of East Stoke
	Real Earl of Warwick paraded at St Paul's Cathedral in London
	Act of Maintenance
1489	Yorkshire rebellion
1495	Arrest of Sir William Stanley before he could join Warbeck
	De Facto Act
1497	Cornish rebellion
	Warbeck rebellion
1500	People of Somerset fined for involvement in Cornish rising
1509–47	**Reign of Henry VIII**
1525	Amicable Grant rebellion
1529	Reformation parliament started to meet
1534	Office holders swore oaths of allegiance and supremacy
	Subsidy Act
	Act of Supremacy
1534–7	Silken Thomas's rebellion
1536	Richard Morrison published *A Lamentation in Which is Showed What Ruin and Destruction Cometh of Seditious Rebellion*
	Statute of Uses

	Ten Articles, dissolution of the smaller monasteries
	Pilgrims entered York and Durham
1536–7	Pilgrimage of Grace rebellion
1537	Sir Francis Bigod's men killed when they attempted to storm Carlisle
1538	Cromwell's Injunctions
1539	Six Articles
1540	Statute of Wills
1547–53	**Reign of Edward VI**
1548	Tax on sheep and cloth
1549	First Edwardian prayer book, Subsidy Act
	Rebellion in 26 counties
	John Cheke published *The Hurt of Sedition*
	Western rebellion
	Kett rebellion
	Appointment of lords lieutenant
1550	Execution of Arundell, Winslade, Bury and Holmes for involvement in Western rising
1553–8	**Reign of Mary I**
1553	The 'Devise' was drawn up
	Northumberland issued a proclamation denying Mary's right to the throne
	Northumberland rebellion
	Northumberland abandoned his attempt to overthrow Mary at Cambridge
1554	Wyatt rebellion
1555–6	Crop failure

1558–1603	Reign of Elizabeth I
1558	Reform of the militia
1558–9	Elizabethan Church settlement
1558–67	Shane O'Neill rebellion
1563	Statute of Artificers
1569	Northern earls entered Durham
1569–70	Northern Earls' rebellion
1569–73	Munster rebellion
1570	500 of Lord Dacre's army killed or captured near Carlisle
1572	Council of the North reformed and Poor Law Act
1579–83	Geraldine rebellion
1593	Repeal of anti-enclosure legislation

1595–1603	Tyrone rebellion
1596	Oxfordshire rebellion
1596–7	Crop failure
1597	Acts to maintain tillage and to prevent the decay of towns and husbandry
1598	English forces defeated by Tyrone at Yellow Ford
	Poor Law Acts: Act for the Relief of the Poor and Act for the Punishment of Rogues and Sturdy Beggars
1601	Essex rebellion
	Defeat of Spanish troops at Kinsale
1603	Tyrone's rebellion finally suppressed

Glossary of terms

Act in Restraint of Appeals   The Act, passed in 1533, started to transfer the powers of the pope to the king and made him head of the Church.

Act of Six Articles   This Act upheld the orthodox Catholic faith and remained in force until 1547.

Act of Ten Articles   This Act stressed the importance of baptism, the Eucharist and penance, and put less significance on confirmation, marriage, holy orders and the last rites.

Act of Uniformity   An Act that enforced the Protestant prayer book, which was first introduced in 1549, and modified in 1552 and 1559. It imposed punishments on those who did not conform.

Anabaptists   Radical religious reformers, many of whom also wanted to overturn the established social order and were therefore seen as a threat.

Anglicise   To make English.

Attainted lands   Acts of attainder were passed by parliament on traitors, and their entire property and that of their family were forfeited to the Crown.

Belphoebe and Astraea   Mythical women celebrated for their beauty and sense of justice, respectively.

Benefit of clergy   The privilege of exemption from trial by a secular court that was allowed in cases of felony to the clergy or to anyone who could read a passage from the Scriptures.

Benevolence   A gift that was occasionally requested to help the government overcome a financial crisis.

Billhook   A curved blade attached to a wooden handle that could be used to slash and cut an adversary.

Bondmen or serfs   Slaves.

Bonds and recognisances   Bonds were written obligations binding one person to another (often the Crown) to perform a specified action or to pay a sum of money; a recognisance acknowledged that someone was bound to fulfil a commitment.

Bonds of allegiance   Financial and legal penalties were imposed on rebels and on anyone of doubtful allegiance.

Break from Rome   The name given to Henry VIII's separation of England from the Roman Catholic Church by a series of parliamentary Acts culminating in the Act of Supremacy of 1534.

Bull of Excommunication   In 1570, the pope issued a bull of excommunication which freed Catholics from obeying Elizabeth and allowed them to overthrow her.

Cade's rebellion   Jack Cade led a revolt in Kent that briefly occupied London before being defeated in battle. The rebels were protesting at high taxes and governmental incompetence.

Castleward   Tenants had once been required to defend Norwich Castle but this military service was later commuted to paying a rent.

Catechism and prymer   A catechism was a book of basic religious instruction in the form of questions and answers; a prymer was an elementary book of religious instruction.

Chantries   Chapels where prayers for the souls of the dead were said. Abolished in 1547.

Commissions of array   Authority given by the Crown to nobles to raise troops.

Commonwealth   The 'wealth' or welfare of the common people.

Compositions   Taxes paid instead of having to undertake military service, have soldiers billeted with you, and take part in purveyance or the selling of goods to the Crown at a lower price.

Convocation   The general assembly of the clergy that usually met when parliament was called.

Copyhold and customary rights   Copyholders were tenants who held a copy of their tenancy but in practice had only limited rights. Customary rights were more secure and reflected traditional local practices and customs.

Court of Augmentations   Established in 1536, this administrative and financial court in London handled affairs relating to the dissolved monasteries.

De facto   By deed, as opposed to *de jure*, 'by law'.

Despotism   The government of an absolute ruler who rules without regard for the law.

Devise   The means by which Edward disinherited his half-sisters, Mary and Elizabeth, in favour of Lady Jane Grey.

Embargoes   Trade restrictions such as those imposed on Burgundy in 1493.

Entry fine   A fee paid by tenants when renewing their lease that allowed them to re-enter their property.

Escheators   County officials responsible for overseeing Crown lands and collecting feudal payments such as wardships and escheats.

Factions   A small number of like-minded people who rivalled an established and larger group for political, religious or social power.

Felony   An offence that carried the death penalty.

Feodary   An officer of the court of wards, which looked after the lands of minors.

Feoffees   Property trustees and administrators.

Feudal dues   Financial rights and powers that the king had over the nobility.

Firebrands   People who cause unrest.

First fruits and tenths   Taxes on the first year's income of a new bishop and one-tenth of the value of ecclesiastical benefices received by the Crown after the Reformation.

Flanders   Part of modern-day Belgium and the centre of the cloth trade.

Folding   Allowing cattle and sheep to graze and manure the land.

Gaelic clans   Some native and older Irish families spoke Gaelic, and were distinguished from the families of Norman descent and more recent immigrants who spoke English.

Garrisons   Fortified towns where soldiers were kept.

Great Chain of Being   A theoretical defence of the existing social order, under which all classes were interdependent.

Harness, arquebuses and morions, with matchlight   Body armour, long-barrelled handguns, metal helmets, and fuses to ignite the arquebuses.

Heir presumptive   An heir who it was presumed would inherit unless an alternative claimant was subsequently born.

Homilies   Lessons that could be read directly or improvised into a sermon.

Humanism   The study of architecture, art, language, rhetoric and literature that enabled the individual to become more civilised and better prepared to play an active role in the political life of the state.

Hundreds   Norfolk, like most counties, was divided administratively into hundreds.

Husbandmen   Small farmers or landowners of a lower social standing than yeomen.

Iconoclasm   The smashing and destruction of religious images and icons.

Imperatur   Imperial status, suggesting that there was no greater power in the country.

Inflation   A rise in prices and an accompanying fall in the purchasing power of money.

Inquisition fines   Fees paid for an enquiry and valuation of a deceased person's estate who was believed to hold freehold land in chief of the Crown.

Knight of the Garter   An honour in the gift of the Crown that Henry VIII generously dispensed. The recipient was entitled to wear blue or crimson robes and took precedence over other knights.

Knight service   Men who held land from the king were obliged to do knight service. This entailed fighting for the king and providing troops whenever he went to war or (as was customarily the case) providing sufficient money to hire mercenaries instead.

Laity   People who were not clergy.

Liturgy   An order of church service.

Livery and maintenance   Wearing a lord's tunic bearing his coat of arms, and the practice in which some lords attended a law court in order to influence the judge and jury.

Marches   The lands that bordered either Wales or Scotland.

Martial law   Military law that replaces civil law during a political crisis.

Masterless   Adolescents who were not apprenticed to a master or an employer and so were more likely to be itinerant and ill-disciplined.

Middle march   The marches were the lands between England and Scotland that were divided into three and administered by wardens.

Midland revolt   A serious peasant uprising in Leicestershire against landlords who enclosed common fields and converted them from arable to pasture.

Musters   Summoning soldiers for inspection.

Oak of Reformation   An old oak tree on Mousehold Heath outside Norwich, so called because it was where the rebels held Protestant or reformed services.

Oaths of succession and supremacy   Office holders and other important people had to swear oaths accepting the monarch as Head of the Church, or under Elizabeth as Supreme Governor, and to accept the succession.

Overstocking   Putting too many animals on the land.

Oyer et terminer   A commission directed to justices that empowered them to 'hear and determine' indictments for specific crimes committed in a particular area.

Pale   A region near Dublin that was one of the few well-governed areas of Ireland in the sixteenth century.

Paternalistic   A policy whereby those in power limit the freedom of others, supposedly in their interests.

Peasants' revolt   In 1381, peasants in Kent and Essex led by Wat Tyler and John Ball marched on London, in protest against a poll tax and calling for the abolition of serfdom.

Placards incidents in France   On 18 October 1534, posters supporting the reformed religion and attacking mass were put up in Paris, five provincial towns and even in the royal place.

Plantations   Lands that were confiscated from rebels and granted to English and local landlords at reduced prices.

Polemics   A strong, often controversial written attack.

Popish   A derogatory term for anything that appeared to be Catholic or inspired by the pope.

Prerogative   Powers held by the Crown. Prerogative courts were presided over by royal councillors who dispensed justice in the interests of the Crown.

Prince of the blood   A prince who was a blood relation of the monarch.

Privy Council   The inner ring of councillors who advised the king.

Proclamations   Notices that were publicly issued by the Crown and proclaimed in London and the localities.

Provost marshal   A senior administrative officer, probably a senior magistrate.

Purveyance   The right of the Crown to purchase supplies or to obtain transport for the royal household at prices fixed below prevailing market rates.

Quarter Sessions   General courts held in a county every three months.

Recusant   A Catholic who denied the royal supremacy or refused to attend the services of the Anglican Church.

Retainers   Nobles retained servants in their households who might be used as private armies.

Richard II   In 1399, Henry Bolingbroke had seized the Crown from Richard II. The re-enactment of Shakespeare's play (written in 1595) reminded Londoners that the deposition of Elizabeth I would not be unprecedented.

Sacramentarians   Protestants who denied the real presence of Christ in the Eucharist.

Sanctuary   A place that provided a haven for outlaws. Every parish church, cathedral and monastery had the privilege to offer sanctuary, although in practice certain crimes such as treason were rendered ineligible.

Scutage   Rather than fight in person for the king in times of war, tenants-in-chief could commute their feudal obligations into a tax known as a scutage or 'escuage'.

Seditious   Liable to cause an affray or act of disorder.

Star Chamber   The name given to the place or court where members of the council dealing with legal matters met.

Strategy and tactics   Strategy is an overall plan and the management of troops designed to achieve an objective; tactics are the means by which the plan is carried out.

Tenants at will   Tenants who could be ejected from their land at the will of their landlord when their lease expired.

Tithes   Payments made by the laity to the parish church of one-tenth of their agricultural profits or personal income.

Vicegerent   Someone exercising authority on behalf of a ruler.

Villein   A tenant who was obliged to perform any services that his lord commanded.

Wardship   The Crown acted as the guardian of the son or daughter of a deceased tenant-in-chief until he or she came of age at 21.

Further reading

I. Arthurson, 'The Rising of 1497' in J. Rosenthal and C. Richmond (eds), *People, Politics and Community in the Later Middle Ages* (Sutton, 1987)

I. Arthurson, *The Perkin Warbeck Conspiracy 1491–99* (Sutton, 1994)

B.L. Beer, *Rebellion and Riot: Popular Disorder in England During the Reign of Edward VI* (Kent State University Press, 1982)

M.J. Bennett, *Lambert Simnel and the Battle of Stoke* (Sutton, 1987)

G.W. Bernard, *War, Taxation and Rebellion in Early Tudor England* (Harvester, 1986)

M.L. Bush, *The Pilgrimage of Grace: A Study of Rebel Armies* (Manchester University Press, 1996)

P. Caraman, *The Western Rebellion* (Tiverton, 1994)

J. Cornwall, *Revolt of the Peasantry* (Routledge, 1977)

S. Cunningham, 'Henry VII and rebellion in North-Eastern England 1485–1492', *Northern History*, 32, 1996

C.S.L. Davies, 'The Pilgrimage of Grace Reconsidered', *Past and Present*, 41, 1968

C.S.L. Davies, 'Popular religion and the Pilgrimage of Grace' in A. Fletcher and J. Stevenson (eds), *Order and Disorder in Early Modern England* (Cambridge University Press, 1985)

S.G. Ellis, *Tudor Ireland: Crown, Community and the Conflict of Cultures 1470–1603* (Harlow, 1985)

G.R. Elton, *Policy and Police* (Cambridge University Press, 1972)

N. Fellows, *Disorder and Rebellion in Tudor England* (Hodder & Stoughton, 2001)

A. Fletcher and D. MacCulloch, *Tudor Rebellions* (Pearson Longman, 2015)

P. Griffiths, A. Fox and S. Hindle (eds), *The Experience of Authority in Early Modern England* (Macmillan, 1996)

S.J. Gunn, *Early Tudor Government 1485–1558* (Macmillan, 1995)

C. Haigh, *Reformation and Resistance in Tudor Lancashire* (Cambridge University Press, 1976)

R.W. Hoyle, *The Pilgrimage of Grace* (Oxford University Press, 2001)

M.E. James, *Society, Politics and Culture* (Cambridge University Press, 1986)

M.E. James, 'Obedience and dissent in Henrician England: the Lincolnshire Rebellion', *Past and Present*, 48, 1970

S.K. Land, *Kett's Rebellion: The Norfolk Rising of 1549* (Boydell, 1977)

D.M. Loades, *Two Tudor Conspiracies* (Cambridge University Press, 1965)

D.M. Loades, *Power in Tudor England* (Macmillan, 1997)

H. Miller, *Henry VIII and the English Nobility* (Oxford University Press, 1986)

G. Moorhouse, *The Pilgrimage of Grace* (Weidenfeld & Nicolson, 2002)

D.M. Palliser, *The Age of Elizabeth 1547–1603* (Longman, 1983)

E. Shagan, 'Protector Somerset and the 1549 rebellions', *English Historical Review*, 114, 1999

H. Speight, 'Local government and the South-West Rebellion', *Southern History*, 18, 1996

P. Thomas, *Authority and Disorder in Tudor Times* (Cambridge University Press, 1999)

A. Wall, *Power and Protest in England 1525–1640* (Arnold, 2000)

J. Walter, ' "A rising of the people". The Oxfordshire rising of 1596', *Past and Present*, 107, 1985

P. Williams, *The Tudor Regime* (Oxford University Press, 1979)

J. Youings, 'The South Western Rebellion of 1549', *Southern History*, 1, 1979

Index